NATIONALISM & SOCIALISM

NATIONALISM & SOCIALISM

*Marxist and Labor Theories
of Nationalism to 1917*

HORACE B. DAVIS

MONTHLY REVIEW PRESS
New York and London

ACKNOWLEDGEMENTS

Numerous scholars have advised and contributed information at various stages in the preparation of this study. Bert Andréas of Geneva has furnished many details for Chapters I–III out of his vast store of information. He has also read the whole manuscript and made numerous constructive suggestions, in addition to harmonizing the footnote references to the writings of Marx and Engels.

Dr. Roman Rosdolsky very kindly made available the manuscript of his study which has now been published, on Friedrich Engels and the theory of the "Peoples Without History." Dr. Dirk J. Struik and Daniel B. MacGilvray opportunely supplied materials which I would otherwise have missed. Indeed it was the former who helped to formulate the project originally.

I wish especially to express my appreciation for the services furnished by the staff of the International Institute for Social History in Amsterdam, and to thank the Louis M. Rabinowitz Foundation which made it possible for me to visit the Institute in the summer of 1965. Dr. Arthur Lehning kindly made available the proof of his forthcoming volume on Bakunin. I have received devoted assistance from my daughters—Wilhelmina Stocking, Barbara Crowley, Esther ("Terry") Radinsky, and Quentin Bassett—in preparing the manuscript. Wilhelmina Stocking did much of the research for Chapter VII. Dr. Olga Lang contributed her time to help resolve some difficult problems.

Needless to say, none of the above is responsible for the shortcomings of the study which remain the writer's own.

CONTENTS

FOREWORD

Democracy, nationalism, and socialism, the three great movements of the 19th century, must be understood in relation to each other in order to be understood at all. Socialism was originally an offshoot of democracy, and many studies have been devoted to the relation between socialism and democracy. But on the relation between socialism and nationalism, although some excellent monographs have appeared, there has been as yet, so far as we have noticed, no comprehensive treatment in English.* The present study represents a first attempt at filling this gap for the early period. Since the whole question took a new turn with the establishment of the first socialist country, the Soviet Union, we have, perhaps arbitrarily, wound up our story with the year 1917. Thus we shall not be attempting to state or appraise the Soviet Union's theory of nationality as such.

Our purpose is rather to test the opinion, which has gained some currency in recent years, that Marxism is not adapted to handling the problem of nationalism.† It would be easy to point out that most non-Marxist theories of nationalism are completely unsatisfactory for various reasons, but we believe it is possible to show that Marxism not only offers the most

---

* We mention two outstanding monographs. The study by Solomon F. Bloom, *The World of Nations: A Study of the National Implications in the Work of Karl Marx* (New York, 1941), is the necessary take-off point for any discussion of Marx's work in the field. This study is hereafter referred to as "Bloom." Very well informed on Eastern Europe, and on Engels' work in general, is the monograph by Dr. Roman Rosdolsky, "Friedrich Engels und das Problem der 'Geschichtslosen Völker,'" *Archiv für Sozialgeschichte*, IV (Hannover, 1964), which unfortunately is not available in English. The author's indebtedness to these two sources will be evident. A pioneer work in the field which deserves to be noted also is A. S. de Leeuw, *Het Socialisme en de Natie* (Amsterdam, 1939).

† Thus Borkenau states: "In the political field nationalism is the fact against which Marxist theory breaks itself."—F. Borkenau, *World Communism* (New York, 1939), p. 94. Cf. also Louis Fischer, p. 207 below.

fruitful technique for analyzing this thorny topic, but that the essential elements of a sound theory of nationalism and nationality problems had already been developed by 1917—this in spite of the fact that the ideas of Marx and Engels on the subject had become largely outdated, and Lenin, their most illustrious successor, confined his writings in the field to articles which, though numerous, were repetitive and unsystematic.

The word "nation" and its derivatives "national," "nationality," and "nationalism" are used in different senses by different writers, or even at different times by the same writer. Often the conclusions that are reached concerning nationalism and nationality problems derive directly from the particular definition that is used. It is possible to set up a self-consistent group of meanings for the several terms, as is done for example by the writers of the standard work on the subject, *Nationalism: A Report by a Study Group of Members of the Royal Institute of International Affairs.*[1]* The word "nation" refers to those persons who compose a political community or other ethnic aggregation of individuals having particular characteristics, while "state" refers to the sovereign power or government.[2]

Nationalism means devotion to the interests of a particular community, whereas patriotism may mean that or devotion to the interests of a particular state. Neither nationalism nor patriotism is necessarily aggressive; but when they become so, and especially when they take such forms as jingoism and chauvinism, they are recognized as vices. Thus the patriotism which is cherished by war has been described as "ordinarily false and spurious, a scourge to the world, a narrow, unjust passion which aims to exalt a particular State on the humiliation and destruction of other nations."[3]

Patriotism and nationalism do not necessarily imply policies which are hostile to other nations. They may refer merely to

---

* Numbered references, which represent source notes, can be found at the end of the book, pp. 215–236. References marked with an asterisk indicate explanatory notes, and are placed at the bottom of the relevant text pages.—Ed.

the most suitable policy to advance the welfare of one's own group. Nationalism and patriotism are quite compatible with socialism, in the opinion of Francis W. Coker. He states:

If patriotism and socialism are understood in the ways in which they operate in ordinary practice—the former as devotion to a particular community, the latter as a particular program to further the welfare of such a community—then clearly the two are mutually compatible.[4]

However, numerous problems arise in connection with defining the community; and when welfare ceases to be the criterion of action, Coker's proposition is no longer relevant.* The kind of nationalism propagated by jingos, chauvinists and fascists is clearly not compatible with socialism.

Nationalism was described by Lenin as "a broad and very deep ideological current."[5] Indeed there is none deeper. Devotion to one's community has always been the prerequisite for man's survival as a group, and man survives, if at all, as a group. Thus, while nationalism has been used as a cloak to cover up some of history's greatest crimes, it has also inspired constructive movements. The problem of the Marxist is to distinguish between these two aspects of nationalism—to learn to harness nationalist movements where possible to serve the interests of progress while condemning and curbing them when they are used for anti-social ends. For this purpose a correct theory of nationalism is indispensable.

Nationalism could be counted a progressive force when it was serving to unite the hitherto scattered units of the post-feudal economy into viable units for production and trade. Elizabethan England deserved the dithyrambics of Shakespeare and Marlowe. The nationalism of the Dutch helped them to shake off the throttling hand of reactionary Spain and to take the lead in European commerce. Nationalism in France, taking shape incipiently with Joan of Arc, reached full self-conscious expression at the time of the Revolution and was

* Cf. Lord Acton, p. 15 below.

even "exported" to the rest of Europe, whose countries came out of the Napoleonic wars committed to national development in their respective areas. Nationalism in the American colonies helped to start them on a course of phenomenal advance; ever since, nationalist movements in colonial areas have been accounted progressive for both political and economic reasons. The national unification of Germany and Italy was applauded by all who valued economic progress.

Imperialism, by contrast, is by its very nature unprogressive and anti-social. The European peoples who first attained national unity—the English, the Spanish, the Portuguese, the Dutch—proceeded to use their new-found strength for expansive nationalism of the most unsocial kind. The rest of the world has suffered for centuries from the exploitative selfishness of the imperialist nations.

Nationalism is today such an all-pervasive phenomenon that we sometimes forget how recent is its emergence, especially in areas such as Asia. The Chinese people in the mid-19th century made a heroic stand against the European invaders in the Opium Wars. Engels described the struggle of the Chinese as a war *pro aris et focis*—for their hearths and homes—which it no doubt was. He added that it was "a popular war" (this too we can accept) "*for the maintenance of the Chinese nation.*"[6] But the Chinese were not then nationality-conscious in the way that most Europeans were, or that the Chinese now are.*

The twofold aspect of nationalism is found most perplexing by those scholars who discuss it at all. Janus-faced, it looks both ways. On the one hand, progressive nationalism beckons to the colonial and semi-colonial peoples to whom it holds out

* We do not at all imply that nationalism was a force without importance in the Taiping rebellion to which Engels refers. But scholars like Joseph Needham stress rather the Chinese tradition of social solidarity: "The problem was how to capture those Artesian depths of a social solidarity emotion which had been one of the main motivating forces of Chinese society for two millennia. *No mere nationalism could ever have done this.*"—Joseph Needham, *The Past in China's Present* (pamphlet published by the *Far East Reporter*, n.d. 1965?), p. 18. Emphasis added.

bright prospects of economic development free of imperialist tributes. The opposite aspect of nationalism is indeed fearsome to contemplate. In its name the most advanced countries plunge into aggressive war against each other and against weaker peoples; and supposedly moral and upright persons find themselves justifying and even committing crimes against humanity more terrible than any that ancient history records. They have no better defense, in the end, than that of Eichmann. Yet what is the alternative? Can nationalism be dispensed with altogether, as some have proposed?*

There are some today who turn to nationalism as a "cure" for alienation. Douglas LePan writes, with specific reference to the new Canadian nationalism: "In a world of rapid change and alienation, and nightmare not far beyond the horizon, nationalism can be a comforting thing." This point of view is similar to that of people who turn to drink as a "comforting thing" when they are unable to face their problems. Nationalism of itself is no cure for the world's ills; it may even, in the wrong hands, be a factor contributing to making that "nightmare not far beyond the horizon" more nearly an actuality. The way out that was suggested by Marx was to cure alienation and remove the dangers of nationalism in the same act—by adopting socialism.

Again, there are some who, in their revulsion against the excesses of nationalism, would condemn it out of hand—who find in it today the greatest menace to civilization.† But according to such a high authority as Max Weber, not only nationalism but political life in general must necessarily be amoral. Weber was indeed an admirer of Machiavelli:

A few weeks before his death [Weber] gave a gripping speech in which he described the tragedy inherent in the fight for a political cause. . . . With great passion he rejected the demand to eliminate the difference between private and political morality. . . . He who enters politics, that is, the realm where power and ruth-

* Cf. below, pp. 16–17.
† See below, p. 209.

lessness alone are valid means, concludes a pact with diabolic forces. Condemning any statesman who hesitates to use unethical means in the pursuit of his ends, Weber takes a strong stand in favor of Machiavelli and admiringly quotes this author's praise for citizens who put the greatness of their commonwealth above the salvation of their souls.[7]

Marx recognized the necessity for using amoral means in the struggle against the exploiting power-holders. But he still thought in terms of a larger morality; power was not an end in itself, any more than the nation was. It is at this higher level that the solution of the paradox of power can be sought. It was his hope that exploitation could be ended and the nation become a vehicle for the advancement of culture instead of a force for oppression and destruction.

In this study we shall trace the early story of how socialism and the labor movement attempted to cope with the problem of nationalism. We shall see how they tried to capture its fine enthusiasm and harness it to constructive ends; and we shall also examine how nationalism sought, sometimes successfully, to use the socialist movement for its own (often nefarious) ends, down to 1917.

Note on the Paperback Edition

In this reissue of my study of six years ago I have not attempted to deal with all the criticisms that have been raised on points of theory. Instead, I have tried to correct errors that crept in, and to obtain greater clarity in certain passages. A full review of the theoretical points will be contained in the second volume, now in preparation, which will include, but will not be limited to, the entire period from 1917 to the present.

I wish to express my special appreciation to those reviewers, such as Jiri Koralka, who have taken the trouble to specify what they considered weak points and errors of fact.

H.B.D.

July 1973

I

FROM NATIONALISM TO INTERNATIONALISM:
THE RECONSTRUCTION OF HEGEL'S THEORY

THE INTELLECTUAL CLIMATE in which Marx and Engels grew up was dominated by Hegel's philosophy. In Hegel the distinction between nation and state is unusually sharp. A people may exist merely as a nation but in that condition it is incapable of contributing to the development of world history, said Hegel. Some peoples even now exist as "savage nations." But in every people there is the urge to form a state and maintain itself as a state.[1]

Freedom is embodied in the state, according to Hegel. World history is the dialectic of the spirits of particular peoples, each of which has a special contribution to make in the realization of reason; afterwards it makes way for the people that has the next contribution to make. The various nations do not contribute equally; some are active promoters of progress. The capacity to build a state which will make a decisive jump to a new and higher form of life depends on such factors as geographical location and also the natural, racial and social qualities of the nation.[2]

The highest duty of the individual, said Hegel, is to be a member of the state.[3] A people for which it had become a matter of indifference whether its state would continue to be a state, would also soon cease to be a people.[4] Individuals and peoples engaged in carrying out the world-historical mission of advancing civilization must necessarily sweep aside those who stand in the way.

1

Hegel believed in the system of private property, but he was well aware of the conflicts of interest which it involved. The state, in his view, was a necessary institution if only in order to control the contending parties and prevent society from flying apart. He thought of the state as an independent and autonomous power, standing in a special, exalted position above the competitive system.[5] Hegel's thought on this point shows an interesting parallel to that of Adam Ferguson, the mentor of the great Adam Smith. Ferguson had found that commerce, taken by itself, is not a state-builder but a state-wrecker: "The mighty engine, which we suppose to have formed society (*viz*: the commercial state), only tends to set its members at variance, or to continue their intercourse, after the bands of affection are broken."[6]

Hegel included the Germans among the world-historical peoples, and said some very uncomplimentary things about the Slavs, especially the South Slavs. He was a traditionalist in some respects, notably in his endorsement of religion; and he glorified the state, which indeed occupied a central place in his philosophy. Thus it was to be expected that the right-wing German nationalists would claim Hegel as their own, and they did so. However, Hegel was not himself a nationalist; and his strong advocacy of the state as such did not include or even connote an endorsement of the actual state of the government of Prussia as it then was. On the contrary, in his 1817 lectures at Heidelberg he made it clear that he detested the absolute monarchy. He said that the reality of reason could be nothing other than *constitutional* monarchy; else it could not be reason.[7]

Part of Hegel's idea was that peoples which have proved themselves unable over a period of time to build a state will never be able to build one. This proposition is indeed somewhat ridiculous, since there must be a first time for everything, and why should a people that has built a state which decayed be in any more favorable position than a people which has never built one? Yet this idea was absorbed by Engels in his younger days.

Writing in the interests of a Greater Germany which had still to be realized, Engels said in 1840–1841:

Perhaps in opposition to many whose point of view I share in general, I am still of the opinion that the reconquest of the German-speaking left side of the Rhine is an affair of national honor: that the Germanization of Holland and Belgium, which have been wrenched away, is a political necessity for us. Shall we continue to let the German nationality be oppressed in those countries while in the East the Slavs are emerging ever stronger? . . . Without doubt it will come to another war between us and France, and we will then see who deserves to have the left bank of the Rhine. . . .

As long as the partition of our country exists, so long are we politically nothing, so long are public life, cultivated constitutionalism, freedom of the press and everything else we demand, only pious wishes, which can be only half realized.[8]

And in 1842 he continued in the same vein:

Königsberg in Prussia has for several years past been acquiring a significance which must be a joy to all Germany. Although formally excluded from Germany by the Act of Union, the German element there has pulled itself together and made a claim to be recognized as German, to be considered as representative of Germany as against the Slavic barbarism of the East.[9]

Engels even called for the purging of unnecessary foreign words from the German language and of "crazy" foreign styles from German art and architecture. This rather extreme type of nationalism was quite rare at the time.

Jingos frequently espouse a reactionary philosophy of society, but Engels was never a reactionary; he always accepted the democratic features of the French Revolution. His biographer Gustav Mayer thinks that Engels gradually eliminated the nationalist element from his thinking.[10] There is no doubt that he tried to do so—with what success, we shall have to examine more closely.

Man and Society

Marx had, like Engels, been a Young Hegelian, but without Engels' jingoism. The reactionary uses to which the philosophy of Hegel was being put, and the inadequacy of the philosophy in certain important respects, made it inevitable that some fundamental revisions would be attempted.

When the publication of the *Deutsch-Französische Jahrbücher* was under discussion in 1843, Arnold Ruge wrote to Marx asking for his advice and cooperation, and proposing that the purpose of the new periodical should be to fight "nationalism and reaction."[11]

Marx did not react to the suggestion as far as nationalism was concerned. He was then working out a new philosophy of society, which was presently to emerge as historical materialism. The main task that he had set himself was to settle the relationship of man to society and to the state—no small task, especially in an intellectual atmosphere which was just emerging from the shackles of religious and mystical conceptions, including Hegel's idealistic conception of the state. Marx was deeply interested in the problem of alienation, which has recently come into renewed prominence in the Western world. Feuerbach with his historic demolition of religion had cleared some of the ground. But much more remained to be done. The egoism of the private property system and the alienation of man from his labor and from the world constituted a problem with which Marx wrestled.

At this time Bruno Bauer wrote two articles raising the question of how man was to free himself, and incidentally attacking the Jews, who he said were farther from freedom than the Christians because they remained immured in their nationalistic religion while the Christians at least aspired to a universal religion.[12] It is interesting that Bauer referred to the Jews as a nationality, but his argument would seem to apply equally to any other ethnocentric group.

Marx replied to Bauer's articles in one of his own entitled "Zur Judenfrage." It seems to be remembered today chiefly for its free-swinging style, of which the Jews were ironically the victims (Marx came of Jewish stock). But the main part of the argument has little to do with the Jews. Religion, in Hegel's works, had been a unifying factor. This might have been true in an earlier age, said Marx; but the type of Christianity that has developed in modern times has had just the opposite effect:

Only under the rule of Christianity, which externalizes all human relationships—national, natural, moral and theoretical—could bourgeois society detach itself entirely from the sphere of the state, destroy all those bonds that link men as a species, replace them with egotism and the demands of self-interest, and dissolve the human world into a world of atomized and mutually hostile individuals.[13]

Man's Relation to the State and the Nation

The essentially anarchic system of private property, in which each man is everyone else's enemy, cannot be held together, said Marx, by the state, which is itself the creation of the bourgeoisie and does its bidding. In the name of freedom the modern state has created new bonds, in that it gives legal sanction to the system of private property, and emphasizes the self-alienation of man that the system entails.

The state is man in his relation to the government, said Marx, but this relationship is "unreal, chimerical." Marx developed this idea further in a series of essays written jointly with Engels between September, 1845, and November, 1846, the full text of which has only recently become available in English, under the title *The German Ideology*. In it we read:

Just because individuals seek *only* their particular interest, which for them does not coincide with their communal interest (in fact the general is the illusory form of communal life), the latter will be imposed on them as an interest "alien" to them and "independent" of them, as in its turn a particular, peculiar "general" interest, or they themselves must remain within this discord, as in democracy.[14]

Elsewhere *The German Ideology* characterizes the state (every state) as a "substitute for community," or as an "illusory community."[15] The road to emancipation, said Marx, is to abolish the egoistic system of private property, and to substitute common ownership; but this change can only be brought about through the revolutionary action of the proletariat. A true community (*Gemeinschaft*) can be realized only when classes have been abolished and the state as such has disappeared. Along with classes will disappear other subgroups such as nationalities:

> The communist revolution . . . abolishes the rule of all classes with the classes themselves, because it is carried through by the class which no longer counts as a class in society . . . and is in itself the expression of the dissolution of all classes, nationalities, etc., within present society.[16]*

Did Marx think of the nation as identical with the state? Sometimes it seems so, since he occasionally used the term "nation" to refer to the nation-state of his era. But while Marx was calling for the abolition of the state, which he looked on as a coercive, class-dominated mechanism, and while he expected, as just noted, that nationalities would be absorbed in the community after classes were abolished, he always refused to be drawn into any attack on the nation as such.† On the contrary, he insisted that nationalism was the necessary condition and prerequisite for the true internationalism which he envisaged for the future.

Even if it were freed of the incubus of the class state with its illusory solidarity, would not society need some organizing principle which could embody real solidarity under communism? What would be the political unit—assuming some such unit to be necessary—which would replace the state when the state had withered away?

Was Marx perhaps suggesting an answer to this question when he mentioned, in the little-noticed passage quoted above,

---

* Marx here speaks as if the working class already dissolves the several nationalities within itself in the existing society, and the constant effort of Marxists like Lenin was to make this aspiration an actuality (see Chapter VIII). To the extent that this dissolution was not accomplished before the proletarian revolution, we take this passage to mean that nationalities would be absorbed soon after.

† See below, p. 17.

the bonds—*national*, natural, moral and theoretical—that link man as a species? Would it not be in the spirit of Marx to look on the nation—not the nation-state, but the nation without the exploitative aspects of the state—as the possible organizational form of the future?

Of course, we should avoid constructing an elaborate super-structure on an admittedly exiguous base. It is not even clear that Marx intended any theory of the nation at all. But it is surely high time that Marxists face up to the question, which was barely touched on by Marx and Lenin, of what is supposed to remain when the state withers away. If not the classless nation, then what?

Free-Trade "Internationalism" vs. Nationalist Protectionism

The decade in which Marx and Engels formed their ideas concerning nationalism and nationality was the decade in which the doctrine of free trade reached its peak intellectually and politically. Even a protectionist economist like Friedrich List, who propounded his doctrine of the need of manufacturing industries for a protected home market, was obliged to pay lip-service to free trade as an ultimate ideal. The decade of the 1840's saw England repeal her corn laws, and by this time the philosophy of Adam Smith (which had been popularized by Bastiat and J. B. Say) had made such headway in France that Napoleon III later made some show of adopting the same economic philosophy as England.

Adam Smith, whose ideas thus seemed to have swept the board, was of course also the great partisan of the doctrine of *laissez-faire*, which had originated in France and was still immensely popular there. The tremendous advances of England under the degree of *laissez-faire* then practiced—much more than in any other country—seemed to stamp this as the political philosophy of the future, as free trade was the progressive economic philosophy of the day.

These ideas had their effect on Marx and Engels. Not that

they were free-traders of the school of Cobden and Bright; on
the contrary, they supported the Chartist rivals of that school,
and their chagrin was profound when the British working class
abandoned Chartism and accepted the leadership of the free-
traders. But Marx could not see the advantage of protectionism
either. He contended that under free trade wages would sink
to, or remain at, subsistence level, by the doctrine of the
classical economists themselves, and so he declared that he
favored free trade—in effect, as a means of showing the futility
for the workers of trying to advance under capitalism.[17] Engels
accepted the "infant-industries" argument for countries like
Germany and the United States, but thought that after, say,
25 years they would do better to adopt a system of free trade.[18]
Thus Marx and Engels lacked one of the motives for boosting
nationalism that affected some other thinkers, namely a belief
in the system of neo-mercantilism, or economic nationalism.

Marx, while not accepting any economic system as "natural"
in the sense used by the classical economists, still regarded a
competitive economy as the most advanced form of capitalism;
and the analysis in *Capital* of the capitalist economy is based
on the purest *laissez-faire* assumptions. For the "national"
economy of List, with its protective tariffs, its subsidies and
regulations, and its creation of domestic monopolies, Marx had
nothing but contempt. That system was outmoded; France and
England had passed through it in the 17th and 18th centuries,
and here was poor Germany just getting ready to adopt it.
Marx was in favor of the *Zollverein* (customs union)—by
means of which Prussia had united with many of the small
German states economically in a kind of common market many
years before it absorbed them politically—for the *Zollverein*
extended the market and broke down feudal restrictions. But
in other respects the "system of national economy" ties society
up in knots, in Marx's view, knots which the English and
French had been trying to untie for decades. In one of those
epigrams which he loved so well, Marx wrote that in France
and England the problem is "political economy or the rule of

society over wealth," whereas in Germany it is "national economy or the mastery of private property over nationality."[19]

The philosophy underlying the *Communist Manifesto* (1848) assumes that the trend toward free trade is in effect irreversible. The bourgeoisie will continue to break down barriers and extend the world market; it will ever draw new peoples into the ambit of capitalism. But the proletariat will not share in the gains of this development, or will share only inadequately and incompletely. Beginning with the most advanced countries, the working class will demand a larger share for itself; eventually, owing to the inability of the capitalist system to do other than act as the tool of the bourgeoisie, the system will develop fatal weaknesses and the working class of the advanced countries will lead the colonial peoples into socialism and freedom.

History decided otherwise. Not the free trade of England but the protectionism of Germany won the day at least temporarily. After Germany and the United States had developed their industries to the point where they could challenge England's dominance of the world market, England itself reverted tamely to protectionism. Yet the world market continued to develop; and some doctrinaire Marxists, like Kautsky, continued to preach the virtues of free trade and a kind of bourgeois version of pseudo-internationalism, long after it had become evident that this was not the "wave of the future." Before modern Marxism could cope seriously with the problem of nationalism, it had to rework this part of Marx's theory completely.

Marx's acceptance—grudging, it is true—of the principle of free trade, and his description of the protective tariff system as an antiquated reactionary system (in the early 1840's) arose out of the conditions obtaining at that time. The nation-state was being soft-pedaled or disregarded while business (the bourgeoisie) was given full credit for whatever happened. Marx's conception of the nation was colored by this environment.

The expansion of trade over the whole world, the "breaking down of barriers" and the incorporation of backward areas into the world market, the spread of western civilization over the world—these are enthusiastically described in the *Communist Manifesto* but are said to be the work, not of the advanced peoples as such, much less of their respective governments, but of the bourgeoisie. The state is hardly mentioned. Hence the class struggle is described as taking place on an international scale, without much reference to the intervention of the political power. The common action of the bourgeoisie in opposition to the international working class is mentioned as a major reason for the international organization of the proletariat. The authors add, more or less as an after-thought, that "since the proletariat must first of all acquire political supremacy, must constitute itself the nation, it is, so far, itself national, though not in the bourgeois sense of the word," and "the proletariat of each country must, of course, first of all settle matters with its own bourgeoisie." More important, in the view of Marx and Engels, was the statement that "united action, of the leading countries at least, is one of the first conditions for the emancipation of the proletariat."

This emancipation, Marx and Engels fully believed, might take place *at any time*—the sooner the better. Whenever they saw a commercial crisis approaching, or the (capitalist) governments of Europe seemed to be getting into deep trouble, Marx and Engels asked each other whether *this* was to be the "final conflict." As late as 1890, Engels still expected the German workers to take over power before he died, say by 1900. Furthermore, when the proletariat did "acquire political supremacy" this would be for the purpose, not of exercising "hegemony" within the capitalist state, as Rosdolsky has recently expressed it, not of "taking a dominant position" in state and nation, as the social-patriot Cunow put it during the First World War, but of abolishing classes, constituting itself the nation, and setting up its own dictatorship, as described by Marx in his *Critique of the Gotha Programme*.[20]

Marx and Engels in the *Manifesto* called on the workers to unite internationally in order the more effectively to combat the international organization of the capitalists.

It is no doubt true that in certain circumstances the capitalist nations may unite to suppress a working-class movement, as in the case of the Paris Commune, or the Russian Revolution. But more usually the capitalists are divided into warring nation-states, each of which seeks (as Marx and Engels noted) to enlist the workers of its respective country in its international adventures.

The "internationalism" brought about by the bourgeoisie was for Marx and Engels a very partial internationalization of certain parts of the culture—nothing more. True internationalism, they contended, can come about only through the victory of the proletariat in the leading countries, when national differences will cease to be important. Marx scouted the idea that the capitalist nations might get together and agree to abolish war, or to disarm, or even to exploit the backward areas more efficiently. Such internationalism is impossible, a mirage.

Marx and Engels contended that it was only the proletariat that could make an end of national divisions and conflicts of peoples and create true internationalism in the world: "In proportion as the exploitation of one individual by another is ended, is the exploitation of one nation by another ended too. . . . With the end of the class war within a nation the hostile attitude of nations to one another disappears."[21]

Workers' Attitude to the "Fatherland"

The statement in the *Manifesto* that "the workers have no fatherland"[22] has been interpreted by some, like Jean Jaurès, as mere sarcastic rhetoric. If taken seriously it is susceptible of at least three different interpretations.

First, it may refer to the proposition that the proletarian under capitalism is so downtrodden and degraded that he is incapable of absorbing, much less developing, any national culture at all. The general misery has no specific national character: "Laws, morality, religion are for him so many bourgeois prejudices, behind which lurk in ambush just as many bourgeois interests."[23]

Second—and this is the context in which the passage actually occurs—it may mean that the workers have no stake in the country until they control it or at least have a voice in its control. This idea was developed at some length by Villegardelle in a book which appeared just before the *Manifesto* was drafted; Marx read the book and made notes on it. The second proposition is not inconsistent with the first, and indeed both ideas are developed simultaneously by Villegardelle.[24] But they are logically distinct.

In these days it may seem strange that the working class should be disaffected and unpatriotic, but the idea is not in itself unreasonable; everything turns on the degree of exploitation. The American Negro is a case in point.

Many white people were unaware of the extent of sympathy for the Japanese which existed among the American Negroes at the beginning of the Second World War. More recently, in 1963, a select group of American Negroes astounded and shocked Attorney General Robert Kennedy by stating that it would be difficult to persuade many Negroes to fight for the U.S. against Cuba. James Baldwin quoted a Negro boy in San Francisco as saying, "I got no country. I got no flag."[25]

If this interpretation is given to the *Manifesto*'s proposition, then the corollary later drawn by Bernstein is hard to avoid. He wrote in 1896:

The saying that the worker has no fatherland is modified from that moment and in that degree that he participates as fully equal citizen in the control of the government and the making of his country's laws, and can influence its institutions according to his wishes.[26]

Third, the proposition that "the workers have no fatherland" may mean that the class-conscious worker feels himself to be more a member of the working class than an Englishman, a Frenchman, a German or a Russian. This interpretation had some currency in Germany in the 1920's, when the slogan, "The Soviet Union is the workers' fatherland," was frequently heard. Bakunin wrote to Marx in 1868: "My fatherland is now the International."[27]* This interpretation also is consistent with the wording of the *Manifesto*, which emphasizes at one point, "United action at least of the civilized countries is one of the first conditions of its [the proletariat's] liberation."

Bloom feels quite certain that Marx and Engels did not intend to imply that proletarian internationalism excluded a decent affection for one's own country, even if not for the bourgeois version of it.[28]

In order to understand what Marx and Engels meant by proletarian internationalism it is necessary to keep several points in mind.

First, internationalism is not cosmopolitanism; it is based on nations. If the nations did not exist, they would have to be created. Great national states in Europe, wrote Engels, are "the unavoidable precondition for the harmonious international cooperation of the peoples" under the rule of the proletariat.[29]

Second, much depends on the timing and sequence of events. Marx and Engels hoped and expected to see socialism in their time, beginning with the most advanced nations, economically speaking; but with the failure of the revolutions of 1848 and later of the Paris Commune of 1871, they became resigned to what they had considered all along as a possibility—namely, that other countries would have to pass through the stage of capitalism before arriving at socialism.† As between capitalism and pre-capitalist feudalism or barbarism, there was simply no choice at all in their view; capitalism with all its faults was

* Bakunin's sincerity has been questioned; see Boris Nicolaievsky & Otto Maenchen-Helfen, *Karl Marx: Man and Fighter* (1936), p. 289. On Bakunin see further Chapter II, below. But many workers, members of the First International, could have held and probably did hold the point of view claimed by Bakunin.

† On this point see further below, Chapter III.

immeasurably superior, if only because of the way it revolutionized production.

Third, internationalism did not necessarily imply national equality. Marx and Engels early showed a preference for large states as against smaller, because the large internal market represented a more progressive form and gave the large countries not only greater power but greater viability and a more advanced system of production. Marx and Engels were impatient with small nations and would-be nations that stood in the way of economic progress as they saw it. Engels at one time had a brief period of belief in the rights of small nationalities, but Marx was never interested in the principle of self-determination as such,[30] and Engels eventually favored stronger countries against weaker in a positively breathtaking manner.

Fourth, and consistent with the previous idea, the internationalism contemplated by Marx and Engels was an internationalism of the advanced industrial nations. For many years they defended the ruthless expansion of imperialism, provided only that it brought economic development in its wake.*

Proletarian internationalism was a system in which such words as freedom, equality, democracy, justice and morality would have real meaning for the workingman. But devoid of socialist content these "eternal principles" were a sham and a delusion, and Marx and Engels never tired of denouncing the hypocrisy of the bourgeoisie, whose morality rested on a foundation of exploitation and brutality. If the policies that Marx and Engels advocated seemed to fly in the face of some one of these "eternal" principles, their answer was that sacrifices are sometimes necessary; the important thing is to have a correct policy and follow it regardless. Since nationalism was not one of the principles that they recognized as valid for its own sake, they were prepared to sacrifice it at any point in the interests of the larger policy.

* See Chapter III, below.

Do the "eternal principles" have validity in the long run? The answer is that they do, and Marx and Engels never pretended otherwise. They contended that they were fighting, not against the great principles, but for them.

What then of the principle of nationalism? Is it eternal, as Hegel implied?

By no means. Not only is it not eternal, it is not even consistent with the principles listed above. On the allied principle of nationality, a distinguished contemporary of Marx and Engels, a Roman Catholic and vigorous anti-socialist, Lord Acton, wrote in 1862:

The theory of nationality is a retrograde step in history. . . . In proclaiming the supremacy of the rights of nationality, the system of democratic equality goes beyond its own extreme boundary, and falls into contradiction with itself. . . . The principle of nationality is a confutation of democracy, because it sets limits to the exercise of the popular will, and substitutes for it a higher principle. . . . Nationality does not aim either at liberty or prosperity, both of which it sacrifices to the imperative necessity of making the nation the mold and measure of the State. Its course will be marked by material and moral ruin.[31]

Positive Aspects of Nationalism

This sweeping condemnation found no echo in the writings of Marx and Engels. Not only was their attitude to the nationalist aspirations of oppressed peoples generally sympathetic, but they recognized that nations were necessary and desirable, and had certain essential functions to perform. The nation is not only the bearer of culture, but it is a unifying influence around which men's efforts may suitably crystallize for the benefit of man's individual and collective development. When Marx and Engels wrote of the "withering away of the state," they had in mind the state as coercive mechanism, the organ of a dominating class. The *nation*, in their view, should survive as the unit around which would be built the international society of the future.

It remained to work out in detail the conditions and situations in which the principle of nationalism and the principle of socialism coincided, at least temporarily. Engels developed his position in 1845 in connection with a gathering in London, where English, French, German, Italian, Spanish, Polish, and Swiss democrats and workers celebrated the anniversary of the establishment of the French republic in 1792. In an enthusiastic article on this meeting for a German paper, Engels begins by telling off the German "true socialists" who sought to dilute and spoil French socialism and the English labor movement with German-philosophical phrases. This literary "clique," he said, had sought to dispose of nationality and the national question for good and all, saying: "Of what importance is the nation? Of what importance is the French republic?" Engels answered them:

Be calm, dear Germany! The nation and the French republic are of great importance to us.

The brotherhood of nations, as it is now everywhere practiced by the most radical political party in contrast with the old, elemental national egoism and hypocritical private-egotistic cosmopolitanism of free trade, is worth more than all the German theories on "true socialism."

The brotherhood of nations under the flag of *modern democracy*, as it originated in the French Revolution and has developed in French communism and English Chartism, shows that the masses and their defenders know better what the score is than does German theory. . . .

In truth the words democracy and brotherhood of nations have at present a social sense, and contain a political meaning. . . . *Democracy today means communism.* . . . Democracy has become a proletarian principle, a principle of the masses. . . . Finally, the brotherhood of nations has today more than ever a social significance. The imaginings of a European republic and universal peace through a political organization have become as ridiculous as the phrases about brotherhood of nations under the aegis of universal free trade; and while all chimerical sentimentalities of this sort are falling out of use, the proletarians of all countries, without too much fuss, are beginning *to practice true brotherhood* under the banner of communistic democracy. The proletarians are the only ones who can really do this; for the bourgeoisie has special interests in each country, and since these interests are for them the most important thing, they can never advance beyond nationalism.[32]

This statement by Engels shows clearly that he considered that the interests of the proletariat lay, not in assisting the business elements in their respective countries to gain special advantages at the expense of other countries and peoples, but in establishing socialism at the earliest feasible moment. The greater productivity of socialism as a system would be enhanced by the combination of economic forces made possible through proletarian internationalism. The policy to be followed by the workers in each country is that which will most advance the cause of the proletarian revolution. However, the bourgeois state is not something that can be disregarded; there is no trace of that "national nihilism" which was later to bedevil the Second International.

In 1866 certain French members of the First International announced that the nation as an idea was obsolete: the nations should be dissolved into little "groups" which would then form an "association" in place of the State. Marx heaped scorn and ridicule on their idea.[33]

Not only is the existence of nations a prerequisite for internationalism—it is a prerequisite for socialism, too, said Engels. The socialist polity must be viable; it must be large. Furthermore, a subjugated people that is large enough to be constituted into a state with prospects of survival must first concentrate on winning its independence; it cannot think about anything else until this all-important goal has been gained. With special reference to Poland, Engels wrote to Kautsky on February 7, 1882:

It is historically impossible for a large people to discuss seriously any internal questions as long as its national independence is lacking. . . . An international movement of the proletariat is in general only possible between independent nations. . . . To get rid of national oppression is the basic condition of all healthy and free development. . . .

It is not our job to hold back the Poles from efforts to win the conditions of their future development, or to tell them that from the international standpoint their national independence is an entirely secondary matter, when it is on the contrary the condition of all international collaboration.[34]*

Nationalism in the Foreign Policy of Marx and Engels

Marx and Engels, like their contemporary Bakunin, were in a sense protected against unconsciously adopting a nationalist point of view by the fact that they spent most of their mature lives as expatriates. Marx had been banished from his homeland, but even so the Prussian police at first pursued him with demands for his extradition; so in order to get a respite from their attentions Marx renounced his Prussian citizenship even before he found a safe and lasting refuge in England. Engels had family and business connections in Manchester and easily adapted to a new life there, but neither of the two was in any danger of becoming an English nationalist. Their theory was, as Engels pointed out, an international product; it was an amalgam of German philosophy, English political economy, and French socialism. Marx retained a lively interest in German affairs and for many years hoped to return there, but his judgments on international politics were at all times motivated by other values and aims than a desire to see Germany come out ahead.

When they began their active political work together, Marx and Engels were immediately confronted with the demands of certain national groups for freedom from their foreign oppressors. Just as they opposed oppression of one class by another, so they opposed oppression of one people or nation by another. Engels went through a period when he sympathized with the South Slavs, held in subjugation by the Austrians and the Hungarians, no less than with the Poles, who were suppressed

---

* Engels did not, of course, include small nationalities in this generalization, not even as important a group as the South Slavs. But as a statement of principle this passage deserves more notice than it has yet received.

by the Germans, the Austrians, and the Russians. The ending of national oppression was advocated for the benefit, not only of the oppressed, but of the oppressors as well. In 1847 Engels launched the slogan: "A nation cannot be free and at the same time continue to oppress other nations."[35] He demanded the freedom of Poland in the interests of German freedom. This same idea was later to be given much wider currency when Marx, as Secretary of the International Workingmen's Association, drafted the famous letter to Lincoln on the freeing of the slaves.*

However, the manner in which oppressed peoples might obtain their freedom was to be determined on the basis of the situation at the time. Under certain circumstances it might even benefit a backward people to be civilized by an advanced nation exercising political or economic control over its destinies. It is impossible to understand the attitude of Marx and Engels to specific situations without studying the various factors involved.

At first, in 1847, Marx and Engels fully expected the socialist revolution to take place very shortly, and demands for national liberation were considered from that point of view. Although they were consistent advocates of Polish independence, they did not, in 1847, advise the Poles to organize a national uprising. The reason was not the fact that such uprisings had been attempted in Russian Poland in 1830 and in Austrian Poland in 1846, and had failed miserably. It was that their thinking had been running along quite other lines—those of proletarian internationalism. So, in the meeting referred to, Marx gave the verdict: "Poland is to be freed not in Poland but in England."[36] How had he reached this conclusion, which at first sight seems at variance with his other famous slogan: "The freeing of the workers can only be carried out by the workers themselves"? Why should not this same slogan be applied, *mutatis mutandis*, to national liberation struggles?

Of all countries, said Marx, England is the one in which the

* On the case of Ireland and the British workers, see Chapter III.

contradiction between proletariat and bourgeoisie is the most developed. Thus the victory of the English proletariat over the English bourgeoisie is decisive for the victory of all oppressed against their oppressors. Let the British workers win their struggle and the old system would collapse on an international scale. Marx concluded: "You Chartists do not have to express pious wishes about the freedom of nations. Defeat your domestic enemies and you will then have the proud consciousness of having defeated the whole of the old society."[37]

But if Marx and Engels professed an internationalist philosophy, in specific judgments they may still have been influenced, especially in their early work, by points of view absorbed from their early environment. They may have been unconscious nationalists.

Their attitudes on nationalism came to a focus at the time of the revolutions of 1848; and to the opinions then expressed they later adhered. The best way to get an idea of their approach to particular problems of nationalism is to study the foreign policy of the *Neue Rheinische Zeitung*, of which Marx was the editor-in-chief and Engels the foreign editor in the revolutionary months of 1848.*

The year 1848 saw the final breakup of the "Congress system" devised by Metternich at Vienna in 1815. The reactionary regimes installed throughout Europe at the conclusion of the Napoleonic wars had teetered before, but in 1848 there seemed to be a real possibility that they would all collapse, one after the other. When Metternich fell and fled to England, a round of revolutions seemed to have started.

Marx and Engels believed that the socialist revolution would be made by the working class, meaning the class of wage-earners evoked by modern capitalism. Since England was the

---

* The foreign policy of the *Neue Rheinische Zeitung* has been analyzed in detail by Roman Rosdolsky in "Friedrich Engels und das Problem der 'Geschichtslosen Völker,'" *Archiv für Sozialgeschichte*, Bd. 4 (Hannover, 1964), pp. 87–282. Also excellent is the treatment by A. S. de Leeuw, *Het Socialisme en de Natie* (Amsterdam, 1939), pp. 56 ff.

most advanced industrial country and had the largest and most significant working class, they expected all through the 1840's that the Chartists would give the lead to the revolutionaries of Europe. When the Chartists instead lost the leadership of the working class to the free-traders, Marx and Engels still thought that the French workers, with their revolutionary tradition and their techniques of street-fighting, would pick up where Babeuf had left off and bring the proletarian revolution to France. The *Communist Manifesto* was intended for use in the uprising which was anticipated in 1848 in Paris and in other countries. When the French movement took a different course from what they had expected and hoped for, they pinned their hopes on Central and Eastern Europe.

Here, however, the situation was rather different from that in France and England. In the first place, capitalism and the factory system were too little developed to have created an urban proletariat of any size except in a few cities. Manual workers indeed there were; but the decisive strata of the handworkers were artisans, relics of the Middle Ages and not very advanced in their point of view. There was also a socialist movement, but it was dominated by middle-class intellectuals such as Marx and Engels themselves, and the kind of communism that flourished among them and among certain small groups of handworkers was largely of the Utopian variety, divorced from the main stream of history. At the same time the bourgeoisie—instead of being securely in the saddle as in England and, to a degree, in France—was in central Europe still overshadowed by the landed nobility and the army, which had retained some of their privileges and whose power constituted a fetter on the full development of capitalism. Marx and Engels realized the impossibility of making a proletarian revolution on the narrow basis that then existed, and advised the workers to help the middle class sweep away the feudal remnants and only later, in the relatively freer air of a bourgeois republic, to organize and carry through the proletarian revolution.

The other important point that distinguished Central European problems from those of France and England was the national question, which was bound to be in the front of peoples' minds as long as the Poles and other Slavs were held in subjection, and Germany and Italy were not unified. The policy of the *Neue Rheinische Zeitung*, as the extreme left wing of the democratic party, was to unify Germany under the leadership of the progressive bourgeoisie rather than under that of militarist Prussia or reactionary Austria.

Tsarist Russia was at this time the "gendarme of Europe"; Russian troops were being used to crush democratic revolutions and perpetuate the rule of reaction. Hungary was shortly to furnish an example of a progressive government suppressed by the Russians, and everybody knew that the same thing could happen to a Germany that set up a progressive democratic government. Accepting this probability, Marx and Engels sought to bring about a war between Germany and Russia, since a war against Russia would mobilize all the progressive forces in Germany and enable them to seize leadership. In the war with Russia the Poles were to be allies, with their freedom and independence as one of the goals. As explained by Engels many years later:

The petty-bourgeois democratic movement was then divided into two parts: the North-German, which would have accepted a democratic Prussian kaiser with pleasure; and the South-German, then under the leadership of Baden, which sought to make Germany into a federative republic on the model of Switzerland. We had to oppose both of them. Both the Prussianization of Germany and the perpetuation of the small-state confusion were against the interests of the proletariat. These interests called for uniting Germany at last into a nation, which alone could set up, free from all small-spirited survivals, the lists in which the bourgeoisie and the proletariat could try their strength. But these interests forbade equally the formation of a Prussian hegemony; the Prussian state with all its institutions, its tradition and its dynasty was precisely the first serious domestic enemy which the German revolution had to defeat; besides, Prussia could only unite Germany by tearing Germany in pieces—by excluding German Austria. Dissolution of the

Prussian state, dividing up of the Austrian state, the true uniting of Germany as a republic—we could have no other revolutionary program, and this was to be accomplished by war against Russia and only by that.[38]

Marx and Engels, then, favored splitting up the Austro-Hungarian monarchy, with the Austrians, the Czechs and neighboring groups going into an enlarged and progressive Germany, the Poles in Galicia going to a reconstituted Poland, and the Hungarians forming an independent state together with adjacent nationalities.

The other major point in the foreign policy of the *Neue Rheinische Zeitung* was an uncompromising opposition to Panslavism, the movement which the Russian Tsar was sponsoring in order to secure the leadership of the Slavs in Central Europe and the Balkans. Bakunin had no more use for the Tsar and his government than had Marx or Engels, but Bakunin's different approach to the question of Panslavism brought on a major debate in which the whole question of nationalism got a working over.

Postscript

Heinrich Cunow, writing during the First World War, tried to maintain that Marx and Engels were really saying in the *Manifesto* that the workers *do* have a nation, or at least that they will have one when they have "constituted themselves the nation," even without the establishment of socialism.

The relevant passage is: "Since the proletariat must first of all acquire political supremacy, must constitute itself the nation, it is, so far, itself national, though not in the bourgeois sense of the word."

Lenin took this passage to mean that *in the early stages of capitalist development* the workers become strong by consolidating their forces, by developing themselves as a nation (though not in the bourgeois sense of the word). But as the development of capitalism breaks down national boundaries, the workers develop class consciousness in preference to national consciousness, and the workers more and more "have no fatherland."

Rosdolsky points out that Cunow's interpretation overlooks the phrase "*so far,* national"—the workers are national only insofar as they have constituted themselves as a nation; they are not expected to remain national forever. But how can the workers have no country, and yet, after acquiring power, remain "so far, national"?

The answer is to be found, says Rosdolsky, in an analysis of the terms used for "nation" and "nationality." The former term is used by Marx and Engels to refer to the people of a sovereign state, while the latter is used for the "historyless peoples" who have a language and a common background but no state. Marx and Engels approved of the "national" struggle of the workers in a certain sense, but disapproved of the "nationality." The struggle of the proletariat for power can only be successful if it is organized on a *national* basis instead of as numerous local struggles. The "national" struggle is equated with the class struggle and is approved *in that form.*

Rosdolsky slips on one point. He speaks of the proletariat rising to be "the leading class of the nation," as having "hegemony" after its victory. It is not stated where these passages are to be found in the writings of Marx and Engels. It seems clear from the wording of the *Manifesto* that when the proletariat "acquires political supremacy" and "constitutes itself the nation," it is expected to do so by emerging triumphant in the class struggle, and by abolishing the bourgeoisie as a class. There is then only one class, the working class, and it will proceed to abolish national distinctions even faster than this has been taking place under capitalism.

Cunow was attempting to salvage the idea that the workers would continue their allegiance to the (capitalist) state even after they had won political power within it. This seems natural enough if the workers forget about the socialist revolution. But that was not what Marx and Engels had in mind, and Marxists of a later age cannot attribute this idea to them. Rosdolsky is correct in thinking that Marx and Engels looked on the socialist state as a transition stage on the way to the classless world of the future. But the workers cannot "constitute themselves the nation" without abolishing classes. That would be a contradiction in terms.*

* See Rosdolsky in *Science and Society*, vol. XXIX, No. 3 (Summer, 1965), 330–337. The quote from Lenin is from *The Teachings of Karl Marx* (1930), p. 31.

II

MARX AND ENGELS:

DIFFERENCES WITH BAKUNIN AND LASSALLE

WHILE MARX AND ENGELS differed from Bakunin and Lassalle on various other points of tactics and philosophy, their major split with both men was on the question of nationalism. Marxists have understandably taken the part of the founders of scientific socialism and have sometimes done less than justice to their opponents. Bakunin particularly had some points which Lenin was afterwards constrained to adopt. But Bakunin was far from being right on all counts.

A polemic between Engels and Bakunin began in 1848 and continued off and on for many years. Engels favored what has been called a "West European" solution to the nationality problem of Eastern Europe. He pointed out that, in the national unification of France, the various provinces had been obliged to drop their several dialects and adopt the language of the center; at the same time, the Anglo-Saxon language which developed in England had spread to cover most of Great Britain. This trend he welcomed since it assisted the growth of large economic units.

In the middle of the nineteenth century the Slavs of Central and Southeastern Europe were being held in subjection. The Czechs, in Bohemia, had no access to the state offices, which were monopolized by the Südeten Germans and the Austrians. The Croatians were governed by the Magyars. The Turks still retained jurisdiction over some millions of Slavs in the Balkans. The Poles were in bondage to the Prussians, the Austrians, and their fellow Slavs, the Russians.

In each of these areas the ruling nationality insisted on the use of its own language for the transaction of official business. This was a grievance primarily of the Slavs of the lower middle class who were not bilingual and who might otherwise have hoped to gain a share in administration. The poorer classes found themselves at a disadvantage because the courts and public authorities in general used a language other than that of the proletariat. The peasants for their part were by no means free of feudal dues and exactions. The economic or class division frequently corresponded to an ethnic (nationality) division, as when the peasants were of Slavic stock and the landowners were Teutons, Magyars, or Turks. Sometimes the peasants and landowners were of the same stock; but where they were not, "it was the national question that made the economic question intolerable."

When towns had grown up in the Slavic areas of Central Europe in the 13th and 14th centuries, the craftsmen and artisans had come largely from Germany, and the urban middle class in these areas was still heavily Germanic in the 19th century. The movement of Germans and Jews into Poland had been deliberately fostered by the Polish king, who took this method of building up and modernizing the country.

The renewed interest in Slavic literature and history that was led in Bohemia, for example, by Palacky, thus had an economic base, though it took the form of a cultural revival with emphasis on development of Slavic institutions of learning and folk arts. This resurgence of ancient nationalities or birth of modern ones was not confined to Eastern Europe; it affected Ireland, Catalonia, the Basque country, and even Provence, and eventually the submerged nationalities of Asia, Africa, Mexico and Peru. It was a world movement.

The Russian Tsar sought to cash in on the Slavic revival and offered himself as the protector of oppressed Slavs everywhere. Marx and Engels looked on Austria-Hungary as a barrier to the reactionary Russian Tsar and his Panslav aspirations. It would be a more effective barrier if it were ruled by the Germans and Hungarians, whom Marx and Engels considered to be the natural leaders anyway by virtue of their greater degree of civilization. The two favored the absorption of the Austro-Hungarian Slavs by the Germans and Hungarians, with "democracy as a compensation," in the same way that Southern France finally lost its separate nationality in the Revolution of 1789.[1]

The revolutions of 1848 forced Marx and Engels to take a position. While the Frankfurt Assembly was in session, in June 1848, an uprising took place in Prague, but the Austrians quickly put it down. The *Neue Rheinische Zeitung* (Marx and Engels) at that time looked on the Germans as the leaders of the democratic revolution, though the actions of the Frankfurt Assembly gave little ground for such hope; and Engels on June 18 wrote an hysterical article, not condemning the Czechs as such—he maintained that the paper had always supported Czech national aspirations—but taking the position that peaceful coexistence of the Czechs and Germans was no longer possible:

A new blood-bath is being prepared in Bohemia. The Austrian soldiery has drowned in Czechish blood the possibility for a peaceful coexistence of Bohemians and Germans. . . . No matter how the uprising ends, a war of extermination of the Germans against the Czechs remains now the only possible solution.[2]

Engels later said that he had meant not that all Czechs should be exterminated but that Czech nationhood was doomed. The reason for this gruesome outcome was, said Engels, that the Bohemians had been driven into the arms of the Russians. Therefore:

. . . their downfall is certain. In the great war between East Europe and West Europe which will break out in a short time—perhaps in a few weeks—an unhappy fate has lined up the Czechs on the side of the Russians. The Revolution will win, and the Czechs will be the first to be overcome by it.[3]

His attitude to the Croats was even more severe. The Croats were dominated in Hungary by the Magyars, whose language was the official language. The liberal Kossuth regime which came to power there in the 1848 revolution did not liberalize the nationality strictures. When the Russian army approached to upset Kossuth, sentiment among the Croats was divided. Some favored resistance, while others could not stomach fighting on the same side as their oppressors, the Magyars. The effect was to take the Croats out of the fight, and the Russian "pacification" proceeded with less than total opposition.

Engels condemned the Croats and called for "the most determined terrorism" against all the South Slavs, in which category he included also the Czechs. He meant the leaders, but this might not have been plain to the Czechs and Croats generally. The attitude of the *NRZ* to nationality questions at this time is summarized by Rosdolsky as follows:

The fact of national oppression *alone* does not by any means create a duty for democracy to take the part of the oppressed nationality; such a duty emerges only when the political actions of this nationality have a revolutionary character and thus serve the special interests of democracy; otherwise the "so-called" national movement can have no claim to protection.[4]

This is a strong statement—perhaps too strong. But in any case, Marx and Engels separately modified their position on this point during the 1850's. We shall presently cite instances of each man separately taking the part of oppressed nationalities *as such*, not merely when their political actions had a revolutionary character.

Engels has been criticized severely for the *NRZ*'s attitude on the South Slavs, for which Marx as editor was of course jointly responsible. In the first place, Engels' whole argument hinges on his analysis of the political situation, and when this proved to be defective (the war with Russia was not joined by Germany), he was left in the position of winking at injustice in the interests of a larger good which did not and could not materialize. But a leader who winks at injustice is preparing a bed of nettles for his followers.

In the second place, Engels was working on the basis of ethnological information which proved to be inaccurate, as he himself admitted not very long afterwards.[5]

Third, Engels was using the theory of "historyless peoples," according to which peoples that have never formed a state in the past cannot be expected to form a viable state in the future. This theory was one of the weaker features of Hegel's philosophy of the state, with which theory both Marx and Engels had broken explicitly. It is the more surprising to find Engels reviving Hegel's idea so soon afterwards.

Fourth, Engels had to distort history in order to apply even this theory to the Czechs, who were by no means a people without history in Hegel's sense. Engels himself called attention in another connection to the "Czechish national peasant war under a religious flag (Hussite) against the German nobility and German imperial overlordship."[6]

Fifth, Engels attempted to justify his support of the Magyars as against the Croats on the basis that the Magyars were economically developed. In fact, they were less developed economically than the Czechs, and no more so than the Croats; they had learned their methods of agriculture, such as they were, from the Slavs in the first place. (Herman Wendel quotes Mijo Radošević to the effect that the words for agricultural implements in the Magyar language were borrowed from the Slavic.[7]) The Magyars were still pre-industrial and almost pre-commercial, as were the Poles, whom Engels also favored.[8]

The assumption that the Slavic peoples of Austria would become cat's-paws for the Russian Tsar was perfectly arbitrary. A Slavic Congress was held in Prague on May 31, 1848, attended by 340 persons, of whom 237 were Czechs and Slovaks, 42 South Slavs, 60 Poles and Ruthenians, and one Russian (Bakunin), who did not represent Tsarist Russia. Palacky in signing the call to this Congress had made clear his attitude to Tsarist Panslavism:

We are resolved to remain faithful to the hereditary house of
Habsburg-Lorraine . . . and to maintain the integrity and independence of the Empire by all means in our power. . . . We therefore reject all accusations of separatism, of Panslavism or Russian-
ism, which might be brought against us by ill-intentioned accusers.[9]

The Czech nationalist leaders of 1848 such as Palacky,
Havlicek and Rieger were thus not Panslavs; they were relatively progressive in their outlook.[10]* Rosdolsky thinks that a
few judicious concessions to their budding national aspirations
plus some overdue economic reforms would have lined them
up on the side of the revolution and against Russian reaction.
The concessions which the Magyars did make to the Croats
were too little and too late.[11]

It has usually been assumed that Engels' harsh judgment
of the Croats was due to the participation of Croatian soldiers
in the suppression of the October Vienna revolt, although
German-speaking soldiers also participated in the suppression,
and it has never been explained why he should have been so
much harder on the Slav privates than on their Germanic
officers. Later investigations have indicated that his unfavorable judgment was formed earlier. The Pest correspondent of
the *NRZ*, on whom Engels and Marx depended for their information on the situation in Hungary, presented from the beginning the point of view then characteristic of the Magyar propaganda, denying all South Slav claims to have a nationality of
their own and assuring the South Slavs that they need have no
fear.[12] The editors did not correct his point of view.

A sixth and serious criticism of the attitude of the *NRZ* is
that it supported the decision of the Vienna Reichstag (Sept.
11, 1848) to make German the only official language of that

* However, as Otto Bauer was to point out much later, the members
of this group did not rise above their class origins. Palacky was an
opponent of the unrestricted franchise, fought communism with the old
argument about the inequality of mankind, and spoke of the proletariat
as the danger of the times. Havlicek also fought against socialism, and
while he declared for the unrestricted franchise, he thought that it
should be accompanied by a property qualification. (Otto Bauer, *Die
Nationalitätenfrage und die Sozialdemokratie*, 2d ed., Vienna, 1924,
pp. 233–234.)

body. Many dozen Polish, Ukrainian and Rumanian deputies were deprived of an effective voice by this resolution, though to their credit they did manage to participate in the debates to some extent. A Galician peasant, Sawka, blamed the nobility for the fact that the peasants could speak only their own idiom; they had had no chance to go to school and learn German. In the French Revolution certain Jacobin leaders had connected the minority tongues with superstition and reaction, and these tongues had been barred in the 1893 Convention. Engels favored barring the minority tongues at Vienna; but the circumstances were different.[13]

Confronted with a difficult choice, the Czech and Croatian leadership had made a wrong decision; in fighting for the preservation of the Austro-Hungarian monarchy and against the German and Hungarian revolutions they were fighting against their own liberties. But Engels in condemning them went much farther than the occasion warranted. The Slavs had reason to mistrust the German bourgeoisie, which had a rather great-German platform; some of the German democrats even contemplated a Germanic empire extending to the Black Sea. Marx and Engels lost no opportunity to criticize and ridicule the bourgeois leadership in the Frankfurt Assembly; but they were still associated with the national-democratic fraction—as its extreme left wing—and it has been charged that they did not sufficiently dissociate themselves from its nationalistic aims, that they brought forward no positive program for the Czechs or the Croats.

Lichtheim thinks that the confusion over where they stood on the question of nationalism was a major cause of the split in the German labor ranks into a pro-Prussian and an anti-Prussian wing, which persisted until 1875.[14] This carries the criticism too far; Marx deplored the Austrophilism of Wilhelm Liebknecht and the Eisenachers no less than the Prussian nationalism of Lassalle.*

By the middle of the 19th century the South Slavs had begun

* See below, p. 87.

to penetrate the cities of Eastern Europe, though they still did
not hold skilled jobs. According to Rudolf Schlesinger, Engels'
attitude to the South Slavs gave aid and comfort to the Germans who wanted to preserve their monopoly of the skilled
jobs, and tended to line up Marxism on the conservative side
of this unprincipled struggle.[15] Surely this is a far-fetched,
tendentious charge.

As noted in the preceding chapter, Marx and Engels favored
splitting up the Austro-Hungarian monarchy, but not on the
lines ultimately adopted. They had no special objection to the
dual monarchy continuing, and considered the possibility that
it might become a unitary state through the unifying influence
of transport and trade. Thus Engels wrote in January, 1848:

The granite walls, behind which each province had defended a
separate nationality, a limited local existence, are ceasing to be an
enclosure. The products of big industry, of machines, penetrate
suddenly and almost without transportation costs into the farthest
corner of the monarchy, destroy the old hand labor, uproot the
feudal barbarism. The trade of the provinces with each other, the
trade with the civilized outside world gains a significance never
before known. . . . Participation in the total interests of the state,
in the events of the outside world becomes a necessity. Local
barbarism disappears.[16]

Marx occasionally speculated along the same lines.[17] But
when a committee of the Landtag in 1849 proposed granting
autonomy to the Croats, Slovenes and Dalmatians within the
Austro-Hungarian monarchy, the Neue Rheinische Zeitung
scornfully rejected the initiative.[18]

Rudolf Schlesinger thinks that Engels eventually retreated
somewhat from his unfavorable opinion of the South Slavs,
including the Balkan Slavs.[19] This is hard to take. As late as
1882 Engels in a letter to Bernstein reproduced all the
unfavorable judgments and defended his indefensible attitude
of 1848.[20] And in 1885 in a letter to Bebel he repeated Hegel's
slanders against the Balkan Slavs.[21] To Kautsky in 1882 he
remarked that no Slavic state in the Balkans should be allowed

to stand in the way of through rail connections between Germany and Constantinople.[22]

Engels did consider what might be the future of the Austro-Hungarian Empire in case of a victorious social revolution in Russia. In that case, he said, the dual empire, which had been held together first by the need for resisting the Turks and later through fear of domination by Russia, would disintegrate of itself.[23]

Engels considered the possibility that a new Slav state might coagulate around Serbia. He was not apparently afraid of such a state being drawn into the orbit of Panslavism; he pointed out that it would have interests opposed to those of the Russian Tsar.[24] The inability of the Turks to develop the area had been sufficiently demonstrated.

Engels' conclusions on Panslavism did not seem to follow from the data he presented. He fully recognized that the South Slavs were weak and divided:

Austrian Panslavism was destitute of the most essential elements of success. It wanted both force and unity: force, because the Panslavic party consisted of a portion of the educated classes only, and had no hold upon the masses, and withal no strength capable of resisting both the Austrian government and the German and Hungarian nationalities against which it entered the lists; unity, because its uniting principle was a mere ideal one, which, at the very first attempt at its realization, was broken up by the fact of diversity of language.[25]

Were these the dangerous elements who at a word from the Tsar would unite, according to various forecasts of both Marx and Engels, and sweep over Europe?[26]

Marx's abiding fear of Panslavism and distrust of the Russian Tsar should not, of course, be interpreted as a permanent opposition to Russia or the Russians. Thus a recent small volume, *The Russian Menace to Europe*, which reprints some of Marx's more violent attacks on Tsarist Russia as if they applied today, is simply laughable.[27] Equally amusing is the editing of another selection, *Marx vs. Russia*.[28]

Both Marx and Engels seem always to have retained a certain belief in the German civilizing mission in Eastern Europe. Engels even wavered in his devotion to the ideal of an independent Poland which he and Marx had favored in the days of the *NRZ*. In a well-known letter to Marx, Engels spoke of Poland as a *nation foutue* and after various sarcastic judgments concluded with the remark that he and Marx had not assumed any positive obligations toward Poland except the unavoidable ones.[29]

Even then, Engels was far from believing in a "master race." The Germans in the Polish towns he frequently referred to as "Spiessburgers," a term of contempt applicable to stodgy middle-class burghers in Germany. However, he lapsed into chauvinist jargon on more than one occasion. In 1852 he wrote in the *New York Tribune*:

The history of a thousand years ought to have shown the dying nationalities of the Bohemians, Carinthians, Dalmatians, etc., that if all the territory east of the Elbe and Saale had at one time been occupied by kindred Slavonians, this fact merely proved the historical tendency and the *physical and intellectual power of the German nation* to subdue and assimilate its ancient neighbors, and this tendency of absorption on the part of the Germans had always been, and still was, one of the mightiest means by which the civilization of Western Europe had been spread in the east of that continent, and that it could only cease when the process of Germanization had reached the frontier of a large, compact, unbroken nation, capable of independent national life, such as the Hungarians, and in some degree the Poles, and that therefore the natural and inevitable fate of these dying nations was to allow this process of dissolution and absorption by their stronger neighbors to complete itself.[30]

There is then a temptation to look on Marx and Engels as unsympathetic to the problems and aspirations of the small nationalities of Central and Southeastern Europe, and this is certainly the point of view of some of the best-informed of modern scholars, including some Marxist ones. The alternative view looks on Marx at any rate as understanding the national aspirations of the Slavs in that area (Central Europe and the Balkans) but believing that great-power rivalries precluded the success of any independence movement there, at least for the time being.

In order to settle this question, we may take a peep at Marx's notes on Rumania, prepared for use in connection with his articles for the *New York Tribune,* of which he was a correspondent in the 1850's. These notes are now available, written in Marx's polyglot idiom where English, French, and German are used together, sometimes all three in a single sentence. Marx was preparing background material for a discussion of the intrigues of the Tsar in the Balkans.

It becomes plain at once that Marx was deeply sympathetic to the struggles of the exploited peasants of that area. He traced the way in which they had apparently thrown off one oppressor (Turkey) only to fall prey to another (Tsarist Russia). With regard to nationalist aspirations, Marx noted how there had been a Rumanian nationalist literary movement going back to the 18th century: "When the Rumanian language was suppressed in Wallachia and Moldavia, the Rumanians of Transylvania faithfully preserved the tongue of their ancestors."[31] Does this sound like the thought of one who expected the "ruins of small nations" to be absorbed by their "more progressive" great-power neighbors? We think not. The basic sympathies of Marx were never in question, no matter how the exigencies of great-power politics might have affected his judgment of particular situations. The weak and exploited must be supported and encouraged in their resistance—this is the message that shines out from every page of these highly significant notes. Engels, by contrast, scoffed at the claim entered by the Roumans of Wallachia to have a separate nationality and a separate national existence.

Engels, who deserved many of the strictures that have been levelled against him in relation to Eastern Europe, often erred through unfamiliarity with the area rather than through concern with the fate of the Slavic inhabitants. He was even

rather shocked when he discovered that in demanding for
Poland the frontiers of 1772 he had in effect been calling for
Polish hegemony over areas not predominantly Polish. He
apologized, in effect, in a letter to Weydemeyer:

> As for the former Polish provinces this side of the Dvina and the
> Dnieper, I have not wanted to hear anything more about them ever
> since I learned that all the peasants there are Ukrainians while only
> the nobles and some of the townsmen are Poles, and that for the
> peasant there the restoration of Poland would mean merely the
> restoration of the old rule of the nobility in full force, as was the
> case in Ukrainian Galicia in 1846. In all these areas, i.e., outside the
> kingdom of Poland proper, there are hardly 500,000 Poles.*

But 13 years later Engels was back in the Polish imperialist
camp, demanding that reconstituted Poland should have the
borders of 1772!†

Engels indeed saw no particular objection to the multi-
national state as such. He wrote in 1866: "There is no country
in Europe where there are not different nationalities under the
same government . . . and in all probability it will ever remain
so." The inclusion of little sections of one nationality in a
neighboring state from which they do not wish to be separated,
is even an advantage from the point of view of the large nation,
in Engels' view, for this circumstance gives such nations con-
necting links with their neighbors, and varies the "otherwise
too monotonous uniformity of the national character."

But it would be absurd, Engels continued, to demand that
each of the numerous "small relics of peoples" in Eastern
Europe should be constituted into a separate nation. He advocated the re-union of Poles, Lithuanians, White Russians, and
Little Russians into a "state composed of at least four different
nationalities."[31a]

---

* It would seem that Rosdolsky, whose criticisms of Engels are in
general so well documented, might in fairness have called attention to
this letter. See his article, "Friedrich Engels . . .," p. 119, n. 47. Engels'
letter, written April 12, 1853, is in *Selected Correspondence* of Marx
and Engels, Moscow, n.d. (from Russian edition of 1953), p. 91.

    † See further Chapter VI, pp. 134 ff.

Bakunin on Panslavism and Self-Determination

Bakunin had his own ideas on Panslavism. He launched the idea of democratizing Russia and freeing the Slavs in the rest of Europe from their fetters. The result would be a kind of "democratic Panslavism." The Slavs of Central and South-eastern Europe instead of losing their Slavism would be united with their fellow Slavs of Eastern Europe in a democratic federation.

Bakunin came out four-square for the principle of self-determination. His point of departure was ostensibly much the same as that of Marx and Engels. Where Engels had said: "A nation cannot be free and at the same time continue to oppress other nations" (Nov. 29, 1847), Bakunin in his *Aufruf an die Slawen* (Köthen, 1848) wrote: "The welfare of the nations is never assured as long as anywhere in Europe one single people is living in oppression."[32] Since the essence of communism is freedom from oppression and the ending of exploitation, Bakunin in calling for self-determination was in a way applying the principle of standing up for the underdog more consistently than Marx and Engels themselves. But he did so in curiously atavistic fashion: in the name of "natural rights." He declared for the dissolution of all old empires constituted by force, and in their place he sought to erect a federation of European republics:

Down with the artificial boundaries which have been forcibly erected by despotic congresses according to so-called historical, geographical, strategic necessities! There should no longer be any other barriers between the nations but those corresponding to nature, to justice and those drawn in a democratic sense which the sovereign will of the people themselves denotes on the basis of their national qualities.[33]

In the future free society envisioned by Bakunin, the state as a coercive political mechanism would disappear. Nations would indeed exist, but as cultural and economic entities they would not have the mechanism or the facilities to repress other

nations. Patriotism would survive, and it would produce interesting and valuable diversity; but man's true loyalty would be
to humanity as a whole.[34]

The effect of a democratic Panslav movement would of
course be to free the South Slavs and the Czechs from Magyar,
Austrian and Turkish domination. However, Bakunin was not
in favor of a new domination by even a changed Russia. He
wrote in 1862:

> I demand only one thing: that to each people, to each large or
> small tribe or race should be accorded the right to act according to
> its wishes. If a people wishes to amalgamate with the Russians or
> with the Poles, let it amalgamate with them. Does it wish to be an
> independent member of a Polish or Russian joint Slavic federation?
> It should be permitted to become such. Finally, does it wish to
> separate itself completely from all of them and live in a completely
> independent state? So let it in God's name be separated.[35]

Marx and Engels were not likely to be stirred by appeals "in
God's name," nor were their followers. But, further, both Marx
and Engels from their early years had been impatient with the
theory of natural rights. With their schooling in Hegelian
method, the founders of scientific socialism would talk of
rights but not of *natural* rights. Rights as they understood them
were relative to time and place, and were to be estimated in
the light of the contribution they made to the dialectic development of society toward its goal, which for them was communism.

Engels said that the contemplated federated republic of
Europe could be achieved only by bloody battles, and indeed
his criticism of Bakunin's rather nebulous idea was devastating.
But Bakunin was, even so, more realistic than the romantic
nationalists. He saw in nationality a fact, not a principle: "The
right of nationality is to me a natural consequence of the
supreme principle of freedom; as soon as it stands in the way
of freedom, it ceases to be a right."[36]

Bakunin supported the cultural autonomy of the Slavs as
against the attempts of the Germans to acculturate them, an

attempt which had failed after a thousand years. With special reference to Engels, he wrote sarcastically:

> Panslavs are in the eyes of the Germans all Slavs who with anger and contrariness refuse the culture which they (the Germans) wish to force upon them. If *that* is the sense they give to the word "Panslavism," oh! then I am a Panslavist from the bottom of my heart.[37]

In 1848–1849 the objective role of the Germans, Hungarians and Poles was in general revolutionary, while the fight of the Austro-Hungarian Slavs aided the counter-revolution.* Bakunin was ready to sacrifice his Slavism on the altar of the Revolution of 1848–1849 as Engels demanded. His two "Calls to the Slavs" were intended to secure support for Kossuth and the German democrats against the Tsar and the Austrian reactionaries: "The Revolution tolerates no halfwayness, no hair-splitting. . . . It is clear, we must declare ourselves in Hungary for the Magyars and against Windischgrätz."[38] When the Russians marched in, Bakunin cried: "Throw out the treacherous leaders!"[39]

Bakunin thus had the political acumen to avoid the counter-revolutionary consequences which his "democratic" Panslavism might have brought about. But did he still believe in Panslavism for its own sake—Panslavism *sans phrase*?

Bakunin produced some lyrical passages on the qualities of the Russian people which were quite comparable with Hegel's on the Germans. He wrote:

> The Russian is not corrupted; he is only unfortunate. There is in his semi-barbaric nature something so energetic and broad, such an abundance of poetry, of passion and spirit, that it is impossible to know him and not recognize that he has a great mission to fulfill at this time.[40]

In 1861, Bakunin reacted like any Russian nationalist—of course, in the name of his future democratic Russia—to a proposal which was then in the air, to set up Austria-Hungary

---

* Thus Wendel, in his article already quoted, is off on the wrong foot.

as a federal state in which the Slav element would predomi-
nate. If Austria became Slavic, Bakunin wrote to Katkow,
"what would become of Russia? Do you suppose that Poland
would remain divided? That is impossible; it would unite
under the auspices of Slavic Austria and take from us (sic) one
after the other Lithuania, White Russia, the Ukraine, the
whole of Little Russia."[41]

Just as Marx and Engels were associated, however loosely,
with German expansionists who dreamed of a (progressive)
German state extending to the Black Sea, so Bakunin confessed
in 1857 that he had had visions of a "free and unified" Empire
of the Orient, a Panslav federation "whose capital would have
been *Constantinople*."[42] But the Turks were not Slavs! Bakunin
always felt himself to be a Russian; he wrote (also in 1857):
"The more I remained abroad, the more profoundly I felt that
I am a Russian and that I will never cease to be one."[43] This
statement may be compared with that of 1868, when Bakunin
wrote to Marx: "My fatherland is now the International!"*

The London Conference of the First International, in 1865,
had before it a draft program for the Geneva Congress of
1866. This program, written by Marx, referred to the "Muscovite invasion" of Europe in a passage attacking the imperialism
of the Russian Tsar. The passage was criticized by the French
and the Belgians on the ground that it singled out the Russians, whereas all the imperialist powers should have been
condemned. "Muscovite invasion" accordingly became "Russian influence." Bakunin, who joined the First International
only in the summer of 1868, later attacked Marx on the ground
that the latter in the quoted passage had sought to get the
International to take an anti-Russian position.[44]

Just as Marx and Engels were always making plans for the
future of Europe on the basis of a united, democratic Germany,
so Bakunin was always seeking partners in West Europe for
his democratic Slav state of the future. It was from this point
of view that his friendly relations with Italian nationalist

* See p. 13.

leaders such as Garibaldi, Mazzini, and Aurelio Saffi were determined. But Bakunin eventually decided that Mazzini was no friend of the social revolution, and their friendly relations were succeeded by hostility.[45]

Marx criticized Bakunin for having made "the will, and not social conditions" the basis of *his* social revolution: "He wants the European social revolution, which is based on the capitalist mode of production, to take place on the level of Russian or Slavic agricultural and herding people, and not to raise itself above this level."[46]

Marx indeed favored having the peasants participate in a *socialist* revolution; not only that—he considered such participation essential, even in a country as advanced as Germany. He wrote to Engels in 1856: "The whole thing in Germany will depend on the possibility of backing the proletarian revolution by some second edition of the Peasants' War."[47]

This formulation implies that the Peasants' War had been socialist-inclined. But Engels' study of those wars makes it plain that the peasants who revolted against the feudal landlords at the beginning of the modern era had for the most part no well worked out social philosophy nor even much cohesiveness among themselves.[48]

Bakunin was concerned to organize the peasants on a socialist basis; in Italy, where he worked for some years, he devoted much attention to the peasants, and in the North Central part of the country laid the basis for a socialist organization of the peasantry which has persisted right down to the middle of the 20th century. It is true that in the absence of such preliminary organization a peasant uprising in Russia, for example, could only have been a Jacquerie; but to imply, as modern students do, that Bakunin's vision stopped there, is not fair either to his underlying theory or to his practical work.[49] He thought that the rural areas of Italy were from the standpoint of the social revolution more progressive than the cities.[50]

Marx also favored propaganda in the rural areas. "We have been too much concerned with the city workers," say the minutes of the London Conference of the First International, September 1871, in which Marx participated.[51] Engels in 1872 accepted the affiliation to the International of a "Society of Workers and Peasants" of Lodi, and wrote a letter to this new section.[52] Marx's criticism of Bakunin was thus based, not on the latter's being interested in organizing the peasants, but on Bakunin's inadequate appreciation of the importance of large-scale industry.

Marx, Engels and Bakunin as Nationalists

Marx and Engels welcomed the Franco-Prussian War of 1870 not only because they had long been anxious to see Louis Napoleon defeated and removed from the scene, but also because they considered that the German movement, which was already superior to that of France in theory and organization, would thereby receive more scope for development. The French workers, they believed, would also benefit. These views were later reproduced by Guillaume with the remark that Marx and Engels were Pan-Germanists because they sought to assure "the preponderance of the German proletariat over the French," and to "transfer from France to Germany the center of gravity of the European movement."[53]* This is an outright distortion, and was labeled as such at the time (1915).

Bakunin tended to look on the principle of self-determination as an absolute principle, valid regardless of place and time. Marx and Engels did not believe that any one of the principles of democracy, as developed in the 18th century, had validity by itself as long as the system of private property persisted, and so they sometimes gave the principle of self-determination rather short shrift. This was done quite consciously and deliberately, in the interests of the socialist revolution, since only after such a revolution could the "eternal principles" of democracy have real meaning for the exploited section of the population. Even other points in the program of Marx and Engels,

---

* Guillaume is here repeating one of Bakunin's slanderous remarks.

such as that of setting up a Polish state to serve as a buffer against reactionary Russia, might have greater validity, in their view, than the idea of self-determination strictly applied. Thus the projected state of Poland would need to have ports on the Baltic, and to have at least the borders of 1772, even if that meant that it would include in its borders some millions of Ukrainians and White (Byelo-) Russians. They said specifically that the reconstituted Poland would be a *multi-national* state.[54]

The General Council of the First International went on record in favor of self-determination for Poland. Its Report to the Geneva Congress (1866) dealt with the "need for annihilating Russian influence in Europe, through enforcing the right of self-determination, and through the reconstitution of Poland upon democratic and social foundations."[55] In this context, self-determination was entirely acceptable to Marx. He also favored self-determination for Ireland and for the Balkan Slavs—in fact, for all subject peoples whose interests coincided at the time with those of the international proletarian revolution.* Beyond that he did not go; he was not much interested in the principle of self-determination as such.

But were Marx and Engels German nationalists, as Bakunin and others have charged? Actually, the attitude of Marx and Engels in the Franco-Prussian War has usually been taken as proof that they were *not* German nationalists. When the war broke out, it is true, Engels wrote to Marx that Germany had been driven into a war for its national existence; a defeat would set back the growth of an independent German labor movement, perhaps for generations. "Bismarck is now doing a piece of our work, in his own way and without intending it, but he is still doing it," wrote Engels.[56]

But Marx and Engels did not go all out for Bismarck, as the Lassallean Schweitzer did. Neither did they at first call for the defeat of Prussia. Later they did, when Bismarck had shown his intention of annexing Alsace-Lorraine. Engels even sketched a plan by which the French might have regained the

* On Ireland see further pp. 65–66, 119–127.

initiative and thrown the Germans out of France. In view of
Engels' superlative reporting of the strategy of the war, a plan
from him was bound to have importance, if it had been published, but it was not.*

Marx and Engels did not consistently advocate the cause of
Germany in international politics. Riazanov points out that
they had no policy looking toward German expansion in the
Balkans.[57]† Although they were much interested in the rise
of the labor movement in Germany, and looked on it as the
vanguard of the socialist revolution, in international politics
they sometimes took the part of the Germans, sometimes not.
Marx especially contemplated developments in Germany with
a chilly eye, and in letters to Engels in 1856 and 1863 reckoned
with the possibility that he might have to advocate the defeat
of German arms in the interests of the international proletarian
revolution.[58] He favored the annexation of Schleswig-Holstein
by Prussia in 1866, but opposed the annexation of Alsace-
Lorraine by Germany in 1871. Prof. Bloom's conclusion that
Marx "simply was not a nationalist" seems the only judgment
possible on the evidence.[59]

The case of Engels is somewhat different. He was a German
nationalist in his youth, and used nationalist jargon on several
occasions later, in spite of his efforts to maintain an internationalist point of view. The last and most damaging of such
occasions occurred after Marx's death, and deserves a word
of explanation and comment.

Marx and Engels had, of course, been aware all along that a
united Germany under the leadership of the Prussian military
class state could be a menace.[60] They decided to pin their
hopes on the German proletariat as the force that would

---

* Bernstein and Bebel, Engels' literary executors, found this document
among his papers. They destroyed it, allegedly lest the German Social-
Democratic Party, which obviously had had nothing to do with the
matter, might be charged retrospectively with an unpatriotic act.—
G. Mayer, *Friedrich Engels*, II (The Hague: 1934), pp. 197 and
544–545.

† Engels' remark in correspondence to Kautsky, quoted above, was
not part of a general policy of expansionism.

democratize and socialize the new Germany. It was a momentous decision, to which Bakunin for one did not subscribe. The philosophy of Marx and Engels on nationalism, wrote Bakunin, amounts to

establishing big new national States, separate and necessarily rival and hostile, to the exclusion of internationalism, of humanity. For unless they contemplate founding one single universal State, they must necessarily found national States, or else, what is still more probable, great States in which one race, the most important and intelligent, will dominate and exploit other races, so that, without admitting it, the Marxists end up with Pan-Germanism.[61]

The danger, then, as Bakunin saw it, was that the working class, in seeking to make the state the instrument for establishing international socialism, would become so interested in building up the state as such that they would give its interests prior attention, and international socialism would be the loser. That this idea was no mere figment of the imagination was illustrated by the case of Engels himself.

Marx and Engels were acutely aware of the effect of national wars in delaying and interfering with the class struggle. Marx had written in 1871:

The highest heroic effort of which old society is still capable is national war, and this is now proved to be a mere governmental humbug, intended to defer the struggle of classes, and to be thrown aside as soon as that class struggle bursts out into civil war. Class rule is no longer able to disguise itself in a national uniform. The national governments are only *one* as against the proletariat![62]

Engels hoped to see the German workers take the lead in the international working-class movement, but only if they remained true internationalists would he give them his continued support. He wrote in 1874:

For the present moment the German workers form the vanguard of the proletarian struggle. . . However, it is necessary to retain a real international spirit which permits of no chauvinism, which joyfully greets each new step of the proletarian movement, no matter in which nation it is made. If the German workers proceed in this way, they may not march exactly at the head of the movement—it is not in the interest of the movement that the workers of one country should march at the head of all—but they will occupy an honourable place on the battle line. . .[62a]

Engels also warned leaders of the German Social Democratic Party quite sharply in the 1880's against falling in with the imperial expansionist policies of the Reich.

Engels several times expressed a horror of a general European war. Thus in 1882 he wrote to Bebel:

> I should consider a European war to be a misfortune. This time it would be terribly serious; it would set chauvinism going everywhere for years, because every nation would be fighting for its own existence. All the work of the revolutionaries in Russia who are now nearing success would be rendered useless—would be destroyed; our party in Germany would be temporarily swamped and ruined by the flood of chauvinism, and it would be the same in France.[63]

In 1891 Engels wrote a piece for *Die Neue Zeit* which smacked of German nationalism, to such a point that it was later to be used by conservative Social Democrats to justify their participation in the First World War in the Kaiser's armies. He argued that Tsarist Russia was the greatest enemy (a traditional Marxist position) and that in a general war it would be the duty of German Social Democrats to fight against Russia and all its allies. In a war against France and Russia, said Engels, Germany would be fighting for its very existence. If it lost the war and therewith much of its territory, it would be in no position to fulfill the role that belonged to it in Europe's historical development. The Social-Democratic Party would be destroyed. But this party had won for itself a leading position in the international labor movement. Its duty was to defend its position against any attacker "to the last man." He added that a war would so weaken capitalism that socialism would succeed it soon.[64]

It is evident that Engels is here doing no more than applying to Germany specifically the analysis that he had made before, in his letter to Bebel, with reference to all European countries.

The context made it seem like a piece of special pleading on behalf of the Germans. Together with a speech by Bebel just before, in which that leader had argued that German workers should fight in a defensive war, Engels' article caused an uproar in the French Workers' Party, which had been trying to conduct a campaign for disarmament. One of the Party leaders wrote to Engels protesting. Engels replied that if France were invaded by Kaiser Wilhelm's armies, the French workers would and should defend themselves. In October, 1891, Engels wrote to Bebel: "If Germany is attacked from the East and West, every method of defense is good."[65] However, Engels did not advise voting for all war credits, only the defensive ones. He wrote:

If, as the Prussian government says, there'll be war in early 1892, we could *en principe* not declare against voting credits now. This would be a rather *fatale Lage* for us. But what if really there is to be war early in 1892? In this case we'll have to vote for all credits tending to reinforce the *defensive*, and only those. In the *perspective* of imminent war, we can't announce now our army policy (*milice*, democratization of the army, new armaments, etc.—this army reform costs too much time), but must try to temporize and vote only those army credits which go to change the character of the army in the sense of a people's army.[66]

Engels was thus restating the position that Marx had taken at the time of the Franco-Prussian War of 1870–1871—in favor of a defensive war when the result would be to preserve the labor and socialist movement. This position was unsatisfactory, and became more so in the epoch of imperialism, when the major European powers were engaged in aggression over a period of years against the less developed peoples of the world, and there was no such thing as an innocent party. But Engels was plainly not engaged in special pleading for the Germans or for the German Party, according to his own explanation.

Engels in practice, in his daily life, was a revolutionary socialist and an internationalist, and continued as such until the end of his life. He gave unstintingly of his time and energy

to help the leaders of the struggling labor and socialist movements of European and overseas countries. Samuel Gompers
looked on "Fred" Engels as a friend of the labor movement.[67]
It is impossible to overlook forty or fifty years of such work
and put Engels down as a nationalist.

Engels chose as his literary executor Karl Kautsky, who at
the time was taking a strong internationalist position. Two
other literary executors, Bernstein and Bebel, had not then
come out as open German nationalists, as they did later.

Right-wing Social Democrats tried to argue in 1914, on the
basis of Engels' ill-judged article, that he would have supported
Germany in the war. This contention overlooks the fact that
the developments of the 30 years before 1914 had rendered the
earlier analysis by Marx and Engels out of date. Marx's opposition to the Russian Tsar as gendarme of Europe, and to all
kinds of Panslavism including Bakunin's, was based on two
assumptions: that Russia was the dominant power in Eastern
Europe, and that it had no revolutionary labor movement. By
the turn of the century revolutionary socialists in Eastern
Europe like Rosa Luxemburg and Lenin were showing that
these assumptions were no longer correct, and were revising
Marxist analysis and Marxist policy accordingly. It is impossible to believe that Engels, if he had been able to live another
20 years and apply his mind with its customary acuteness to
the problem of international relations, would have maintained
his position of 1891. Already in 1893 he had taken a decisive
step in the direction of a new position.[68] He then said that
Russia was hardly capable of waging a defensive war, let alone
of attacking Germany. The right-wing Social Democrats were
disingenuous, to put it mildly, when they made Engels into a
supporter of an imperialist war. Whether he would have called
for the "defeat of the fatherland" with Lenin is of course
another question.

Marx and Engels may indeed have both been unconscious,
or subconscious, nationalists in that they hoped Germany

would take the lead in establishing socialism.[69] This desire is comparable with Bakunin's wish that a democratized Russia might give such a lead. It is impossible to imagine the two great Rhinelanders offering a program for Europe in which the Russians would have pride of place, and equally impossible to cast Bakunin in the role of an advocate of German leadership. Subconscious nationalism influenced the policies advocated by all three. But this is not to say that Marx and Engels would have deplored the socialist revolution taking place in Russia first. At most they might have agreed with Lenin's opinion that "the German revolution is incomparably more important than [the Russian]." Nor would Bakunin have rejected the kind of revolution that he favored if it had come to Germany ahead of Russia. Consciously and basically all three were committed to the international socialist revolution.

The Case of Ferdinand Lassalle

Lassalle, on the other hand, was frankly a German, or rather a Prussian, nationalist. He advocated the "Prussian" solution to the problem of the unification of Germany, even to the point where Marx suspected him of being in touch with Bismarck. Lassalle did secretly establish such a contact, so Marx's opinion was justified; but Marx and Engels had formed an unfavorable opinion of Lassalle much earlier, and the national question was one of several elements in a rather deep-going disagreement.

In the diplomatic maneuvering which accompanied the move for Italian liberation in 1859, the attitudes of both Marx and Lassalle were determined more by their respective conceptions of what would be good for the rest of Europe than by any concern for Italian unification. Lassalle favored the defeat of Austria in Italy because Austria was Prussia's rival in the struggle for hegemony in the approaching unification of Germany. Marx was not in favor of the Austrians in their operations in Italy, but did not strongly oppose them because of his deep distrust of Napoleon III who was then pitted against Austria, and of Russia, with which he suspected Napoleon was allied.

Marx and Engels in England were political exiles; they followed international politics very closely, but were not associated with the day-to-day working of any national party or labor movement. Lassalle, on the other hand, had always known that the rise of national working-class parties was a necessary stage in the international socialist movement; and while he considered himself Marx's friend for many years and sought his advice and approval, he went his own way in the end, while trying to avoid an open break.

Lassalle, while professing an internationalist philosophy, considered things increasingly from the German or even narrowly Prussian point of view. Where Bakunin had hoped to see Russian soldiers in Constantinople, Lassalle in a letter to Rodbertus, another German expansionist, endorsed the latter's hope that Germany would one day become the heir of Turkey, and German soldiers would stand on the Bosphorus.[70] This of course would be after "the Revolution," for Lassalle as for Bakunin. Lassalle's influence was recognized as dangerous and possibly disastrous by Marx and Engels, precisely because of his failure to outgrow the narrow nationalism to which he was clearly committed.

Where Marx and Engels had come to consider the State as the organ of the ruling class, Lassalle seldom let pass an opportunity to glorify the State as such; he pictured it as being in some mystical way above the class struggle. Thus he said at one time: "The State shall be the institution in which the whole virtue of mankind shall realize itself."[71] Hegel can almost be heard applauding from his grave. In his famous article on the Indirect Tax, in which he called the State "the immemorial vestal fire of all civilization," Lassalle further developed his conception:

To the *State* I ascribe the high, the powerful task to develop the germ of humanity, as it has done since the beginning of history and will do through all eternity, and as the organ which is there *for all*, to bring the condition of *all men* under its protecting hand.

Bernstein, in editing Lassalle's works, added a reproving footnote at this point.* Lassalle's policy—mistaken, in Marx's view—was to attack the liberal bourgeoisie and seek to ally the proletarians whom he led with Bismarck, who was then backed primarily by the army and the landed aristocracy. This policy earned him the applause of a certain section of the intellectuals, who sought afterwards to build up the nationalist Lassalle at the expense of the proletarian internationalists Marx and Engels. Bernstein, while not attacking Marx and Engels, tried to rescue Lassalle's reputation with the Social Democrats by showing that his nationalism had been misunderstood; Bernstein quoted from Lassalle's correspondence with Marx to show that Lassalle was really an internationalist at heart and only had different ideas as to the tactics to be followed at the time of the Italian war in 1859. But even Bernstein is obliged to admit that Lassalle was "still in practice pretty much imbued with Prussian jingoism," and he adds: "Lassalle's conception of the State is the bridge that was one day to bring together the Republican Lassalle and the men fighting for absolute monarchy, the Revolutionist Lassalle and out-and-out reactionaries."[72]†

Marx and Engels had advocated that the proletariat should ally itself with the liberal bourgeoisie to sweep away the "feudal remnants" and break the power of the army and the big landowners. Lassalle's successor Schweitzer, by contrast, continued Lassalle's disastrous policy of playing up to the reactionaries. Lassalle's Socialist Party was split several times. Even the union of the Lassalleans with the "Eisenachers" (Bebel, Wilhelm Liebknecht, *et al.*) and the formation of the Social-Democratic Party in 1875, did not furnish an adequate

* Bernstein was working at the time under the general supervision of Engels.

† This passage also is to be seen as possibly due to the influence of Engels, who undoubtedly saw the manuscript in advance of publication.

challenge to the old order; the "feudal remnants" survived, and
the system of (bourgeois) liberty was never fully introduced
in Germany at all. The German socialist movement on which
Marx and Engels pinned their hopes had within it from the
beginning an unrepentant nationalist element which for the
sake of temporary gains was quite prepared to make common
cause politically with the greatest enemies of international
socialism. "Eisenachers" were not entirely devoid of nationalist
sentiment, as we shall see.*

The First International

The socialist and trade union movements of Europe were
international before they were national. When the International Workingmen's Association was projected in the 1860's,
the labor and socialist organizations were few and scattered.
There were no national union organizations, and, on the continent, few unions. The Chartist agitation in England had
attained national scope; but the Chartist organizations had
ceased to exist. Lassalle had founded the General German
Workers' Union (ADAV, after its German initials) in 1863,
but it had hardly attained national stature even within Prussia.

In the absence of national federations of organized workers
(union federations or national political parties), the representatives in the International came from a variety of groups.
Some British unions participated primarily because of their
fear of immigration of European workmen into England; but
others, like George Odger, were much more sophisticated
politically and more aware of movements abroad than most
pure-and-simple unionists of a later day.† Some groups of

---

* Chapter IV, pp. 85 ff.

† "Political rather than industrial questions were uppermost in the
minds of those Englishmen who became members of the Central Provi-
sional Council of the International. Had this not been the case, they
would hardly have tolerated Marx's Inaugural Address which contained
not a single reference to trade unionism . . ."—Royden Harrison, "The
British Labour Movement and the International in 1864," in *The
Socialist Register 1964* (New York 1964), ed. by Ralph Miliband & John
Saville, p. 294.

national refugees came, and the first Congress, as already noted, went on record for the freedom of both Poland and Ireland. There were also ideological groups, socialists and anarchists of various persuasions, followers not only of Marx and Bakunin, but also of Proudhon and Blanqui.

The First International furnished a stimulus to the formation of national parties and union groups, and it was a deep-going disagreement on the extent of control to be exercised by the international organization over these rising national groups, rather than the widely advertised personal feud between Marx and Bakunin, which led to the collapse of the I.W.A.

Marx had wished to build a highly centralized international organization to which the workers of all countries would owe their first loyalty. However, when the movement for independent national parties of the working class gained momentum toward 1870, Marx favored a resolution to endorse this movement. Such a resolution was actually presented to the London Conference of 1871 by Vaillant—Resolution IX, calling for the formation of independent political parties of the working class—and was adopted over the protest of Bakunin's friend Guillaume. At the Hague Congress of 1872, Resolution IX was incorporated into the Rules of the Association, to Marx's entire satisfaction.

Meanwhile, however, the disagreement between the centralists (Marxists) and the autonomists had reached the breaking point, and the organization split. The centralist federation moved its headquarters to New York and presently passed out of existence. The leading group in the autonomist international was that of the Belgians; in 1870, some 70,000 Belgian workers had belonged to groups affiliated with the International.[73] They eventually became so interested in the advances made by the German Social-Democratic Party that they decided to imitate it, and this led to the collapse of the international federation to which they belonged.

Engels afterwards commented to Sorge on the reasons for the demise of the First International. He said that its death was due to its very success. As long as the labor and socialist movement was suppressed and persecuted throughout Europe, the oppression gave the movement unity and prescribed abstention from inner polemics. The common cosmopolitan interests of the affiliates could occupy the foreground of attention. But the first great success was bound to break in pieces this "naive conjunction of all fractions."[74] This success was the Paris Commune. All schools wanted to exploit it for their own uses, and the crackup came.

This result was ironic in that the Paris Commune was the work of the Parisian proletariat and not directly of the International at all. Marx had advised against it. But the event was associated in the public mind with the International; so it would have been futile, and poor policy besides, for the International to try to disclaim responsibility.

The First International marks the last and only attempt, in our period, of Marxism to assume direct control of events in the labor movements of the several countries, as distinguished from the giving of advice. From that time on, the power and responsibility in the several countries of Europe rested in the hands of the national parties. The international proletarian revolution remained as an objective, but one which did not enter into the lives of the workers in a day-to-day, organizational way. Labor leaders in small countries might continue to look back wistfully to the days when the International used to hold out a helping hand, however remote.[75] In modern times, help extended to labor movements across international boundaries has been due more often to interested nationalism than to proletarian internationalism.

And yet, the idea that the struggle against imperialism is and necessarily must be international is by no means dead. From opposite sides of the globe came this idea in 1965—from the Guatemalan guerrillas and from the government of the Peoples' Republic of China.[76]

The collapse of the First International coincided with the unification of Germany, following soon after the unification of Italy. Thenceforth the growth of territorial ambitions in Germany and Italy was to involve, not the welding together of separate parts which had been disjoined by the accident of history, but the incorporation of new territory then under alien rule. Expansive nationalism had become imperialism, for *all* the *leading* countries of Europe. Marxism had still to define, or rather redefine, its position in relation to imperialism.

For some other countries, nationalism still meant struggling for national unification, as with the East European countries from Poland to the Balkans; or fighting for national independence against the imperialist powers, as with the Irish, the Czechoslovaks, and the oriental and African peoples. Marxism had still to answer the questions of how far these nationalist movements were justified, how far they were a legitimate concern of the working class, and what attitude the proletariat of all countries should take to them. Was there a general principle involved? If so, Marx and Engels had not clearly enunciated it, and Bakunin's approach was ambiguous. All branches of the socialist movement were agreed on the virtues of proletarian internationalism. Did this philosophy imply opposition to nationalism as such? Should aggressive, imperialist nationalism be opposed? Should constructive, anti-imperialist nationalism be supported? The failure to come up with a clear and early answer to these questions was to cause a split in the socialist movement.

Proudhon Opposed the Nation-State

Pierre-Joseph Proudhon (1809-1865) differed with Marx on many subjects. Where Marx saw the size of industry increasing, Proudhon was the apostle of small-scale production. Marx was a centralist, Proudhon an extreme decentralist. Marx called for a workers' government. Proudhon would have preferred to get along with no government at all; but having recognized, toward the end of his life, the need for some authority, he sought to dilute it by a system of federalism. Proudhon liked to think of himself as an anarchist, though not of the same variety as Bakunin. Although he had once written a slashing attack on (big) property, he was no socialist, but rather a distributivist, or mutualist; his solution of the social question was in terms of mutual associations financed by a (central!) bank. The attempts of the French CGT after the First World War to build him up into an authentic prophet of the labor movement must be put down to a misunderstanding, deliberate or otherwise, of the essential nature of his message.

Yet Proudhon participated in the uprising of 1848 as a revolutionist; tried, though unsuccessfully, to use the dialectic analysis; and was treated with respect by Marx, who, though he called Proudhon a petty bourgeois, still thought it necessary to expose in a book (*La Misère de la Philosophie*) what he took to be Proudhon's fallacies. In the still decentralized, still small-production economy of early nineteenth-century France, Proudhon, an eloquent writer and skillful demagogue, had a working-class following.

Consistent with his opposition to authority in general, Proudhon, almost alone among the thinkers of his day, opposed the unification of Germany and Italy, on the ground that this would lead to the growth of new power centers.

Proudhon's working-class followers were organized into unions, mutuals, cooperatives, or political groups, and some of these appeared after his death at the Congresses of the First International, where they created confusion by refusing to recognize the existence of national states; in their extreme cosmopolitanism, they acted as if the International was the only government. Marx was able to laugh them out of court; but the battle over decentralization continued throughout the life of the International, as already noted.

III

NATIONS, COLONIES AND SOCIAL CLASSES:
THE POSITION OF MARX AND ENGELS

MARX AND ENGELS thought that social development involved a dialectic progression from stage to stage on the road to socialism and communism; that each step in this progression represented an advance as compared with the preceding one. They deprecated slavery on humanitarian grounds, but still thought that it represented an advance over earlier systems in that it made possible the accumulation of a surplus, and this surplus could be used to move on to a higher stage of development; without such a surplus, progress would have been slow and difficult if not impossible.[1]

Marx and Engels on Imperialist Domination

Countries that had been left behind in the race for development would have to catch up the best way they could. The quickest way might be to have the backward country fall under the domination of an advanced country, which would break the shell of custom and introduce free enterprise, thus launching the area on the path toward greater productivity and eventually socialism.

Marx and Engels were much interested in the work of the American anthropologist Lewis H. Morgan, which presented an elaborate classification of cultures by stages. Engels' famous monograph on the *Origin of the Family, Private Property and the State* used Morgan's material.* The attitude of Marx and

---

* Engels made use of Marx's notes on Morgan's work in preparing this monograph, which appeared after Marx's death.

Engels toward colonies and backward areas was determined at first by their belief in the theory of economic stages.

The true nature of imperialist domination began to show itself more clearly in the second half of the nineteenth century, and opinions that Marx and Engels had expressed earlier about particular areas were sometimes modified or even reversed in their later writings. In the present chapter we shall attempt to trace these shifts, some of which seem to have escaped attention up to the present. Indeed, by quoting passages from the writings of Marx and Engels out of context, it has been possible for one school of writers to make them out as apologists for slavery and imperialism, while another school has set out to prove that Marx was not only omniscient but could foretell future events with exactitude. It is hard to tell which school has done more to render difficult a correct understanding of Marx's ideas.

In their early writings, Marx and Engels showed much enthusiasm for large political units as such; small states were a block on the road to progress. Engels even went so far, in his condemnation of small states and nationalities, as to reproach the Swiss retrospectively for having won their independence from Austria. According to Engels, Austria at the time (13th century) was for once in its history a progressive state, and nothing must stand in the way of a progressive state.[2]

Robert Grimm was to give much later a quite different version of the Swiss independence struggle. For him it was a fight of free Swiss farmers with a communistic system of land ownership against subjection to the feudal lords of Hapsburg.[3] One wonders what Engels would have said about that.

A pamphlet, *Po und Rhein*, written in 1859, shows most clearly Engels' attitude in favor of the absorption of small nations by larger ones. In this pamphlet he indicates the futility of trying to draw boundaries based on the supposed necessity of each nation for militarily defensible boundaries. He then continues:

All changes [in the map of Europe] if they are to last must in general start from the effort to give to the large and viable European nations more and more their *true* national boundaries, which are determined by language and sympathies, while at the same time the ruins of peoples, which are still found here and there and which are no longer capable of a national existence, are absorbed by the larger nations and either become a part of them or maintain themselves as ethnographic monuments without political significance.[4]*

Engels had already pointed out that questions like that of the rights of nationalities were not likely to receive much attention when it was a question of war or the threat of war, when "one is defending his own skin."[5]

Underdeveloped peoples generally received harsh treatment at the hands of both Marx and Engels in their early years. The Montenegrins were "cattle robbers" and "pious freebooters" (Marx); the Mexicans were "lazy" (Engels) and *"les derniers des hommes"* (Marx).[6] The idea that the "backward" peoples might get farther faster if they resisted the encroachments of Saint Bourgeois, and made their own selection of the blessings of civilization in their own time, was indeed slow in penetrating Marxism.

Just to show that he played no favorites as between backward small peoples and backward large ones, Marx loosed some of his choicest shafts at the Chinese at the time of the Opium Wars; he suggested: "It would seem as though history had first to make this whole people drunk before it could rouse them out of their hereditary stupidity."[7]

Even Tsarist Russia was capable of exercising a civilizing influence in the East, according to Marx and Engels. The latter defended the operations of the Tsar in Central Asia in the following terms: "Russia . . . is really progressive in relation to the East. For all its baseness and Slavonic dirt, Russian domination is a civilizing element on the Black Sea, the Caspian Sea and Central Asia and among the Bashkirs and Tartars, etc."[8]

* The Marx-Engels-Lenin Institute (Moscow) dissociates itself from this conclusion of Engels, which the Institute describes simply as erroneous.—*Werke.* XIII, 678.

Where two advanced countries contended for the hegemony over a backward area, Marx and Engels favored the more progressive. England was more progressive than Tsarist Russia, and so its influence in Central Asia was to be preferred to that of the Russians. Engels wrote in 1853: "It is evident that not only a very large trade, but the principal intercourse of Europe with Central Asia, and, consequently, the principal means of re-civilizing that vast region, depends on the uninterrupted liberty of trading through these gates to the Black Sea."[9]

Incidentally, this passage puts in question the opinion expressed by Professor Bloom, that Marx accorded no civilizing power to "capitalism of a purely commercial character," which, in Bloom's phrase, "fattened on backward countries without helping to transform them."[10] The operations of the British in Central Asia were of a purely commercial character.

Still more progressive than the British, in the view of Marx and Engels, was the United States. Thus the U.S. aggression against Mexico in 1847 was condoned on the ground that Mexico was bound to come under the domination of some advanced power, and it was better all round that that power should be the United States rather than England. It was obvious in any case, they said, that the "energetic Yankees" would develop California better and more quickly than the "lazy Mexicans" could or would, and the world economy would be the gainer.[11]

Taken by themselves, such passages make Marx and Engels seem like imperialist apologists, and later publicists have so interpreted them, right down to the present day. Marx and Engels did indeed accept imperialism and colonialism as facts of life in their early years.

But this interpretation of the over-all views of Marx and Engels has not gone unchallenged. In later writings, both men showed much more hospitable consideration to the claims of small and backward nationalities. Cunow during the First World War attempted to use the attitude of Marx and Engels regarding the U.S. aggression against Mexico to prove that they sometimes sanctioned aggressive wars. Kautsky retorted that they had changed their minds, and he offered as proof Marx's condemnation of wars of conquest in his address to the First International.[12]

Marx had indeed condemned what he took to be the aggression of Napoleon III against Prussia in 1870, and the General Council of the First International had adopted a statement to that effect.[13] Whether this incident can be taken as a general statement of Marx's position is another question, which is discussed further below (Chapter VIII). For our present purpose the important point is that later Marxists, not only Kautsky but also Lenin and others, have shied away from defending the position that Marx and Engels took on the U.S.-Mexican War.

The duchies of Schleswig and Holstein had been wrested away from Denmark and attached to Prussia in 1867, with Marx's approval.* In 1891 Engels favored a referendum to see whether Schleswig-Holstein inhabitants wished to remain attached to Germany, even though the outcome of such a vote might have been to detach the provinces and turn them over to the tiny state of Denmark.[14]

A particularly striking illustration of the development in the point of view of Marx and Engels—specifically, Engels—is furnished by the case of Algeria. In order to establish themselves in Algeria, the French had to overcome stubborn and long-continued resistance on the part of the native tribes. When one of the chiefs, Abd-el-Kader, was taken, Engels was in Paris, where he acted as the Correspondent of the *Northern Star* (London). His reaction—or the reaction of the author of the Correspondence, if it was not Engels—was quite in the spirit of the remarks of Marx and Engels just before on the Mexican War. He wrote:

The struggle of the Bedouins was a hopeless one, and though the manner in which brutal soldiers, like Bugeaud, have carried on the war is highly blameworthy, the conquest of Algeria is an important

* See above, p. 46.

and fortunate fact for the progress of civilization. The piracies of the Barbaresque states, never interfered with by the English government as long as they did not disturb their ships, could not be put down but by the conquest of one of these states. And the conquest of Algeria has already forced the Beys of Tunis and Tripoli, and even the Emperor of Morocco, to enter upon the road of civilization. They were obliged to find other employment for their people than piracy, and other means of filling their exchequer than tributes paid to them by the smaller states of Europe. And if we may regret that the liberty of the Bedouins of the desert has been destroyed, we must not forget that these same Bedouins were a nation of robbers, whose principal means of living consisted of making excursions either upon each other, or upon the settled villagers, taking what they found, slaughtering all those who resisted, and selling the remaining prisoners as slaves. All these nations of free barbarians look very proud, noble and glorious at a distance, but only come near them and you will find that they, as well as the more civilized nations, are ruled by the lust of gain, and only employ ruder and more cruel means. And after all, the modern *bourgeois*, with civilization, industry, order, and at least relative enlightenment following him, is preferable to the feudal lord or to the marauding robber, with the barbarian state of society to which they belong.

Some ten years after he had, in effect, endorsed the French occupation of Algeria, Engels had become aware that things were not working out for the best interests of the Algerians. In an article written in 1857 for the *New American Cyclopedia*, he even paid tribute to the "intrepidity" of Abd-el-Kader, while condemning the inhumanity of the French tactic of *razzias*, or raids accompanied by the destruction of native villages which resisted the conquerors. "The indigenous population is still governed by a hand of iron," he wrote, and the legal proceedings against Captain Doineau in 1857 "revealed the cruelty and the despotism which the French officials, even those of minor rank, habitually use in their administration of power." Very significantly, the *Cyclopedia* article described the birth of a national spirit among the Algerians as a result of the French occupation, in such terms as the following:

From the first occupation of Algeria by the French . . . the unhappy country has been the arena of unceasing bloodshed, rapine and violence. . . . The Arab and Kabyle tribes, to whom independence is precious, and hatred of foreign domination a principle dearer than life itself, have been crushed and broken by the terrible razzias. . . . The tribes still assert their independence and detestation of the French regime. . .

The same volume of the *Cyclopedia* contained a laudatory article on Abd-el-Kader, who was depicted as a kind of "father of his country." This article may also have been written by Engels.

Of course, it must not be assumed that the progressive American editors of the *Cyclopedia*, George Ripley and Charles A. Dana, got their anti-colonialism from Engels. It could have been the other way around. It was not until the 20th century that anti-imperialism finally ceased to be fashionable in the United States, in liberal circles. But it is known that Engels wrote the first draft of the article on Algeria, and he is said to have complained later to Marx that parts of his description of the movement led by Abd-el-Kader were edited out.[15]

In the 1840's Marx had advised the Irish workers to make common cause with the Chartists, whom he expected to stage a workers' revolution that would result in freeing Ireland. Later, he favored using the Irish nationalist movement to break the power of the British landed aristocracy, first in Ireland and then in England. He contemplated independence for Ireland regretfully, and thought it might be followed by federation.[16] The main consideration here was economic development, which would be facilitated by retaining large units where they existed (and forming new ones where possible).

But here as elsewhere, realism and willingness to learn featured the writings of both Marx and Engels. The latter learned about Fenianism from his common-law wife Lizzie Burns, visited Ireland, and became so interested in the country that he set out to write its history.[17] Marx became aware of the

prejudice against the Irish that had grown up in England during the 1850's, when the British workers resented the arrival
of the new immigrants; this factor weakened his faith that the
freedom of Ireland would be achieved in England.

In the end, Irish liberation came to occupy a leading place in
Marx's thinking. It was not only an important issue for the
British workers—it was *the most* important issue. When the
International Workingmen's Association was founded in 1866,
Marx was tireless in rallying the General Council, including
the very moderate trade union leaders in Britain, on the side
of the Irish national struggle.[18] Marx and Engels, against violent opposition, persuaded the Council members to regard
Ireland as an independent nation.[19] In November, 1867, Marx
wrote and the Council adopted a resolution addressed to
Gathorn-Hardy, Home Secretary, protesting against the condemnation to death of three Fenians. Marx kept continental
Europe in touch with the Irish situation; he published two
articles in the *Internationale*, Brussels, in 1870, denouncing
police methods in Ireland; at the same time he helped his
daughter Jenny with eight articles on Ireland published in
Rochefort's *Marseillaise*. The Council adopted numerous resolutions on Ireland; one especially, dated January 1, 1870, contained the apothegm: "The people which oppresses another is
forging its own chains."[20] Marx wrote at this time a letter to
S. Meyer and A. Vogt in which he commented: "The national
emancipation of Ireland is [for the English workers] no question of abstract justice or humanitarian sentiment, but the first
condition of their own social emancipation."[21]* The Council's
resolution points out that England's only excuse for maintaining a large standing army—which could be used against the
English workers—is that this army might be needed in Ireland.

---

* Engels had written already in 1856: "Ireland may be regarded as
the first English colony. . . . The so-called freedom of English citizens
is based on the oppression of the colonies."—Letter to Marx, May 23,
1856.

Some development may also be traced in Marx's point of view regarding India. Contrary to a commonly accepted view, Marx did not in 1857–1859 advocate independence for India, any more than Cobden and Bright did. At most, he considered the possibility that India might win its independence before the social revolution took place in England.[22] And he still thought that British capitalism would perform a useful function in India, even if at tremendous cost, in shaking that country out of its centuries-old conservatism and backwardness. In 1862 he quoted with approval the hyperbolic language of Mazzini, who had said that the English soldier seemed a demigod during the Indian insurrection![23]

It is perhaps taking an unduly narrow point of view to say, as Marx and Lenin did, "We will not support reactionary movements," meaning that a war against imperialism or occupation would not be supported if it was led by a reactionary class.* But it is impermissible to read back into Marx points of view that were developed by Marxists after his time. Thus a booklet appeared in Moscow in 1959 entitled *The First Indian War of Independence, 1857–1859,* in which the Marx-Engels-Lenin Institute pictures the revolt of those years in the Indian army as an incipient nationalist revolt which was greeted as such by Marx. This interpretation of Marx's writings is downright misleading. The Sepoy "mutiny" had quite other causes than nationalism, which developed later in India.

The Indian-British Marxist R. P. Dutt had earlier given an interpretation of the 1857 uprising which is free of the objections that can be raised to the Institute's treatment. He pointed out that in the first half of the 19th century "the rising middle class in India, typically represented by Ram Mohan Roy, supported British rule, and sought to assist its endeavors; it was the decaying reactionary elements, the discontented princes and feudal forces, which led the opposition, and whose leadership culminated and foundered in the revolt of 1857."[24] We

* On this point see further Chapter VIII.

would only add at this point: the British still had no business
to be ruling India, even if their rule was challenged by the
"wrong" people—that time.

In his writings at this period Marx did not make as much
use as the little-Englanders and free-traders did, of the figures
showing the annual tribute levied on India by England. In
1881 he had begun to use these figures.[25]

The opinion of Marx, according to which England's presence
in India could be expected to have a constructive effect, was
based on the assumption that India, like other Asian countries,
was still suffering under fossilized "oriental despotism"; that in
order to progress it would have to pass through a capitalist
stage; and that England would supply the impulse to that
capitalist transformation. Later, however, in 1877 and after,
with special reference to Russia—which they believed to be
also an "oriental despotism"—Marx and Engels considered the
possibility that this capitalist stage of development might be
skipped, and the village commune might be reorganized
directly as the kernel of a socialist society. Marx wrote to Vera
Sasulich on March 8, 1881:

> The analysis presented in *Capital* gives reasons neither for nor
> against the vitality of the village community, but the special study
> which I have made of it, and for which I have searched for the
> materials in original sources, has convinced me that this community
> is the strategic point of social regeneration in Russia.

To be sure, this development was to be conditioned on the
previous victory of the socialist revolution in Europe.[26] For
Marx and Engels still believed that the main liberating force
would be the labor and socialist movement of the European
countries, which would free the colonies while the latter were
still not sufficiently developed to adopt socialism. The question
then arose: what would be the effect on socialist Europe of all
these increasingly powerful capitalist nations on the outside?
Marx wrote to Engels October 8, 1858:

> The weighty question for us now is this: On the continent the
> revolution is imminent, and will, from the first, take on a socialist

character. But will it not inevitably be crushed in this small corner, since the movement of bourgeois society is still ascendant on a far wider area?[27]

Engels does not seem to have suggested his answer to this question at the time; but in 1882 in a letter to Kautsky he speculated as follows:

In my opinion the colonies proper, *i.e.*, the countries occupied by a European population, Canada, the Cape, Australia, will all become independent; on the other hand the countries inhabited by a native population, which are simply subjugated, India, Algiers (*sic*), the Dutch, Portuguese, and Spanish possessions, must be taken over for the time being by the proletariat and led as rapidly as possible towards independence.[28]

While Marx was at first inclined to give capitalism more credit than it deserved for developing the backward areas of the world, his slashing attack on colonialism in the first volume of *Capital*, fully documented as it was, plus his well-known articles on India, gave such a strong—indeed, unanswerable— condemnation of colonialism on purely humanitarian grounds, that Marxism has ever since, and rightly, been considered to have opposed the colonial system as such.[29] Even before the new outburst of colony-hunting that set in around 1870, international socialism had given notice of just what to expect. So it was, that soon after the Second International was founded in 1889, it went on record as strongly condemning the colonial system, and this remained its position, in spite of attacks from the right, down to the First World War.* The reasons for the new outburst of colonialism had still to be given a Marxist interpretation, and the rights of colonial areas to national movements and governments of their own had to be integrated into Marxist theory, but this was not too great a task for later generations to shoulder. Marx's genius and industry had indeed given capitalism a staggering blow at its weakest point.

The tart remarks of Marx and Engels about various small and underdeveloped peoples should not be taken as implying

* See below, pp. 128–132.

any special prejudice against these peoples, specifically or in general. Both men were if anything more acid in their condemnations of advanced peoples, and it was always possible for them to document their diatribes, for what people has pursued through history a course marked by high-mindedness and progress? Marx and Engels were never tired of castigating the Germans, the French, the English, the Austrians, in fact just about every nationality with which they dealt at all. Thus Engels wrote bitterly of the Germans: "The Germans have never been national where the interests of nationality and the interests of progress coincided; they were always national where nationality came into conflict with progress."[30]

Both Marx and Engels, in their characterizations of advanced and backward nations, laid about them with gleeful abandon. Thus Marx wrote in *The German Ideology* (1845) of "the two most scoundrelly nations on earth, the patriarchal swindlers— the Chinese, and the civilized swindlers—the Yankees."[31] And Engels wrote concerning the Scandinavians, who today are sometimes referred to as the most civilized people in the world:

Scandinavism consists in enthusiasm for a brutal, dirty, piratical, old-Nordic nationality, for that deep inwardness which is unable to express its extravagant thoughts and feelings in words, but unquestionably can do so in deeds, namely, in brutality towards women, chronic drunkenness, and teary sentimentality alternating with berserk fury.[32]

Engels' endorsement of the imperialistic expansion of France and the U.S.A., and Marx's delay (if it can be called such) in calling for India's independence from England, were the result of their particular conception of the probable order of events in the evolution of the respective countries.

If socialism was to be reached only by a country's first passing through the purgatory of capitalism; if capitalism was a progressive stage in comparison with the pre-capitalist (feudal or primitive) stage; if the quickest way to launch a backward country on the path of economic development was to have it fall under the domination of an advanced country that would develop it—then the endorsement, however unwilling, of the subjection and domination of the backward areas follows naturally. It was only later, when the unreality of these various assumptions became clear with the revelation of the true nature of imperialist exploitation, that Marxism dumped this whole approach and called for determined resistance to imperialist expansion all along the line, and for the quickest possible ending of imperialist domination in those areas on which it had fastened itself.

One tool in this campaign, the slogan of the self-determination of peoples and the appeal to the nationalist sentiment in the subject areas, was only beginning to show its usefulness when Marx and Engels began their work. The independence of Poland and Ireland was thus demanded (when it was) not on broad general principles of the rights of man, but because *in relation to the whole politico-economic situation of both the imperialist country (or countries) and the oppressed area* this step seemed to be a progressive one. Hence the relatively slight attention paid to nationalism by Marx and Engels in this connection.

Marx and Engels apparently never did reconsider their early endorsement of slavery as a historic stage. But later Marxists have been busy showing that the surplus generated by slave economies is seldom used for industrial development—rather it goes back into the expansion of the slave economy as such, or is expended on undemocratic lobbies, or is hoarded, or used up in wars or unproductive show. The charismatic qualities of nationalist slave revolts like that in Haiti have also received recognition at the hands of later Marxists. The "stages" of Lewis H. Morgan have not withstood criticism, and Engels' system of stages is admittedly out of date.

Marx and Engels as Racists

Marx has been accused of anti-Semitism on the basis of his essay *Zur Judenfrage* (1843), in which he charged the Jews with having introduced to capitalism all the typical capitalistic vices; he said that the true religion of the Jews was money-grubbing.

This essay needs to be read as a whole. When we do this we perceive that Marx says nothing of the Jews that he does not say also of the Christians, who are stated to have taken over the capitalist ethics of the Jew and made them their own. "Christianity sprang from Judaism; it has now dissolved itself back into Judaism," wrote Marx. Even as to the responsibility of the Jewish religion for the mercantilist ethics of capitalism, it would seem that the position of the Jews as the pioneers of the money economy in the Middle Ages, rather than their religion, was the real reason for their association with the particular characteristics that Marx disliked. Marx indeed suggests that the cause-and-effect relationship was from the economic to the moral and ethical rather than the other way round; he writes: "Bourgeois society continuously brings forth the Jew from its own entrails."[33] Marx naturally dissented from Bruno Bauer's contention that Jews should be denied civil rights.

If Marx's attacks on the Jews were unfair and in bad taste— and who can deny that they were?—the attempt by certain of his modern detractors, like Dagobert Runes, to associate him with Nazis and other professional anti-Semites is, to say the least, much more so.[34] Marx did not consider the Jews' shortcomings to be innate; he wrote: "Here again the supreme condition of man is his *legal* status, his relationship to laws which are valid for him, not because they are the laws of his own will and nature, but because they are *dominant* and any infraction of them will be avenged."[35]

Just as Engels' writings on the national question sometimes seem, in Riazanov's words, "very impulsive,"[36] so Marx's leanings toward racism were held in check through his association with Engels. Marxism was thus saved from meandering down some of the blind alleys of mid-nineteenth-century pseudo-science. Marx was ready at first reading to adopt in 1866 an idea of the French writer Trémaux, who had sought to trace differences in national character to differences in the geological properties of the soil. Engels, who knew something about geology, set Marx straight. Trémaux had also launched an elaborate theory of the origin of human races, in which he attempted to show that "the ordinary Negro type is only the degeneration of a much higher type," and this line of thought also Marx was prepared to accept; but Engels again had the equipment to refute Trémaux and he even chided Marx gently for having been so incautious.[37]

In their use of racist epithets Marx and Engels were both impolite and unscientific, and they appear especially so in these days when genocide is at last recognized as an international crime. To say that most of the leading intellectuals of their day shared the same prejudices is not so much a defense of Marx and Engels as a criticism of their epoch. Their occasional use of the word "nigger"—in private correspondence—should not be allowed to obscure their extraordinary services during the American Civil War. At a time when the dominant manufacturing and trading interest had almost committed England to the side of the Confederacy, and the labor aristocracy and labor press leaned to the Southern side, Marx got the First International to give strong moral support to the North, and helped organize mass meetings where rank-and-file workers could express their sentiment against slavery.

Nationalism and Social Class

It is in the field of social classes and their relationship to the problem of nationalism and nationality that we look most hopefully to Marxism for guidance, since Marx put the class struggle so dramatically in the front of his analysis of past and contemporary history. But just as Marx never finished his analysis of classes as such—the third volume of *Capital* breaks off tantalizingly just as he seems about to delve deeply into the subject—so the references to class in the discussions of nationality problems are few and disappointing.

When the sentiment of nationalism is enlisted in a worthy cause, it rates a favoring adjective. When on the other hand nationalistic sentiment holds back progress, it is dismissed as "prejudice." Occasionally these two uses occur in the same passage. Thus when Marx was discussing the attitude of the French and British workers and peasants to the Crimean War, he wrote: "Both British and French proletarians are filled with an honorable national spirit, though they are more or less free from the antiquated national prejudices common in both countries to the peasantry."[38] When does "antiquated national prejudice" turn into an "honorable national spirit"? Surely Marx refers in both cases to nationalist sentiment. Does he mean that the proletariat is always right? If so, we cannot credit him with sufficient scientific caution.

Once Marx and Engels had become committed to the philosophy of proletarian internationalism, they seldom referred to nationalism without some deprecatory adjective, usually "narrow."

Thus, Engels in 1848 complained that the Belgian Government had appealed to the "narrow sentiment of nationalism" prevalent among a certain class of the population in order to arouse the people against the German rebels, such as Marx, and secure their expulsion.[39] Marx reproached the German philosophers for being narrowly national without realizing it:

If national narrow-mindedness is everywhere repulsive, it becomes actually loathesome in Germany, for there it is coupled with the illusion that the Germans are above nationalism and practical interests, in contrast to those nations that have the frankness to admit their national narrow-mindedness and their dependence on practical interests.[40]

But while the proletariat might be credited with an "honorable national spirit," its mission in history, as seen by Marx and Engels, was to overthrow the bourgeoisie and establish proletarian internationalism. Thus the long-run sentiment of the proletariat would be not nationalist but internationalist, and this was the point of view that Marx and Engels and their associates consciously sought to profess. They thus easily slipped into the position of attributing internationalist sentiment to the proletariat as something natural to it, in contrast to transitory nationalist sentiment or "prejudice." Thus Engels wrote in 1845: "The proletarians are in the great majority already by nature without national prejudices, and their whole education and movement is essentially humanitarian, antinational."[41] And Marx wrote about the same time: "It is, of course, true of every nation that insistence upon nationality is now to be found only among the bourgeoisie and their writers."[42]

Marx and Engels seized on any evidence which might show that the proletariat was more international-minded than the bourgeoisie. Marx cited fraternal statements from both sides of the border in 1870 as evidence that the workers of France and Germany showed less nationalistic sentiment than the respective upper classes. This sentiment of the proletariat he attributed to the advanced state of their class consciousness. Concerning the nationalist demonstrations in Germany, he wrote to Engels in July, 1870:

Fortunately this whole demonstration stems from the middle class. The working class, with the exception of Schweitzer's immediate followers, are taking no part in it. Fortunately the *war of classes* [English in original] in both countries, France and Germany, is far enough advanced so that no war *abroad* [English] can seriously turn back the clock of history.[43]

Unfortunately for the theory of proletarian internationalism, the growth of nationalist sentiment in the late 19th and 20th centuries did not pass the proletariat by. The syndicalist Lagardelle in an article in 1902 called attention to the fact that the masses of the workers were chauvinistically inclined, and somewhat sadly expressed the wish that the Socialist Party would fight wholeheartedly against the patriotic demagogy of the bourgeois parties, all of which were nationalistic. "But unfortunately," he concluded, "this is not the case."[44]

The "National" Class

Since society is divided into classes, now one and now another exercises the dominant role in determining policy. Can any one class be considered the "national" class? For considerable periods one class may exercise control, in the view of Marx and Engels; and when it exercises its power in such a way as to develop suitably the forces of production, it justifies its claim to be considered the "national class." Engels wrote in 1888: "The English capitalists in the early nineteenth century had become the leading class in the nation, the class whose interests were for the moment the national interest."[45]

Some writers, such as Solomon Bloom, have taken this concept of the national class to imply that "to speak at all of national wants or the welfare of a nation argued a potential common purpose hovering, however tenuously, over the battlefield of contending classes." He adds: "Otherwise, the idea of the nation and the idea of the class excluded each other."[46] The implication of Bloom's argument is that when the leading or "national" class is following a policy which is in the national interest, the other classes should follow its lead, and especially in times of national crisis should submerge their particular class interests temporarily.

This was not the meaning that Marx and Engels gave to the terms. There was for them no "idea of the nation" as such; those who used this term could be accused of "idealism" as found in unreconstructed Hegelianism. There was also no national interest superior to the interests of the proletarian revolution, although, as we have seen, Marx and Engels did think that it was in the interests of all concerned that there should be nations to develop the productive forces.

The "national class" during the period of its dominance no doubt conducted public affairs in such a way that it as a class was benefited. But it always maintained even so that the interests it represented were national interests and that its administration was being conducted in the interests of all the people. When it favored its own class too obviously and unashamedly, Marx, who spent much time writing for the general press, used to call it to task and charge it with putting its class interests above the general interest. In his articles in the *New York Tribune*, for example, Marx once wrote: "As for the British aristocracy, represented by the Coalition Ministry, they would, if need be, sacrifice the national English interests to their particular class interests."[47]

Bloom, ostensibly expounding Marx, writes: "If one class leads, other classes must follow."[48] Marx surely never said that. The examples which Bloom gives prove the opposite. They show that the workers and peasants in the French Revolution, mentioned by Marx, were by no means content to leave the conduct of the revolution to the bourgeoisie, even though it was then the leading class and was developing the productive forces. On the contrary, the workers and peasants subjected the bourgeoisie to continuous pressure; and this pressure, in Bloom's own words, "supplied the guarantee that the bourgeoisie would not place its own interests before the common cause."[49]

It might be possible to use the "national class" idea to defend the ruling class in a society which, though caste-ridden and undemocratic, is making rapid economic progress.[50] But whether used in this way or in the way employed by Marx and Engels, the concept of the "national class" seems to add nothing to the already existing framework of analysis. It has caused unnecessary trouble.

According to Marx and Engels, modern society tends to split up more and more into two main classes, the bourgeoisie or middle class and the proletariat or working class. Since in some countries, such as France, the majority of the population did not belong to either of these classes but consisted of small farmers (peasants), and since Marx elsewhere recognized the persistence of a class of large landowners, the division adumbrated in the *Manifesto* is intended to apply to the future more than to the present. But as between the two main classes, there was no question in Marx's mind that the only one that had the right to be considered the "national" class in the long run was the proletariat, and only then because after the social revolution it would absorb the other classes which it would first have defeated.

The bourgeoisie had been a progressive force in the immediate past, and indeed Marx thought that it would continue to be a progressive force in backward countries even after socialism had won out in Europe; and in such countries, as in Europe where the bourgeoisie found itself still in conflict with feudal reaction, it was the interest and the duty of the workers to aid the bourgeoisie—although Lenin later added the qualification that where the workers were strong enough they should take the lead in this struggle.

For Marx, "national interest" was a bourgeois term, used to mask the real state of affairs. Since he believed that the theory of increasing misery ruled out a *more rapid* improvement of the condition of the workers than of the middle class, he lost no opportunity to emphasize that the interests of the bourgeoisie coincided with the interests of the people at large only partially or temporarily.

It is evident that Marx in discussing nationalism had to take account of the psychology of the several strata of society. This need follows from the proposition, enunciated so clearly by Bakunin and accepted in practice by Marx, that class consciousness and the sentiment of nationalism are alike facts and must be dealt with as such. The dialectic method of Marx and Engels does not deny the existence of such facts, even when they run counter to what the theorist might have predicted. If it did it would not be a scientific method. At most the materialist approach can *explain* ideas, and it does this often in a way that would be completely impossible for historians who give to ideas a natural history of their own, divorced from their social context. Of course, Marxists can also propound policies and predictions which have then to vindicate themselves in practice like any others. But as Croce points out, the materialist conception of history does not necessarily embody any particular solution to the problems of history.[51] Thus Marxists are in frequent disagreement not only as to policies but as to facts and the interpretations which should be placed on these facts.

Contradictions in the Marxist Position

We have already noticed that the attitude of Marx and Engels was not always consistent on problems involving the national question. When they abandoned their early pro-imperialist line and sharply criticized the exploitative activities of the colonial powers, this shift represented progress and is surely commendable. But on some other points, such as self-determination, the future of the South Slavs, the permissibility of offensive wars, the protective tariff, and so on, we have observed contradictions and inconsistencies in their treatment. The unifying thread, as we would expect, was in general opposition to exploitation and a vindication of the rights of the underdog; but even this guiding principle is not always adhered to.

The real problem of interpreting the attitude of Marx and Engels on nationalism arises when the several strands of their thought on nationalism clash, or when events fail to bear out their predictions, so that we are left to wonder which of several suggested alternatives they would have chosen. These problems began to arise already during the lives of both men.

According to the *Manifesto*, the workers have no stake in capitalist society and hence no feeling of patriotism for it. But suppose they get a stake in it, through the acquisition of suffrage, an improvement in their scale of living and an old-age pension? Do they then have a fatherland, and are its interests their interests, country by country?

Marx and Engels had stated flatly in the *Manifesto* that the workers' level of living in capitalist countries would deteriorate further, and this position was maintained long afterwards by doctrinaire Marxists.[52] However, Marx and Engels themselves quietly abandoned this untenable position and in the late 1860's were emphasizing *relative* misery of the workers, whose *absolute* condition had improved. Marx in the first volume of *Das Kapital*, published in 1867, mentioned the possibility of real wages rising; and Engels in 1869, recalling the condition in which he had found the British working class at his first arrival in Manchester, was forced to recognize that they had made advances.

By 1891 Engels had abandoned completely the idea of increasing *absolute* misery of the proletariat. A conference of the German Social-Democratic Party, which had just emerged from illegality, had been called to meet in October, 1891, and the program to be adopted there would, it was realized, set policy for years to come. A draft of the program proposed by the party executive was sent to Engels in June. It stated among other things that the suffering of the proletarians was getting ever greater—a thoughtless parroting of the language of the 1848 *Manifesto*. Engels objected to this passage on the "suffering." He commented: "Expressed in this unconditional form, this is incorrect. The organization of the workers and their constantly growing resistance will possibly stem the *growth of misery* to a certain extent. But the *insecurity of existence* will certainly grow."[53] The criticism was accepted. The program finally adopted at Erfurt in October eliminated the reference to "suffering"; it stated instead that "general insecurity has become the normal state of society."

Bourgeois economists in the third quarter of the 19th century had attributed the improvement in the workers' condition to free trade. When free trade gave way to protectionism, and imperialism became the order of the day, the continued (though slow) improvement of workers' standards was attributed to imperialism, and Engels could do no better than fall in with the current idea. He foresaw the growth of a "bourgeois proletariat" in England and considered such a development not surprising in "a nation which was exploiting the whole world."[54] We have shown elsewhere our reasons for considering this analysis to be incomplete, since it did not consider the alternative theory that the improvement was due to improving techniques and greater productivity both at home and abroad.[55] According to this alternative approach, the economic improvement which was noted in the period to 1914 took place *in spite of* the system of imperialism and nationalist rivalries.

Marx and Engels, by their insistence on the importance of developing large economic units, especially through national unification, had implied that the workers had a stake in nationalism. On the related point—whether the workers had a stake in imperialism—Marx and Engels were not so explicit, but they stated that the skilled workers had been bought off by the super-profits of imperialism and implied by the use of phrases like that of Engels on the "bourgeois proletariat" that the unskilled had benefited too.

The question of whether the workers should work through their respective national governments and through trade unions to secure for themselves a share of the increasing national prosperity was answered by Marx and Engels in the affirmative. It was only when the "national interests" of two different countries clashed that a problem was posed for the workers of the countries concerned. It was not possible, in the light of their other theories already mentioned, for Marx and Engels to deny that there were such "national interests" nor even to contend that these were exclusively class interests of the bourgeoisie, as they had maintained at first.

Do the workers then have an interest in supporting the bourgeoisie in the national struggles of the latter? The guidance given by Marx and Engels on this point was inconclusive, owing to their failure to develop fully the economic implications of the imperialist movement. Their general position, however, was never in doubt: in any given war, the defeat of one or another national bourgeoisie (ruling class) would be in the interests of the proletarian revolution, and the workers should accordingly support or oppose their respective bourgeoisies, including in wartime.

The question as to what attitude the working class of a colonial or semi-colonial country should take towards a national-liberation movement led by the national bourgeoisie cannot be answered for a Marxist by simple reference to the works of Marx and Engels (if indeed that method is ever correct). Marx and Engels wrote before the emergence of an industrial proletariat in the colonial countries, so the question hardly arose for them. Any attempts to attribute a position on this question to Marx and Engels on the basis of their supposed belief in the charismatic qualities of the "national class" must founder, as indicated already, on the fact that leadership by such a class in Marxist theory is an apocryphal misinterpretation.

The idea that the workers of one nation have a stake in the interests of that nation as opposed to other nations has to be considered in three parts. When both the countries are capitalist countries, a true Marxist position would be one of opposition to the imperialist aims of each bourgeoisie; such a line was taken by Karl Liebknecht, Rosa Luxemburg, Lenin, Connolly, and others during World War I. Where one of the countries is socialist and the other capitalist, the problem is relatively simple to answer. When both countries are socialist, the question should not, in strict theory, arise; certainly Marx and Engels would have been shocked and horrified at the thought of their followers falling out to the extent that war between two socialist countries could be contemplated. But proletarian internationalism is a difficult philosophy to apply—especially since not all those who call themselves socialists or communists are Marxists.

IV

FROM INTERNATIONALISM TO NATIONALISM: THE PERVERSION OF GERMAN SOCIAL DEMOCRACY

In the generation before the First World War, nationalism and the national question impinged on the life of the socialist and labor movement at a dozen points. The rush to divide or redivide the world among the great powers caused a sharp division of opinion within the movement on the subject of imperialism and colonialism. The rise of new nationalities dominated the politics of Austria-Hungary and posed problems also in other European countries such as the Russian and Turkish empires, Germany and even Scandinavia. International frictions increased sharply, and armaments and militarism became an issue, while various proposals for heading off the approaching war were discussed. The issue of social revolution vs. reformism involved the national question inasmuch as Marx had insisted that true internationalism was possible only after socialism should have been achieved. The movement had not fully made up its mind what attitude to take toward the (bourgeois) state and nation as such.

The position adopted by the several leaders on the issue of evolution vs. revolution served to classify them into left and right wings, and there is a temptation to use the same classification with regard to the national question, since anti-colonialism, anti-militarism, and a favorable attitude toward the claims of subject peoples generally went together with a Marxist-Leninist revolutionary approach. But such classifications have to be used with caution. In the Netherlands, where the issue between left and right first reached the breaking point, so that a secession from the Social-Democratic Workers Party took place as early as 1909, the colonial issue was not a factor; left-wing leaders split among themselves on the attitude to be taken to the colonies.[1]* Jean Jaurès was extremely active in opposing militarism but on other issues was rated as a moderate. Bebel, who was quite a militant in some respects, favored sweeping nationalist and colonial issues under the rug. Rosa Luxemburg, an outstanding left-wing leader, was opposed to the principle of self-determination; while in the United States Eugene Debs, in most respects a militant left-winger, thought that imperialism was an issue with which the working class should not concern itself. In England, some of the most vocal socialist leaders were among the outstanding British patriots and jingos. Also some leaders, like Kautsky, shifted their positions both before and, especially, after August 7, 1914. Thus the position of each leader has to be considered on its merits. It is noteworthy also that with regard to certain of these issues more effective leadership was given in developing what would now be considered a good Marxist position, by non-Marxists than by Marxists, and some revisionists posed as Marxists while preaching a non-Marxist philosophy. But the attitude taken by any given leader on questions of nationalism and imperialism is itself an element in determining whether he should be considered a left-wing Marxist or a reformist. Thus the contention of one recent writer, that certain "left-wing" leaders of German Social Democracy were in favor of imperialism and even of collaboration with the reactionary upper bourgeoisie and the landed interests, has to be received with some reserve.[2]

The debates in the German Social-Democratic Party during this period were of special importance to the international movement for their intellectual content, which was in general high, and also for other reasons. After its legalization in 1890, the Party grew so rapidly that by 1914 it was the largest single party in Germany. Democratic reforms were proceeding apace,

* The secessionists at first took the name "Social-Democratic Party"; later—Nov. 17, 1918—the group was rechristened the "Communist Party."

and the time seemed not far distant when this important country would be ruled by the Social Democrats, with or without an absolute majority. In international relations, Germany was in the position of challenging established powers such as England; hence any proposals for disarmament or arbitration, such as were frequently brought forward, would obviously require German assent. The influence of German ideas and policies was very strong on the neighboring countries. Thus the statement of their position by German representatives in the international congresses such as those of the Labor and Socialist International was listened to with much attention.

The Social-Democratic Party had been declared illegal in 1878, but was legalized again in 1890. At Erfurt the following year it adopted an electoral program which remained, with few changes, until 1914. The attitude to militarism and war was indicated in Point 3, which called for a citizens' militia in place of the standing army, and for arbitration of international differences. There was also a demand for a referendum before war should be declared; but this provision disappeared at the next Congress and was not heard of again until after World War I.

The question of what attitude to take to the Kaiser's government was debated at Erfurt, and the decision was to have as little as possible to do with the government. As between those who believed in working with and through the bourgeois state (the *staatserhaltend* position) and those who believed in opposing it at every point (the *staatsfeindlich* position), the victory rested at first with the latter.

Early Leaders

This battle had indeed begun in Marxist circles even before the formation of the first Social-Democratic Party. Where von Schweitzer and the Lassalleans were ardent protagonists of the Prussian state, and of the German Empire as constructed by Bismarck, Wilhelm Liebknecht took just the opposite point of

view. His slogan was: "No peace with the present state." Together with Bebel and the Eisenachers he waged a continual
war against it. The reconstruction of Poland was for him a
holy duty. He rejected the name of Deutsche Arbeiter-Partei
which was proposed for the united party in 1875, on the ground
that the name was too nationalistic.[3]

Julius Motteler, speaking on behalf of six Eisenachers and
three Lassalleans, had said in the Reichstag in 1874: "We
are opponents of the Reich insofar as the Reich represents
certain institutions under which we feel oppressed, under
which we suffer. We are no opponents of the Reich as such—
as a national, as a state whole."[4]

The distinction which was thus presented in somewhat
blurred and equivocal form, tended to become even less sharp
as the Reich developed some features of a social state.

Wilhelm Liebknecht was an opponent of the Prussianized
German state, but not of *a* German state. He was indeed a German expansionist, seeking to advance the power of the
German people at the expense of the Slavs. He always re-
gretted that Prussia had defeated Austria in 1866; he regarded
Austria as "the German frontier which we had pushed into the
Orient, in the direction of Constantinople and the Mediter-
ranean Sea," and which through the war of 1866 had been
"delivered over to the Slavs." Like Rodbertus, like Lassalle—
whom he opposed on the issue of Prussian leadership in the
German Reich—Liebknecht would have liked to see German
soldiers stand at Constantinople.[5]

Wilhelm Liebknecht was a pioneer socialist. But the Union
of German Workers' Unions (1863), of which he was a leader, was not socialist in the sense that Lassalle's party was.
It joined the First International, with reservations, in 1869, at
which time it was reorganized as the German Social-Democratic Workers' Party. Liebknecht was known as an internationalist, but he did nothing to build up the International.
Bebel and Liebknecht, says a modern scholar, wanted to use
the prestige of the International's name without giving up their

freedom to organize the Party according to purely German needs, and also without fully acknowledging the International's program, or even paying membership dues.[6] This indeed was Engels' judgment at the time.[7] Marx was just as much against the Austrophile nationalism of Wilhelm Liebknecht as he was against the Prussian nationalism of Lassalle. Thus non-Marxist German nationalism affected both wings of the German movement before their union in 1875, at Gotha.

August Bebel, who with Wilhelm Liebknecht had participated in the founding of the International Workingmen's Association in 1863, was like him at first a firm opponent of the Prussian state and of Bismarck's German Reich. The war of 1870, like the War of 1914, was presented in Germany as a defensive war, but Bebel was skeptical and together with Liebknecht refrained from voting on the war credits in 1870, in the North German Reichstag. In 1871, after the removal of Louis Napoleon, Bebel decided that the war was one of aggression and voted against the war credits. Like the rest of the world, he had been misled by Bismarck's falsification concerning the start of the war (Ems telegram, etc.); he said later that if he and Liebknecht had known the real facts, they would have voted against the war credits in the first place.[8] However, in the course of time he came to accept the monarchy, as nearly everyone did. At the Amsterdam Congress of the Second International in 1904 he said the monarchy was not as bad as it had been painted. He gave it credit for having brought about "something the French had never had, namely national unity."[9] He came to the point of view that the Fatherland was the same for the working class as for the other social classes, since all lived on the same soil, spoke the same language, and had the same customs.

A leading opponent of Bebel in the SPD was Georg von Vollmar, who was frankly conservative and no less nationalistic than Bebel. In 1907 he said, "International is not anti-national. It is not true that we have no fatherland." And again, he said that we cannot imagine the dissolution of nations into a "formless mixture of peoples" (*Völkerbrei*).[10] This opinion, like the quoting of it by Herman Heidegger in a recent study, is apparently intended as a criticism of Marx's theory of internationalism, which Heidegger finds to have been inadequate.[11] But Heidegger, and probably Vollmar too, misunderstood the theory of proletarian internationalism. Marx always contemplated the survival and development of national culture and national organization, but thought that true internationalism could be attained only on the basis of socialism. The attempt to develop a system of internationalism while capitalism still prevailed, which was in the minds of some of Marx's alleged disciples, was doomed from the start. Marx cannot be made responsible if this idea, which he never held, was discredited by the events.

Position of the Unions

Within the labor and socialist movement the German trade unions represented a stronghold of state-supporting and nationalist sentiment. Although collective agreements did not come into general use until the end of the First World War, the union leaders had necessarily to adapt themselves to and even participate in government institutions. The scale of living of the German workers was not high in any absolute sense, but it was rising, and the idea gained ground that the workers had a stake in the country. Revisionists had close connections with the union movement and conducted a number of trade-union schools. When war was declared in 1914, the whole "free" trade-union press without a single exception called for support of the government.[12]

The smaller group of "Christian" unions from their first congress in 1899 were at least as nationalist as the "free" (Social-Democratic) unions, while the very small Hirsch-Duncker unions were explicitly nationalist from their foundation in 1868. German syndicalists had appeared before World

War I, but at the peak of their strength, in 1922, they numbered no more than 200,000.

The labor and socialist leaders could not in practice be consistently *staatsfeindlich* and still do their job. In local and national assemblies, in the cooperatives and trade unions which had constant relations with the authorities, in the local governments, the sick-benefit *Krankenkassen* of the social insurance system, and many other connections, the Social-Democratic activist had to work with the government institutions and even to help make them work. The boycott of the state was never taken seriously in South Germany, and became less and less effective in the country as a whole. The Social-Democratic Party (SPD) did not enter the government, even when it had become the largest party in the country, but it did participate in the Reichstag, and finally in 1913, conversations began between government spokesmen and the conservative SPD representatives in the Reichstag.

The official position on the relation to the State was at best equivocal. During this period the Party was campaigning for freedom of the unions to organize, for the unrestricted franchise, and for the full democratization of the governmental machinery. The rank and file worker could not be blamed for thinking that these demands if won—and they were being won, one after the other—would benefit him, or for thinking that he was getting a form of government worth having: a state worth supporting and participating in. Thus the very idea of boycotting the state had in effect been abandoned before 1914.

The general strike as a means of upsetting governments and stopping international wars was much discussed after the Russian strikes of 1905 had shown spectacular results. The German union leaders made it quite clear that the organized labor movement in Germany would have nothing to do with any such affairs. Rosa Luxemburg speculated on the possibility of a general strike of the unorganized workers[13] (the Russians in 1905 had been largely unorganized); but the idea had to be dismissed as chimerical, since unorganized workers are poor material for any but a completely spontaneous popular movement. Thus the discussion of the revolutionary general strike somewhat abated after 1907.

The demand for the establishment of a citizens' militia met a fate similar to that of the general strike against war. In the military class state of Germany, the standing army was a sort of sacred cow, and attacks on it were difficult and dangerous. When the Social Democrats demanded a citizens' militia in place of the standing army, they were frankly seeking to weaken the government, a demand which of course ran contrary to the demand for defense of the fatherland in which most Social Democrats were joining.* Thus the citizens' militia remained a sort of shibboleth—something to talk about, but not intended for serious implementation. The SPD continued to vote against increasing the standing army, but in 1913 did vote for the first time in favor of increasing taxes for military purposes.

Left-Wing Leaders

The left wing in the SPD, from 1900 to the end of the First World War, was represented by Karl Liebknecht and Rosa Luxemburg, who were opposed to the state and all its works. Karl Liebknecht was anti-militarist to the extent of being anti-patriotic; he declared flatly that the workers had no fatherland.[14] However he attacked Hervé as unrealistic. He did not seriously advocate the general strike against war, since he was forced to recognize that the great majority of the proletariat was not prepared for such an action; he thought that the workers were not class conscious or socialist-minded, to that extent.[15] Alone of the 111 SPD members in the Reichstag, he voted against the war credits on Dec. 2, 1914.

---

* "The militia demand is in order to weaken the government," wrote Kautsky in 1911. —"Der erste Mai und der Kampf gegen den Militarismus," in *Neue Zeit* 1911–1912, Bd. II, p. 98.

Rosa Luxemburg said that in the imperialist environment there could no longer be such a thing as a war of defense. It was either patriotism or class struggle, imperialism or socialism.[16] She considered the SPD's support of the war to be treason to the international movement, and set forth her views in a flaming series of articles (the Junius pamphlets).[17]* The group to which she and Karl Liebknecht belonged called at that time for a frontal attack on the bourgeois ideology of nationalism:

The next task of socialism is the spiritual liberation of the proletariat from the tutelage of the bourgeoisie, which expresses itself in nationalist ideology. The national sections have to direct their agitation in the parliaments and in the press to denounce the phraseology of nationalism as an instrument of bourgeois domination. The only defense of all truly national freedom is today the revolutionary class struggle against imperialism. The fatherland of the proletarians, to whose defense everything else must be subordinated, is the socialist Internationale.[18]

Of course, there were other writers who at one time or another were classified as left-wing, and it is to them, or some of them, that Abraham Ascher referred, in his opinion already quoted that certain "left-wing" leaders of German Social Democracy were in favor of imperialism and even of collaboration with the reactionary upper bourgeoisie and the landed interests.†

It is possible to show from Ascher's own data that this statement is a slander on the left wing.

The three writers that he selects for treatment are Anton Pannekoek, Paul Lensch, and Heinrich Cunow.

It appears that Pannekoek before the First World War (1912) had contended that imperialism would add to the

---

* The International Group (Spartakusbund) adopted on Jan. 1, 1916, a resolution drawn up by Rosa Luxemburg which stated: "In this era of unchained imperialism there can be no more national wars."—Rosa Luxemburg, *Ausgewählte Reden und Schriften* (Berlin, 1951), I, 395.
† Cf. above, p. 84.

burdens on the proletariat and work it up to the point where
it would rebel against capitalism. He did not advocate that the
Social-Democrats should openly espouse imperialism, but he
did favor relaxing opposition to it (says Ascher), on the theory
of "the worse the better."

Lensch is another pre-war radical of the left cited by Ascher.
He anticipated Lenin in calling imperialism the highest stage
of capitalism, through which capitalism must pass in order to
reach socialism, says Ascher. It was Lensch who supposedly
advocated collaboration with reactionaries.

The third of the pre-war radicals to come out for imperialism,
in Ascher's account, was Heinrich Cunow, who during the war
was to succeed Kautsky as editor of *Die neue Zeit*.[19]

The refutation of Ascher's slanderous contentions is not
difficult. Pannekoek was Dutch, but let that pass. Before the
left-wing group to which he belonged had time to take action
against him, he had shifted his position and was campaigning
(in 1915) for the independence of Indonesia from the Netherlands (Holland).*

As for Cunow, by the time he espoused imperialism he had
ceased to be considered a member of the left wing, as Ascher
also shows. But Lensch is the most striking example to disprove
Ascher's point. His progression toward adoption of imperialism
was so marked that it took him not only out of the left wing
but out of the Social-Democratic movement altogether. Like
Hervé in France and Mussolini and Corradini in Italy, he went
into the pay of the reactionaries. He became a writer for the
Deutsche Allgemeine Zeitung, owned by Hugo Stinnes.

All that Ascher has proved is that certain writers theretofore
known as left wing adopted at a certain time a pro-imperialist
approach. But he does not tell what attitude the left wing took
toward these writers. Thus his story is incomplete. We can only
assume that the incompleteness is deliberate, since in most
respects his study is well informed.

* Cf. below, p. 119.

Colonialism

When the Kaiser's Germany had first embarked on an expansionist course, with a program of building a big navy and going after overseas colonies, the Social-Democratic Party was strongly opposed, and it might have been expected that this opposition would continue. Several factors favored the anti-colonialists.

First, they had the advantage of an early start. Kautsky, who had founded *Die neue Zeit* in 1883 and had continued as its industrious editor, had been at first a strong opponent of colonialism and armaments. He even brought in question the morality of the treatment of the North American Indians.[20] For him colonialism was exploitation by definition. When Germany began to acquire colonies in Africa, Kautsky was in the forefront of the opponents. He traced the degrading effect of colonialism on the Europeans, and concluded: "We don't bring civilization to the Africans: we take over barbarism from them."[21] Even this statement, incidentally, was not fair to the Africans, since as Kautsky relentlessly recounted, the subjugation of the Africans, like that of the Indians, was one long history of duplicity and brutality in which the Europeans far outdid their underdeveloped victims—underdeveloped in this as in other respects.

The Mainz Party Congress of the SPD (1900) adopted a resolution against colonialism, which it said derived in the first instance from the grasping demand of the bourgeoisie for new opportunities to increase its ever-swelling capital as well as from the pressure for new markets. This policy (continued the resolution) rests on the forcible appropriation of foreign territories and the ruthless enslavement and exploitation of the peoples living in them. It brutalizes and demoralizes the exploiters themselves, who carry on their robberies by the most reprehensible and even inhuman means. Social Democracy, the resolution concluded, demands that the desirable and necessary cultural and trade relations be established in such a way that the rights, freedoms, and independence of these peoples are guaranteed.[22]

Beside the arguments from general democratic-socialist principles (humanitarianism and self-determination) the German anti-colonialists had the strong point that the colonies and the big armaments were a financial burden on the taxpayer, especially on the workers because of the unjust system of regressive taxation.[23] The point about high taxes affected other classes too and was fully appreciated by the business community, which was by no means unanimous at first in endorsing colonialist policies. The anti-colonialist Social Democrats also pointed out that development of the colonies might involve building up industries that would compete with home industries—the "coolie labor" argument. To be sure, the German colonies never came close to that degree of development.

Still another argument against colonies arose out of the breakdown controversy. The question whether capitalism would collapse as a result of its inner contradictions was much debated, and some maintained that colonialism would postpone the inevitable collapse by furnishing capitalism with an outlet for surplus goods and surplus capital. This argument was two-pronged. Thus, Paul Lensch in 1912 wrote that imperialism was the highest stage of capitalism and that it was therefore futile to talk about disarmament in existing conditions; the only correct policy was a frontal attack on imperialism as such.[24]*

However, one wing of the German Social-Democratic Party had favored German colonialism from an early date. Eduard Bernstein, who had enjoyed the confidence of Engels and was one of his literary executors, wrote an article in defense of colonialism in 1896. Although cloaked in Marxist and even humanitarian terminology, the import of the argument was clearly imperialist. Bernstein began by saying that the Social-

* The article from which this opinion is taken was cited by Ascher to prove that Lensch had gone over to the imperialists! This illustration may indicate how completely unreliable Lensch had become.

Democratic Party had opposed the annexation of Alsace-Lorraine to Germany in 1871, as indeed it had. The Party, continued Bernstein, was in favor of the peoples' liberation struggles everywhere. However he proceeded to list a number of exceptions to this rule. Exempted are African peoples who carry on traffic in slaves, or who claim the right to fall on their peaceful neighbors and plunder them. Also, "to support savages and barbarians who resist the penetration of capitalistic civilization would be romantic." Bernstein contended that "higher" civilizations have rights superior to those of "lower" ones. He spoke out in favor of diplomatic intervention for German (capitalist) interests abroad.[25]

Herman Wendel, by quoting selected passages from this article, was later able to present Bernstein as an internationalist and defender of the rights of backward peoples, while Abraham Ascher has more recently described Bernstein as a "sincere humanitarian."[26] If these opinions are correct, then there is no such thing as insincerity or double-talk.

In another article a little later, Bernstein defended the role of the British in India, contending that everything there was for the best under the best of all possible imperialisms. If the Indian peasant had not benefited as much as he might have, this was largely his own fault; he was a difficult man to help. And Bernstein ended by blaming the Indians themselves for their poverty in the same way that Malthus had defended poverty in England—the people of India insisted on having too many children.[27]

Already in 1896 Bernstein wrote as a "patriotic German." By 1898 he had formulated his philosophy as an advocate and defender of German capitalist interests everywhere. Where "really important national interests" are at stake, he wrote, as in China for example, "Germany should secure herself a position." The acquisition of colonies, he said, claiming to represent the views of Marx and Engels, is not in itself wrong:

It is neither necessary that the occupation of tropical lands by Europeans should injure the natives in their enjoyment of life, nor

has it hitherto usually been the case. (!) Moreover, only a condi-
tional right of savages to the land occupied by them can be
recognized. The higher civilization ultimately can claim a higher
right. Not the conquest, but the cultivation, of the land gives the
historical title to its use.[28]

To such uses had the work of Marx and Engels been turned.

Yet curiously, when the English Socialist Belfort Bax wrote
an article for *Die neue Zeit* upbraiding Bernstein and contending that Socialists everywhere should oppose colonialism,
Kautsky came to Bernstein's defense in an editorial note.[29]
Belfort Bax in his article had included Kautsky with the
defenders of colonialism, though without giving the grounds
for such inclusion.

During the Boer War (1899–1902) the sympathies of the
German Social Democrats were divided. Some attacked the
Boers on the ground that they were slaveholders and agrarians,
while England represented industrialism, capitalism, and free
labor—in a word, progress. Kautsky answered that as between
patriarchal and capitalistic exploitation of forced labor the
latter is undoubtedly the worse. The real issue, said Kautsky,
is national independence, which in South Africa as in any
modern community is the precondition for its normal and
quick development.[30] This was almost exactly the position that
Engels had taken in 1882 with regard to Poland, with this
difference: in Poland the indigenous population was not being
exploited by two competing groups of Europeans.*

Bernstein at times recognized that there had been outrages
in the colonies, but he contended that they were "heavily outweighed" by the benefits that imperialism had brought.[31]

The ranks of the Social Democrats were indeed badly split.
Richard Calwer, a strong nationalist, and a group including
also Ludwig Quessel and Gerhard Hildebrand advocated
colonialist and expansionist policies in *Sozialistische Monatshefte*, a theoretical journal second in importance only to the
official *Neue Zeit*. The policies advocated by Hildebrand were

* See above, Chapter III.

not in any sense socialist but he was not expelled from the Party until 1912. This group was from the beginning allergic to the charge that the Social-Democrats were unpatriotic. Internationalism was not the same thing as anti-nationalism. They played down capitalist rivalries, which they admitted had existed in the early days; but this period had been succeeded, they said, by one of increasingly close interconnections and the development of a world market. The trusts and cartels, they said, were examples of international cooperation and could become the basis of an internationally organized economy.[32]

The proletariat, they contended, is stateless through the fault of the bourgeoisie. "We, the socialists, will give it a fatherland for the first time."[33]

Their type of internationalism did not exclude the fostering of nationalist animosities in the German working class, which was reminded of the Poles and Russians who were allegedly being imported to take the place of native German workers with a higher living standard.[34] Gustav Noske introduced an anti-Semitic note when he sought to stir up feeling against Jewish teachers who were brought in from the East.[35]

Max Schippel attacked the distinction that was being made by the Social-Democratic majority between settlement colonization, and annexation of populated territories. Settlement colonization, exemplified by the United States, is not any better for the natives, he said; there is no part of the world where immigrants can settle without sacrificing the interests of the original native population.[36]

The members of this school of thought, who contended that colonialism could have a civilizing influence if administered by socialists ("we can do it better"), were eventually dubbed "social imperialists." If they were not expelled, as Hildebrand was, this was no doubt because their ideas were shared by such a large and influential element in the Party. The 1901 (Lübeck) Congress of the SDP did indeed condemn Bernstein's revisionism as contrary to Social-Democratic policy. The

editor of the Berlin *Vorwärts* was replaced in 1906 for being
too revisionist. But even Bebel said that colonial policies could
"under certain circumstances" operate as a civilizing factor.[37]

Victory of the Revisionists

The expansion-minded rulers, who had embarked on a big-
navy, more-colonies policy, sought in 1907 an endorsement of
this policy from the electorate, and heaped scorn and calumny
on all who opposed, meaning principally the Social-Democratic
Party. The Party had supporters from the lower middle class
in the cities when it came to resisting taxes to build the navy;
in fact some students thought afterwards that the small-navy
policy of the Party at this period had been developed by and
for this middle-class element.[38] But the Party was no match for
the big-business campaign. At each election up to that time
the Social Democrats had shown a substantial gain over the
previous one; but in the 1907 elections they barely held their
own in the popular vote, and lost a number of seats in the
Reichstag.

The right wing of the Social-Democratic Party at this point
became very vocal, demanding in effect that the Party should
withdraw from the field of foreign policy and leave it to the
ruling class, in exchange for which the rulers would be expected to pay good wages and grant the working class greater
political rights.[39] This was the old revisionist position, and it
gained ground steadily in the period up to 1914.

The centrists were shocked to see what inroads had been
made in the working class by the propaganda of jingoistic
nationalism. But instead of maintaining their anti-imperialist
position, they gave ground to the nationalists and damped
down the criticism of imperialist expansion. They were re-
warded by a greatly increased vote for the SPD in 1912, when
the Party polled one-third of all the votes. It was said at this
time that the Party was talking internationalism and practicing
nationalism in order to win votes.

Marxist theory did not, however, put the lower middle class down as anti-nationalist. On the contrary, both Lenin and Rosa Luxemburg found that this social stratum was, for certain specified reasons, the special repository and home of nationalism as a social philosophy.*

Misconceptions About Imperialism

With the benefit of our hindsight, we can now see that certain key arguments used by both sides in 1907 and before and after were based on a misconception. Imperialism was presented sometimes as the cause of prosperity and sometimes as its result. Both formulations were partly or wholly defective. With regard to Germany, it should have been obvious that the colonies were not bringing any financial return to Germany or to any Germans; they were draining the treasury of funds while not even benefiting private parties. Thus the argument that the government should develop colonies so as to raise the scale of living of the working class was disingenuous. Even with regard to England, where colonialism had after long experience been made to show some private dividends, the question of whether the gains to the bourgeoisie as a class outweighed the losses was even then being seriously debated.

The theory that imperialism was the result of surplus capital formation had been originally developed by the bourgeois economist Rodbertus, and was given wide currency at the turn of the century by bourgeois economists like Edward Atkinson in the United States and John A. Hobson in England. The Marxists in the German Social-Democratic Party accepted this theory rather too readily. No doubt their method involved a search for an economic cause as the primary explanation of any social phenomenon, and there plainly had been a movement of capital abroad in the 19th and early 20th centuries. The stakes of diplomacy were frequently lush investment opportunities.

* Cf. below, pp. 136, 202. Hitler was later to pitch his propaganda for expansive, imperialist nationalism more particularly toward just this class, with extraordinary results.

The cause-and-effect relation was not fully established, and later researches were to bring a considerable weakening of this theory, which had been so generally held in Marxist and non-Marxist circles alike. The Russian Tsar's aggressions in Asia were plainly not the result of surplus capital formation, since the country was poor and was borrowing money abroad, as the United States had been when it conquered Mexico in 1847. Hobson himself had pointed out that the bankers, who were frequently important gainers from imperialist exploitation, did not typically take the lead; he described them as "the most timid of people" where money was concerned. No doubt the basic cause of imperialism was still economic, in the sense that what was at stake was world leadership in opportunities for exploitation; but the moving force was not immediately an economic one in all cases; the initiative might be taken by a political leader like Kaiser Wilhelm II, or by the military acting on its own. Colonialism as practiced by the first German Reich was not economic; it was uneconomic or anti-economic. The most obvious argument against imperialism was in this case a correct one.

However this argument did not go very far. The German worker, who had been made to feel that he had a stake in the country, was also told that the English worker had a better life than the German because he, the Englishman, had benefited from the successful application of imperialism over a period of time. If the German nation could take over British leadership, the German worker would be correspondingly benefited.

A few doctrinaire Marxists tried to argue that the lot of the working man had not risen, or was not rising, in Germany or in England. Kautsky stated flatly: "The proletariat has no interest in imperialist exploitation."[40] The German however could not but be aware of the economic progress that the world was making; and Engels could be quoted to show that the English worker had indeed enjoyed some improvement in his condition. While the rise in German real wages had not been spectacular, the worker had hopes for the future, and these had been nourished by the Social-Democratic leaders themselves who had urged him to organize and vote.

On the international front, the Franco-Russian alliance had just been supplemented by the understanding of both powers with England, so that the German felt himself encircled. Under these circumstances, no matter who started a war, it could be made to seem that Germany was fighting defensively. The Fatherland was in danger. The appeal to patriotism was very effective. Even Kautsky, then considered a strong defender of orthodox Marxism, wrote in 1907: "Both bourgeoisie and proletariat have a common interest in preventing their subjection by a foreign nation."[41]

Conclusion

The German Marxists had not sufficiently taken to heart the repeated warnings of Marx and Engels about the nature of the Prussian state. Bakunin also had delivered himself of a cogent opinion in 1873: the German government, he said, depended on "the patriotism of its faithful subjects, on the sentiment of boundless national pride and blind obedience, whose origin goes far back in history, as well as on the cult of authority which today characterises the nobility, the small bourgeoisie, the bureaucracy, the church, the whole body of scholars, and often, alas! under the united influence of these, also the people itself."[42] And again, more specifically: "It is clear that so long as the goal of the German workers consists in setting up a national State, no matter how free or how much of a people's State they *imagine* it to be, . . . they will ever continue to sacrifice the liberty of the people to the greatness of the State, Socialism to politics, and justice and international brotherhood to patriotism."[43]

The German socialist and labor movement had thus before World War I been integrated psychologically into the fabric of German society. The *staatserhaltend* position which slips

over so easily into patriotism and unquestioning support of a
country's foreign policy had become characteristic of nearly
the whole of both the SPD and the union movement. There
was no group as important as (say) the French C.G.T. or even
the American I.W.W. to challenge the state as such and
patriotism as such. The anti-nationalists had been all but
silenced. Bakunin's prediction had come true. The German
working class had not fulfilled the historic mission set for it by
Marx and Engels.

In 1912, Charles Andler, professor of German at the Sor-
bonne, wrote a piece for a French newspaper in which he
discussed the action of the SPD which had expelled Gerhard
Hildebrand but had not moved against his fellow-revisionists,
although some authentic Marxists like Plekhanov had been
demanding for many years that they be ejected from the
International. Andler discussed in turn Bernstein, Quessel,
Schippel and others, and concluded that the SPD had become
a patriotic, capitalist party:

In neo-Lassallean German socialism, the working classes are
partisans of capitalism; they are partisans of colonial policy; they
are partisans of a policy of armaments, defensive in principle,
offensive if necessary; and if the German Empire was drawn into
an offensive or defensive war, the German workers could not desire
its defeat. Thus they are partisans of the political constitution established in their country and, literally, interested in maintaining the
ruling dynasty. This socialism is new in its absence of scruples. It
guards vigilantly the immediate interests of the workers. But it is
not ashamed to sacrifice principles.[44]*

* It was this pro-capitalist party, so aptly described by Andler, which,
shorn of its left wing, was to endorse Hitler's foreign policy in 1933 as
its last act before Hitler dissolved it! Explicit repudiation of socialism
and endorsement of the "free-enterprise system" followed after the
Second World War.

V

COLONIALISM, MILITARISM AND ALLIED ISSUES IN WESTERN EUROPE, 1890–1917

THE FRENCH SOCIALIST PARTY, which as a member of the *bloc des gauches* actually participated in several ministries in the early 20th century, did not make disarmament or abandonment of colonies a condition of such participation.

It failed to live up to the principles laid down on colonialism at Romilly in 1895 by the *Parti Ouvrier Français*, one of the predecessors of the French Socialist Party. At Romilly the delegates had adopted a resolution which attempted an analysis of colonialism and which stressed the contradiction between the interests of the workers and those of the ruling class. It had also set a significant precedent in that it had admitted that the interests of the colonial countries should be taken into account.[1]

The violent anti-patriotic propaganda of Gustave Hervé, and the calls for a general strike in the event of war, though they were taken seriously by some, could not succeed in one nation alone, and the general-strike motion always failed in the internationalist socialist congresses where indeed the French delegates were the only ones to give the idea serious support.

The nationalism of the French Revolution was the bourgeois brand, and the French socialists, recognizing it as such, developed an anti-national theory which has cropped up repeatedly ever since. We have already noted Engels' caustic treatment of the anti-nationalists in 1845, and the sarcastic references by Marx to the anti-nationalism of French members of the

First International in 1866.* Marx had charged that the point of view of this group, which included his own son-in-law-to-be Paul Lafargue, amounted to concealed nationalism, since "by the negation of nationalities he [Lafargue] appeared, quite unconsciously, to understand their absorption into the model French nation."

Politically, the issue was drawn between "militarism," meaning large army appropriations, and "anti-militarism," which might mean anything up to and including revolution. All the French socialists from Babeuf to Jaurès emphasized the defensive character of their patriotism.[2] The lineup in the French Socialist Party in the decade before the First World War on the question of militarism is indicated by the voting at the Limoges Conference in November, 1906. Gustave Hervé repudiated "governmental and bourgeois patriotism" and invited the citizens to reply to a declaration of war by a general strike and insurrection; his resolution received 31 votes. Vaillant, Jaurès, Sembat, and others recognized the validity of defensive war but called for the use of all means to prevent war up to the general strike and insurrection. Their resolution received 153 votes and carried. A third position was presented by the Federation of the North, where the influence of the "pure" Marxist Jules Guesde was paramount. This group called for international action of the proletariat to reduce military service and refuse credits for war purposes. Its resolution received 98 votes, and had gained some ground the next year at Nancy, but was still not the majority position. In 1910 all factions were agreed that if war threatened, the bureau of the Socialist International should be called together, and up to 1914 no better course of action had been developed.[3] When war broke out, great pressure was brought to bear on Guesde to join the cabinet in the name of national unity, and he acceded.

As with militarism, so with colonialism. The French Socialists offered little but token opposition at the parliamentary level. However we should not overlook the extremely active

* In Chapter I, pp. 16, 17.

work against militarism and war carried out not only by Hervé, whose influence always remained limited, but by Jaurès. The struggle against war came to occupy most of his time, and he campaigned up and down the country in a vain attempt to head off war and check overgrown militarism. Whether he also would have been overwhelmed by the nationalist wave must remain a matter for speculation, for he was assassinated just at the outbreak of the war.

However, Jaurès had maintained several times that the French workers should fight if France were attacked. He said:

The truth is that wherever there are fatherlands, that is, historical groups having a consciousness of their continuity and their unity, any attack on the freedom and integrity of these fatherlands is an attack against civilization, a relapse into barbarism.[4]

Jaurès also wrote that "a revolution is necessarily active. It could only be so if it defends that national existence which serves as its base."[5]

There is not much question that Jaurès was a patriot, but he was not a conventional one. His particular contribution was a serious effort to work out a citizen militia system, on the model of the citizen armies that defended the French Revolution. He called this idea the *Armée Nouvelle*, or New Army, and elaborated his ideas in a book with that title. Since this project would have involved abolishing the standing army, it had no more chance of adoption in France than the corresponding project had in Germany.[6]

Jules Guesde, considered the most orthodox of the Marxists, said that since he had got the vote, the worker had come to believe that he had a fatherland.[7] Guesde always considered the issue of militarism essentially a bourgeois issue.[8*]

Marx had not given a strong lead on the subject of nationalism, so the Marxists were badly divided, in France as in Germany. Guesde's position was similar to that of Debs in the

---

* Cf. Marx: "It is, of course, true of every nation that insistence upon nationality is now to be found only among the bourgeoisie and their writers."—*The German Ideology*, p. 99.

United States. Others, having in mind no doubt the early writings of Marx and Engels, defended imperialist expansion while still claiming to be Marxists; in this class were not only the German revisionists but Antonio Labriola in Italy. It was only after the outbreak of the First World War that Lenin worked out a differentiated approach.

The French trade-union federation, the Confédération Générale du Travail (CGT), was much more political-minded, or rather anti-political-minded, than its opposite numbers in Germany, England, or the United States. Its biennial congresses from 1902 to 1914 were largely taken up with the question of the fight against war and militarism. The CGT was anti-patriotic. In 1905 it printed and distributed 100,000 copies of the famous *Manuel du Soldat*, which was intended to cause disaffection in the armed forces. Sorel, Berth, and Lagardelle demanded the abolition of the army, and, to undermine its principal ideological support, the abolition also of the idea of the fatherland. Congress after Congress went on record for the general strike against war, though to be sure the vote at Marseille in 1908 was carried only by 688 to 421. In 1912 the CGT called for mass desertions in case of war.[9]

How far the views of the radical majority in the Congresses were shared by the rank and file was always a question, especially as the workers were voting for the French Socialist Party, and this was following a moderate policy. The CGT was against voting, on principle. Lagardelle cited a spot check that he had made of 41 militant union leaders, practically all of whom rejected the fatherland as identical with the system of private property; they answered the question: "Does the worker have a fatherland?" in the negative. But Merrheim, the Metalworkers' leader, always said that the rank and file of the workers were patriotic,[10] and Lagardelle was obliged to admit that the masses were chauvinistically inclined.*

If the French Socialist Party's acceptance of colonialism was

* See his article in *Neue Zeit* (1902), cited in Chapter III, above, p. 75.

immoral and non-Marxist, the position of Jaurès and the CGT was inconsistent. The latter staged their main attack against the army and militarism as such, while according only secondary attention to France's colonial expansion, although this expansion was plainly the main cause of diplomatic friction with Germany and had even brought France into dangerous confrontation with its closest ally, England. While professing to be opposed to war, the French anti-militarists paid inadequate heed to the causes of war. Their views may have been honestly held, but their judgment was open to serious question. They attacked nationalism but had too little to say about certain noxious manifestations of nationalism.

It is generally agreed that the revolutionary fervor in the CGT ebbed somewhat after 1908. On the eve of the war, Léon Jouhaux, the leader of the CGT, met Karl Legien, leader of the German union federation (ADGB) and asked him what the German workers were prepared to do to head off the war. According to Jouhaux's account, Legien met this question with silence. Jouhaux returned; war was declared; Jouhaux joined in its support and so did the French workers.[11]

England

England was not a country where much development of socialist theory took place in the second half of the 19th century. The working class, which had been seething with unrest in the 1830's and '40's, lost interest in socialism when the workers' condition began to improve after the repeal of the Corn Laws. By 1870, the improvement had been sufficiently marked so that Marx and Engels perforce accepted it as a fact. Thus the Social Democratic Federation (SDF), founded in 1881 by H. M. Hyndman with a Marxist program, remained small.* Also small in numbers, though with a certain influence

* The Social-Democratic Federation split immediately after its formation and a group headed by William Morris and others formed, with the support of Engels, a body called the Socialist League. However the Socialist League failed to put down roots and some of its members drifted back to the SDF.

on public policy, was the Fabian Society, founded in 1884, which concentrated its efforts for public ownership largely on the public utilities. Keir Hardie, a miner, founded the Independent Labor Party in 1893 with a vaguely socialist platform. And Robert Blatchford, a lone wolf without an organization, carried on propaganda for socialism through his paper, *Clarion*. In 1899, when the Boer War broke out, the SDF counted 2,680 members, the Fabians 861, and the ILP 7,092.[12]

Hyndman in his early days had been a frank imperialist who believed that British expansion, such as took place on a vastly extended scale after 1870, was "good alike for governors and governed."[13] Later experiences and observations turned him into one of the most incisive critics of British colonial rule, especially in India; alluding to the extreme poverty of the Indian peasants (*ryots*), he wrote that "no such awful crime has ever been committed in the history of the human race as that which England has committed in India."[14]

The Boer War furnished a test, both for the socialists and for the British working class. Would they be submerged in the wave of nationalism which was, of course, whipped up partly by Blatchford's *Clarion*, which supported the war throughout?

The SDF sounded the alarm even before the war began; its organ *Justice* said that war was being begun "in the interests of a clique of mine-owners," which, it added (with a dash of irrelevant anti-Semitism), was composed in the majority of foreign Jews.[15] As the paper continued its anti-Semitic hysteria, a group formed inside the SDF to oppose it on this issue. Hyndman attacked the war in public meetings, braving London mobs, for about a year, after which the executive committee of the Federation decided to stop the campaign. During this period there were times when the interests of the black Africans were brought into the spotlight; however for the most part the SDF took the part of the Boers, who it said were victims of an international capitalist conspiracy.[16]

The ILP, meeting during the war, in April 1900, denounced imperialism and declared that the partisans of socialism had the duty to protect less civilized peoples and to aid them to obtain their independence. It also went on record opposing conscription and calling on its members to refuse to bear arms. Keir Hardie, the principal spokesman, took a Christian pacifist position. He tended to idealize the Boers; but he also said that the main purpose of the war was to bring about a reduction in the wages of the indigenous miners.[17] Ramsay MacDonald, an important member of the ILP and like Hardie a pacifist at this time, did not speak out publicly against the war, but visited South Africa four months after the end of hostilities and found that the wages of the African natives in the Rand had indeed been reduced. (The reduction, from 50 or 60 shillings to 30 shillings per month, both with board, proved to have no relation to market realities, and most of the cut was restored!)[18]

The British Labor Party had not been formed at this time, and the political leadership of the union movement was in the hands of the Trades Union Congress. The sentiment of many leaders was against the War for the right reasons. A Manifesto signed by 83 of them was circulated late in 1899; it stated that the object of the war was to enrich capitalists by "cheap and forced labour." The signers included such well-known leaders as Joseph Arch, Henry Broadhurst, Thomas Burt, John Burns, Keir Hardie, Robert Smillie, and Will Thorne; nine of them were or had been members of Parliament.[19] This Manifesto stuck to the strictly labor issue of cheap labor and wage reductions; but it was evident that there was a group of trade-unionists sympathetic to the SDF position operating behind the scenes and not without influence in the union movement, most of whose members were, to be sure, apathetic on the issue. In the 1900 Congress the delegates were treated to a Presidential address which espoused the cause of collectivism and ended with a long quote from Engels. The Report of the Parliamentary Committee chose to play down the war; but a rank-and-file delegate, J. Ward of the London dockers, raised the issue. He moved a resolution regretting that the report did not refer to the disastrous effect of the war upon the trade and industry of the country. The resolution described the war as cruel and unnecessary, and said it was "a blow aimed at the independence of South African labor and against those principles of national freedom which have characterised the history of the close of the century."[20] His speech was interrupted by applause and according to the *Westminster Gazette* met with general approval. The resolution carried "by a small majority," a large number abstaining.[21]

It is evident from this episode that those who attribute Bernstein's conservatism and revisionism to his long association with the British trade-union movement are telling only half the story. The unions had a radical wing, and were not necessarily unsympathetic to the principles of scientific socialism. But the leaders were decidedly coy about expressing in public any sentiment that might be interpreted as derogatory to the Empire. They preferred to stick to so-called "labor issues" like wages, trade and the suppression of the union movement.

On the significant question of whether the skilled workers or the unskilled were more permeated by the jingoistic propaganda which obviously had made inroads in the labor movement, no final judgment can be made. Hyndman sought to show that the mobs which attacked and at first broke up his anti-war meetings were corrupted proletarians who did not have the support of the mass of the workers. But an analysis of the trade-union press has led F. Bealey to the opinion that if anything it was the poorest and least educated among the workers who were the most chauvinist.[22]

The Fabian Society split on the issue of the war. G. Bernard Shaw's defense of the war, which was adopted by the Society, justified it as a means of protecting the native Africans from enslavement by the Boers; it called for ownership of the mines by an international consortium, but also said that the British Empire "must" develop the area in the interests of all humanity.[23] There was also a section of the Society which opposed the war, and forced a referendum vote on the question whether the Society should take a stand on the question of imperialism as related to the war. The vote was 217 in favor and 259 against. Most of the anti-imperialists left the Society in disgust.[24] Sidney Webb, a leading Fabian, said little in the early part of the war, but he expressed himself on the "rights" of small nationalities in an article published in September 1901. He wrote: "What in the name of common sense have we to do with obsolete hypocrisies about peoples 'rightly struggling to be free'?" He scoffed at "that Fenian abstraction, the 'principle of nationality,'" and added: "What *vieux jeu* all this 'Early Victorian' nationalism now seems!"[25] The reference of course was to the nationalism of the Boers—and Irish.

John A. Hobson was not a Marxist, though he was clearly influenced by Marx and in turn has influenced Marxist writers; there are still economists who thoughtlessly state that Lenin got his ideas on imperialism from Hobson's classic, *Imperialism: A Study*.[26] Hobson, like Adam Smith, was a moderate British nationalist; although he supplied ammunition to critics of imperialism, and gave an economic interpretation of the phenomenon, his failure to condemn imperialism in Africa, even in the later editions of his work, must be considered the result of nationalist blindness, for the excesses of oppression practiced in places like the Belgian Congo and also in British possessions in Africa had become well known early in the 20th century.

The Labor Party from its formation in 1906 until 1914 adopted anti-militarist and peace resolutions almost annually, and the Trades Union Congress also frequently did the same. The 1912 Labor Party Conference adopted by 1,323,000 to 155,000 a resolution calling for an investigation of a general strike to stop war, but that was as far as the matter went.[27]

In England as in all imperialist countries, foreign policy has been continuous regardless of which party was in power. The opposition criticizes on points of detail, but once in power endorses the acts of the previous administration and hitches its own acts on where the other Party left off. Before the First World War the criticism by the opposition had to do with the size of the appropriations for the navy and with minor points in the handling of foreign relations. The Labor representatives in Parliament, from 1880 on, associated themselves with this criticism, more particularly with regard to the enormous appropriations for armaments; Labor was almost alone in opposing the increase in the navy estimates.[28] On the key question of India, the champions of Indian rights in the House of Commons from 1880 to 1905 were non-laborites, but the laborites, whenever they acted, always followed the lead of these men. From 1905 to 1917, Keir Hardie (until his death in 1914) and James O'Grady, both of the ILP, gave leadership in demanding freedom for India which was quite equal to that of the non-laborites. However, the ranks of Labor were not solid on this issue. In 1908 a minority of Labor representatives in Parliament voted for the coercion of India; and the next year also, a minority voted with the Liberal government against greater self-government for India.[29]*

On the other issues connected with Empire the Labor representatives contributed little. The unwillingness of the leaders, even those who knew better, to take any stand against the maintenance and extension of the Empire, had been illustrated during the Boer War. Thus it was not surprising if the British workers before the First World War gave lip service to the cause of peace, internationalism and limitation of armament but remained nationalists. Their psychology was regretfully summed up by the Labor journalist Brailsford, himself a strong critic of imperialist policies, as follows:

Let a group of labor leaders, English and German, address a mass meeting of British workingmen. It can be roused to a real sense of the solidarity between the two proletariats; it can be induced to vote a contribution from its own trade union funds to assist German miners on strike; it will leave the meeting with a real desire for peace and fraternity between the two nations. . . . The same crowd, prepared by the press and artfully stimulated by

* In the period before 1914, the laborites who opposed Indian freedom were most usually members of the Liberal Party—"Lib-Labs."

skillful orators, could also be induced to applaud the speeches of naval scaremongers, and to go away shouting for more dreadnoughts, and looking for German airships in the sky.[30]

Marxists and other left-wingers brought some practical internationalism to the British labor movement by helping the Irish in their struggle for independence. James Connolly paid tribute to them in an article in *Forward*, July 1, 1911:

Keir Hardie was battling for Irish Home Rule when the Liberal Government was filling Irish jails with unconvinced Irish men and women. Bruce Glasier was a member of the Irish Land League in Glasgow in the same stormy time. H. M. Hyndman sat upon the National Executive in Great Britain of the Irish Land League; Edward Aveling, brilliant expositor of Socialist science was the first man outside Ireland to join formally the Irish Socialist Republican Party; his wife, Eleanor Marx Aveling, daughter of Karl Marx, in her *History of the Working-Class Movement in England,* says sympathetically of our national struggle: "It is certain that the hope of 'Ireland a Nation' lies not in her middle-class O'Connells, but in her generous devoted heroic working men and women!" And within a month of its formation in 1896 she wrote to the Dublin organization offering us whatever help it was in her power to give. [The reference is to Connolly's Irish Socialist Republican Party.][31]

It should also not be forgotten that it was in England that Jim Larkin learned of the connection between socialism and nationalism—in Liverpool, where he was raised and where he used to meet with a group of Socialists in the Clarion Cafe.[32]

Eventually, the British Labor Party declared for Irish independence. But for some years after its formation as a separate Party, it had continued to cooperate with the Liberals in support merely of Home Rule for Ireland. The Irish Socialist Republicans would have appreciated a more active pro-labor and pro-independence policy. They pointed out that the social legislation which was being adopted for the benefit of the English working class could have been extended to Ireland if British Labor had been willing to fight for the extension. By following such a policy and supporting the demand for Irish independence, the British Laborites, it was claimed, might have made inroads into the Irish vote in the English constituencies, which continued to support the Liberals because of the latter's traditional espousal of Home Rule. But British Labor would not sponsor reforms for Ireland unless these met with the approval of the Irish Nationalists (Redmond), and the members of the Redmond group were from the Irish middle class and opposed to the demands of Irish labor.[33]*

In the decade before 1914 Hyndman's sentimental attachment to British (as opposed to German) culture came more and more to the fore. As his biographer Gould says, he was convinced that Social-Democracy for Britain was dependent upon appreciation and safeguarding of the British nationality.[34] He brushed aside the pacifism of Keir Hardie, who was arguing that no one would dare to attack a completely disarmed nation. Like Rudolf Hilferding, he perceived quite early that Germany would challenge Britain's imperial domination, and an increasing share of his time was devoted to warning against the "German menace." He became such an ardent big-navy man, advocating a navy large enough to take on any possible combination of adversaries, that he found himself increasingly isolated from other Socialists.† When the war broke out, he was in the front ranks of those advocating a complete military victory. The Social-Democratic Federation finally expelled him.

Keir Hardie, like Jaurès, died just at the outbreak of the war. The other ILP leaders took varying positions. The Secretary, A. Fenner Brockway, went to prison as a conscientious objector. Ramsay MacDonald supported the war, though he was given no responsibility in connection with its conduct. The ILP took the stand that all colonies including Ireland and India should be granted the right of self-determination.

The union movement generally, and the Labor Party, after a period of hesitation lined up for the war.

---

* Connolly criticized Keir Hardie for failing to recognize the middle-class nature of Redmond's Irish nationalism.—Connolly, p. 74.

† Belfort Bax found Hyndman's position jingoistic and reprehensible. See E. Bernstein, *Evolutionary Socialism* (New York, 1909), p. 179 and n.

A little group of labor leaders and intellectuals who resented the general toleration by Labor of the pacifist Left organized in April, 1915, the Socialist National Defense Committee, later the British Workers' National League. This group, which included Blatchford, H. G. Wells, and the steel-workers' leader John Hodge, favored retaining the empire and enlarging it through the acquisition of Germany's colonies. The *British Citizen and Empire Worker*, founded to propagate the group's views, together with Blatchford's *Clarion* "turned a steady fire upon the left, and some of their staffs and correspondents surpassed the stoutest Tories in the violence of their attack."[35]

Italy

In Italy, down to the end of the 19th century, comparatively little Marxist influence could be noted. Andrea Costa, who was elected to the Italian Parliament as a Socialist in 1885, had belonged to the "anti-authoritarian" (Bakuninist) wing of the First International. Costa was confronted with the necessity of taking a stand on imperialism when Italy embarked on its first African adventure. He met the challenge and in the debate of May 6–8, 1885, stated flatly that colonialism was of no interest to the Italian workers: they would have none of it. Instead of wasting its money in expensive overseas wars the government should turn to a solution of the social question. To this argument the other deputies showed comparatively little overt objection, but two years later when Costa maintained that the colonialist adventures had sullied Italian honor, he was showered with vilification and abuse. The metallurgical workers of Terni staged a demonstration against the colonial war.[36]

Filippo Turati, emerging in the 1890's as a moderate Socialist leader, and editor of *Avanti*, was from the first an opponent of colonialism, which he called a "malady"—a "fever"—a "morbid condition" of which Italy should cure itself. Meeting the argument that colonies were necessary to cure Italy's overpopulation, Turati saw no objection to setting up agricultural cooperatives overseas but denied that emigration would cure the poverty at home. Colonialism, he contended, was against the interests not only of the workers but also of the bourgeoisie, whose pacific development would be blocked by military adventures. In 1895–96, when the Italian forces were proving unable to defeat the armies of King Menelik of Abyssinia, the cry "Viva Menelik" was heard in working-class neighborhoods.[37]*

A well-known scholar, Antonio Labriola, had in 1888 announced himself as a Marxist, and his opinion and guidance were eagerly sought both by the younger generation of Socialists and by the rising imperialists. Labriola, following as he said the spirit rather than the letter of Marx, came out for an active expansionist policy and gave his endorsement to the military conquest of Tripoli.[38]

Nationalist sentiment was on the increase, under the leadership of men like Gabriele D'Annunzio and Enrico Corradini. The latter, in a deliberate effort to win followers in the working class, picked up and propagated an idea of Pascoli's according to which the "proletarian nations" of Europe should break the monopoly of colonialism held by the "plutocratic nations." I. Bonomi, a right-wing Socialist, broke with the Party on the issue of "patriotism."[39] Angelo Olivetti, an authentic syndicalist, founded the periodical *Pagine libere* (*Free Pages*) at Lugano in 1907 to prove the advantages of colonialism to the workers.[40] Arturo Labriola (not related to Antonio), one of the most brilliant syndicalist leaders, accepted the concept of the "proletarian nations" and thought in addition that the Libyan War (1911–12) would bring closer the day of the proletarian revolution—a doctrine reminiscent of the theory of "the worse the better" which had sometimes been preached by anarchist leaders.

---

* On the whole period under discussion, new material has been compiled, unfortunately too late for inclusion in the present study. See especially Enzo Santarelli, "Le socialisme national en Italie," in *Mouvement Social*, 1965, pp. 41–70.

Turati showed himself absolutely firm and intransigent against colonialism, even in the face of the Libyan War, when other moderate leaders like Bissolati were prepared to compromise. The Party congresses at Modena and Reggio Emilia maintained the Socialist opposition. Benito Mussolini announced in 1910 that "the proletariat has no fatherland, nor in truth has the bourgeoisie; in case of war we Socialists will not go to the front—we will raise insurrection within our own borders."[41] At the Reggio Emilia Congress in 1912 he launched violent attacks against the Socialists who had defected to the government; he also participated in direct action, tearing up railroad tracks to prevent troops being shipped to their ports of embarcation for Tripoli. As leader of the powerful left wing of the Socialist Party, Mussolini assumed the editorship of *Avanti*, replacing Turati.

But with the advent of the First World War, Mussolini began to preach a strongly "patriotic" line, and with the aid of a million francs delivered to him by the French government, founded his own paper advocating the entry of Italy into the war on the side of the Allies. Turati resumed the editorship of *Avanti*, and the Socialist Party adopted a policy toward the war of "no cooperation, no sabotage." This was essentially the position of Ramsay MacDonald in England and Kautsky in Germany; it was attacked mercilessly by Lenin as giving objective aid and comfort to the war-makers.

The Netherlands

As a small country with a large empire, the Netherlands occupied a special position in Europe during the period before 1914, especially as the Netherlands Indies were a rich and profitable area. The Dutch Social-Democratic Workers Party was among the first to present a program for colonial reform. The reforms, which were proposed by the Party Congress of 1901, included nationalizing "those enterprises which are fit for it," in order to prevent impoverishment of the colonies; and organizing the proletarians in the colonies to enable them to resist the onslaught of capital, to improve their conditions, and to prepare them for democratic self-government.[42]

The Party did not propose immediate independence for the colonies, and one gets the impression that the colonies might have had to wait quite a long time for the Party, if it had been in power, to make up its mind to grant such independence.[43] The Dutch socialist writers were much interested in questions of nationalism, and some of the best pamphlet literature of the period came from their pens. Some were anti-colonialist, but with reference rather to the acquisition of colonies by Germany than to the colonial powers divesting themselves of their possessions. Thus W. van Ravesteyn undertook to prove that colonialism worsens the condition of the working class, which has to pay for the costs of colonial expansion in the form of taxes, and which has to stand the cost of imperialist wars. He did not discuss whether the Dutch colonial empire had benefited the Dutch worker, but he did call for an international struggle against colonialism and imperialism.[44]

H. Gorter, whose reputation as a poet continues undiminished to the present day and who was also an effective pamphleteer, produced a pamphlet in 1915 (described by Lenin as "excellent") in which he discussed the causes of nationalism in the proletariat. The reason, he said, why the proletariat puts itself so completely at the service of the bourgeoisie is that it does not understand how to proceed internationally against the bourgeoisie; it does not know how to fight for distant goals like socialism, but only for its own immediate needs. The worker gets his living from nationalist capital, and works constantly for it; hence he tends to believe that its interests are his interests. He is passively nationalist except insofar as he is actively socialist. Imperialism dominates the politics of capital, which has been constantly busy uniting nations against the proletariat. But "internationalist socialism was a slogan; there was no internationalism in practice." Gorter supported the position of Karl Liebknecht in Germany in voting against the war credits, and called for a mass strike against war.[45]

The left wing of the Social-Democratic Workers Party, which had broken away in 1909 and formed the Social-Democratic Party, rethought its position after the outbreak of the war, and under the leadership of Wijnkoop, Gorter and Pannekoek carried on an active campaign for the independence of Indonesia, with the slogan of "*Indië* [Indonesia] *los van Holland.*" The way had been prepared for a discussion of Indonesian independence by the work of S. J. Rutgers, the Social-Democratic author of a two-volume work on that area. Where Hobson in England had pointed to the corrupting influence of the "nabobs" on British politics, the Dutch left-wing Social-Democrats blamed the class of rentiers that had been created by imperialism for the failure of Dutch capitalism to develop.

Spain

The opposition in Italy to patriotism and colonialism was related to the continuing influence in the working-class movement of the ideas of Bakunin. In those areas of Spain, such as Catalonia and the Asturias, where Bakunin's ideas were likewise on the ascendant, the anarcho-syndicalist movement was linked not only with anti-colonialism, a sentiment which in Spain was strong partly because Spain's colonial ventures worked out so badly, but also with regionalist movements. A further complication was the strong anti-clerical sentiment in Catalonia. In Barcelona the anarcho-syndicalist riots against the Moroccan war of 1909 had strong regionalist and anti-clerical overtones; several convents were burned.

Ireland

While England and the great powers of continental Europe were extending their dominion over those portions of the globe not hitherto subjugated, with only token resistance from the "socialist" movements of the respective imperialist countries, a persistent war for colonial independence was being waged right in England's back yard, in Ireland (now Eire). James Connolly, leader of the working-class wing of this movement, was one of the most remarkable socialists of this epoch, and his theory of what we might call proletarian nationalism was a real contribution to the understanding of the relations between socialism and nationalism. Whereas in Eastern Europe the attitude of the oppressed peasants toward nationality questions depended largely on the nationality of their respective land-lords, in Ireland the British rule was of such long standing and had been so disastrous in its consequences that all social classes had perforce reacted to it. And of those, who better than the proletarians should know of rack-renting, famines, and starvation wages?

The reason, said Connolly, for the lack of success of the Irish independence movements of the nineteenth century was that they had not had a sufficiently broad and dynamic appeal. For his inspiration Connolly went back to the United Irish movement of Wolfe Tone in 1798, and to John Mitchel of 50 years later. Wolfe Tone, said Connolly, "saw clearly, as we see, that a dominion as long rooted in any country as British dominion in Ireland can only be dislodged by a revolutionary impulse in line with the development of the entire epoch."[46]

In 1889 Connolly joined the Socialist League. In May 1896 he founded the Irish Socialist Republican Party. He always considered himself an Irish patriot, but patriotism for him necessarily implied the idea of social equality:

True patriotism seeks the welfare of each in the happiness of all, and is inconsistent with the selfish desire for worldly wealth, which can only be gained by the spoliation of less favored fellow-mortals. It is the mission of the working-class to give to patriotism this higher, nobler, significance.[47]

Like Engels, Connolly had been a rather extreme nationalist at one time in his youth. In the developed philosophy of both men socialism was the more important movement. "We are Republicans because we are Socialists," Connolly wrote in 1898, in the first number of the *Workers' Republic*. He fully realized that political independence could result in a new subservience to the power of foreign capital, unless control over the country's resources passed at the same time to the Irish people. He was against economic imperialism no less than political imperialism:

If you remove the English army tomorrow and hoist the green flag over Dublin castle, unless you set about the organization of the Socialist Republic your efforts would be in vain.

England would still rule you. She would rule you through her capitalists, through her landlords, through her financiers, through the whole array of commercial and individualist institutions she has planted in this country and watered with the tears of our mothers and the blood of our martyrs. . . .

Nationalism without Socialism—without a reorganisation of society on the basis of a broader and more developed form of that common property which underlay the social structure of Ancient Erin—is only national recreancy.[48]

The last paragraph illustrates one phase of Connolly's thought which may have been original but can hardly be considered successful—that is, the attempt to hitch modern socialism onto an early communism which was supposed to have flourished in ancient Ireland.

The reason why Connolly thought that socialism was a prerequisite to real national independence was quite simply that no class but the working class could be trusted to break completely with the British overlords. The middle class, he found, was linked to the British by a thousand ties of an economic nature; "only the Irish working class remain as the incorruptible inheritors of the fight for freedom in Ireland."[49] These are almost the identical words with which Engels described the leading role that the Polish proletariat must play in the struggle for Poland's independence. Connolly found it possible to cooperate with the Sinn Fein (James Griffith) and the Home Rule Party (John Redmond) while differing pro-

foundly with them on tactics and ultimate goals. "We announce
to all and sundry," he wrote in 1913, "that as Socialists we are
Home Rulers, but that on the day the Home Rule Government
goes into power the Socialist movement in Ireland will go into
opposition."[50]

For many years Connolly was an evolutionary socialist. In
1897 he specifically dissociated himself from insurrectionary
socialism and called for the use of the "slower, but surer
method of the ballot-box."[51] Two years later in an article, "The
Re-Conquest of Ireland," he described how in his view the
laborers might

take control of the work of the country from the hands of private
individuals and vest [it] in charge of public bodies representing
the Irish people. . . . By a steady pursuit of this policy the process
of the subjection of Ireland can be, in great part, reversed. . . . In
the course of this socialisation of society, this gradual re-conquest
of Ireland, the public boards in question will eventually find their
paths crossed by the capitalist Imperial government. Then Labor,
from a dominant local, will rise to the position of a dominant
national party, and the fight for complete independence will be
taken up by the working class already in possession of the internal
government of the country.[52]

In 1914 he was still not advocating the use of force to seize
power. He wrote: "The only force available to the worker is
economic force; the capture of political power when it does
come will come as a result of the previous conquest of economic power, although that conquest can be and should be
assisted by the continual exercise of political action."[53]

Yet in the interim Connolly had passed several years in the
United States, and had been one of the earliest organizers of
the IWW.[54] He came back to Ireland in 1910 talking the language of syndicalism, but only in certain respects. The administration of the industries of the country by the Industrial
Unions of the respective industries is there; so are the One Big
Union and the sympathetic strike; and when he speaks of internationalism it is in true Bakuninist phrase, the "free federa-

tion of free peoples."[55] But the revolutionary general strike, the insurrection, is still not there.

James Larkin—or Jim, as he was always called—was another Irish Socialist leader who had importance for our purposes, although he was no theorist and did little writing for the public press. Massive of build and fluent of tongue, Larkin earned the candid hatred of the employers and of middle-class Sinn Fein leader Arthur Griffith because of the effective way he organized the dockers. Coming to Ireland in 1907 after a youth spent in Liverpool, where he had become a trade-union organizer, Larkin found himself at the head of a major strike on the Belfast docks. The working force was composed partly of Orangemen and partly of Irish Nationalists. But in spite of the attempts of the employers to sow the seeds of nationalist distrust in the labor ranks, Catholic and Protestant workers stood shoulder to shoulder through most of six months. If the same spirit manifested at that time by organized labor had been carried into the public life of Ireland generally, the partition of Ireland might have been avoided. It is still believed by some that if the National Union of Transport Workers, with headquarters in England, had supported the strike strongly, a victory might have been won. As it was, the result could best be described as a draw. But the fine solidarity of Protestant and Catholic workers did not survive. Both the political and the union movement were split. The Belfast branches of the ILP concentrated their attention on municipal ownership of public utilities ("sewer socialism," the policy was called disparagingly in England), and remained aloof from the Socialist Party of Ireland.

The General Secretary of the Transport and General Workers Union in England, James Sexton, was opposed to Irish nationalist aspirations. A long period of increasing friction between him and Larkin finally reached the breaking point and Larkin organized a new union, the Irish Transport and General Workers Union, with headquarters in Dublin. From the beginning it took a militant nationalist coloring. In

1913 it conducted, under Larkin's leadership, a historic eight-month strike for union recognition in Dublin, in the course of which Connolly organized the Citizen Army, as a volunteer workers' force. Intellectuals and even many Britishers supported the strike, though Larkin, touring England to solicit funds for the strike—and getting them—often met with stony silence when he tried to present the claims of Irish nationalism.

Larkin went to the United States and threw himself into the work of the IWW as Connolly had done. There was no conflict between the anti-nationalism of the IWW and the Irish nationalism of Connolly and Larkin, for the former was directed against the imperialist nationalism of the United States and Great Britain, and not against the rising nationalist sentiment in the colonial and semi-colonial countries.

Connolly succeeded to the leadership of Larkin's union. He was also a well-known figure in the councils of the Labor and Socialist (Second) International, where he associated himself with the left-wing group. When the First World War broke out, Redmond ostentatiously offered the services of the Home Rule Party to the British, but Connolly called on the Irish workers to revolt against the war. On August 22, 1914, he wrote in the Scottish journal *Forward*:

The war of a subject nation for independence, for the right to live out its own life in its own way, may and can be justified as holy and righteous; the war of a subject class to free itself from the debasing conditions of economic and political slavery should at all times choose its own weapons . . . but the war of nation against nation in the interest of royal freebooters and cosmopolitan thieves is a thing accursed.[56]

Connolly, like Lenin, had really hoped and expected that the workers would rise up against the war and possibly even bring it to a stop. He greatly admired Karl Liebknecht for his stalwart resistance to German participation. He saw no ideological cleavage among the big imperial powers and counselled resistance to the war not only in Ireland but everywhere else.

In the months that followed, Connolly travelled the same

road as Lenin in seeking to end the imperialist war and bring about a civil war. He carried with him the political and union wings of the Irish movement. Lenin with his erudition and great organizational ability was the theorist of this school, but Connolly sometimes anticipated Lenin's thinking with formulations of his own. Lenin first used the slogan "turn the imperialist war into a civil war" on November 1, 1915. Connolly had written in March of that year in the *International Socialist Review*:

The signal of war ought also to have been the signal for rebellion. . . . When the bugles sounded the first note for actual war, their notes should have been taken for the tocsin for social revolution. . . . Such a civil war would not have resulted in such a loss for socialist life as this international war has entailed.[57]

Alone of the trade-union movements of Western Europe, the Irish Trades Union Congress branded the European war a "war for the aggrandisement of the capitalist class." Among the European Socialist Parties, only the Russians and the Serbs took the same stand as the Irish. The Irish nationalist movement was already putting into practice in 1915 the policy that was advocated by the Zimmerwald Conference in September of that year: "Now you must stand up for your own cause, for the sacred aims of socialism, *for the emancipation of the oppressed nations* as well as of the enslaved classes, by means of irreconcilable proletarian class struggle."[58]

It became evident to Connolly that an armed uprising offered the best opportunity for Irish independence. But realizing that the workers could not act alone, he sought to rally all the anti-imperialists under one banner. He adumbrated the conception of the National Front, including all classes which were willing to fight against the foreign ruler for national liberation. The victory of this Front would lead to the establishment of a national revolutionary government.

Connolly had already written off the British Laborites for practical purposes. Soon after the outbreak of the war a bill had been introduced in the House of Commons providing new repressive measures for Ireland, with death sentences by courts-martial as a possibility. Connolly then had said that the British Labor members "like all apostates, are readiest to stab and destroy all those who remain true to that ideal of democratic freedom they have deserted and dishonored."[59] Marx had called on the workers in the colonial and oppressed nations to work with the proletarians of the imperialist country and to follow their lead. A different policy was forced on Connolly by the logic of events and by the attitude of the English workers themselves; and Connolly's view ultimately was accepted throughout the colonial world, and in Marxist theory as well.

In preparation for the armed uprising which he was helping to organize, Connolly arranged the merger of the Citizen Army with the Volunteers. Connolly participated in the uprising, which failed; he was captured and shot, and has been honored ever since as a martyr to the cause of Irish nationalism. The debates still rage over the question of whether he gave priority in his thinking to the national revolution or to the socialist revolution. A recent study concludes:

> At first he was inclined to *identify* them. Later he distinguished them as the political and economic *aspects* of one process. Finally he reached the conclusion that they were two stages of one democratic reorganisation of society, each involving economic changes which it was the function of political change to promote.[60]

Connolly's "first stage of freedom" corresponded to the period just after the success of the nationalist revolution, which was to be brought about by a coalition of classes. It would be a period of dictatorship, when imperialists and their works would be ruthlessly suppressed; but it would not be a proletarian dictatorship—yet. Connolly believed that in the "first stage of freedom" the capitalists who had participated in the nationalist movement would be allowed to keep their capital.[61] The workers would be "in on the ground floor," participating in the nationalist movement and seeking always to lead it. Connolly rejected the idea then held by some of his opponents, that the task of advancing socialism was something separate from the national liberation movement. And here we note a real distinction between Connolly's thought and that of Lenin. For Lenin deprecated labor's participation in national separatist movements, on the ground that these movements were led by the bourgeoisie, and the workers, in participating in such movements, would come under the influence of the bourgeoisie; whereas for Connolly, who never doubted that the nationalist movement must succeed, it would be a fatal mistake for the revolutionary proletariat by concentrating exclusively on socialist propaganda to hand over the leadership of the national struggle to the bourgeoisie.[62] This same issue had of course arisen and been hotly debated in the labor and socialist movements of Eastern Europe, where the decision on the part of left-wing nationalists to join up with the separatist organizations of the middle class was similarly condemned, but later approved, in Marxist circles abroad.

The news of the Irish uprising of 1916 and its suppression was variously received by Marxists in other countries. Some attacked Connolly for having "deserted socialism" for nationalism. All agreed that the uprising was premature. But Lenin showed his greatness by refusing to condemn or blame the participants, just as Marx had refused to condemn the Paris Communards. Lenin saw clearly that this was merely one of many cases where "flames of national revolt have burst out in the colonies *and* in Europe." "The misfortune of the Irish was that they rose prematurely, when the European revolt of the proletariat had *not yet* matured." He continued:

Only in *premature*, partial, sporadic, and therefore unsuccessful, revolutionary movements will the masses gain experience, acquire knowledge, gather strength, get to know their real leaders, the Socialist proletarians, and in this way prepare for the general onslaught, in the same way as separate strikes, demonstrations, local and national, mutinies in the army, outbreaks among the peasantry, etc., prepared the way for the general onslaught in 1905.[63]

Japan

All over the world, in the decade before the First World War, Marxists wrestled with the problem of where their first loyalties lay—with the country or with the international working class movement. Sen Katayama, pioneer of Japanese Marxism who spent many years abroad, wrote in 1904 of the Russo-Japanese War. He had opposed the war from the beginning, he said, and had held anti-war meetings at the height of the war fever; the working class had everything to lose from the war and nothing to gain; why should they shoot down their Russian brothers? Then he added:

"I am opposed to this war, but as a Japanese I do not wish to be beaten by Russia who in the past treated the Jews as she has in Kishineff, and is still dealing with Finns in the most brutal fashion, and moreover she has shot down many laborers during strikes!"[63a]

Katayama wrote "as a Japanese," as it were in spite of himself.

The Second International

It could not be expected that the Labor and Socialist (Second) International would produce a carefully reasoned, compact position on questions affecting nationalism, especially as the representatives came from parties which were after all national and might have been expected to defend the positions of their respective countries in international gatherings. The resolutions adopted were frequently the result of compromise. The debates in open session were sometimes *pro forma*, and took place after the real work had been done in committee behind closed doors, in sessions the records of which have not always been preserved. Since the International had no power, there were some who boycotted its sessions.

Nevertheless the positions taken were frequently in advance of those in the majority of countries; and certain of the leaders, especially of the left wing (Lenin, *et al.*) came to attach considerable importance to the sessions of the International and worked hard for the adoption of a correct position.

The Second International passed anti-militarist resolutions at its Congresses in 1889, 1891, and 1894. At the 1896 Convention, held in London, a resolution on colonialism which had been drafted by George Lansbury, a Christian pacifist, on behalf of the British, was adopted. It read: "Under whatever pretexts of religion or civilising influence colonial policy presents itself, it always has as its goal the extension of the field of capitalist exploitation in the exclusive interests of the capitalists."[64]

This Congress also went on record in favor of the general principle of self-determination of peoples.

The next Congress, held at Paris in 1900, adopted a strong condemnation of colonialism. The reporter, Henri van Kol of the Netherlands, had indeed contended that colonialism was inseparable from capitalism in its existing phase, and counseled trying to improve conditions in the colonies. The resolution adopted not only repeated the 1896 dictum that the purpose of colonies was to increase the profits of the capitalists—it called on the workers everywhere to fight against colonialism. For the first time colonialism was linked with militarism, and the workers were urged to fight against that, too.[65]

At Paris the British were singled out for special condemnation on account of the manner in which they were conducting the Boer War, which was then in progress. Hyndman and Quelch, the British delegates, then compiled a dossier on the other countries which they presented to the Bureau of the International after the Congress, with the demand that it condemn the imperialist policies of "all the countries of European civilisation, including the United States," and this was done.[66]

At Paris the rather paternalistic approach of van Kol had contrasted with the denunciation of colonialism on principle by Hyndman, and both were invited to prepare reports for the Amsterdam Congress in 1904. However, those who expected to see a major debate on the floor were disappointed, as were those who had expected a strong resolution. The Congress made no basic analysis of the colonial question, nor of industrialism and militarism as causes of colonialism. It failed to take a stand even on the question, then much debated, of whether colonialism was a benefit to the natives of the countries concerned. It did set a significant precedent when it invited a representative of a colonial country (India) to address the Congress. For the rest, the Amsterdam Congress condemned colonialism in much the same terms as in 1900.[67]

Colonial revolts, and exposures of the evils of colonialism, as well as the first Moroccan crisis in 1905, had brought the colonial question into the spotlight by 1907. At Stuttgart, the "big names" were not in the Commission, which reported in favor of a "positive" colonial policy, i.e., acceptance of colonialism. Ledebour moved an amendment to reaffirm the Congress' opposition to colonialism, and this was passed 127 to 108, by virtue of the votes of the non-colonizing countries; the majority of the French and English votes, and all of the votes of Germany, Holland, and Belgium were for the Commission report.* The countries, or some of them, must have been using the unit rule in voting since Ledebour and Kautsky, Germans, led the attack on the Commission report.

The extreme right was represented by Dr. David of Germany. Europe, he said, had a civilizing mission, and besides, Europe needed colonies. In the center were van Kol, the Belgians, and Jaurès, aided by Bernstein, Rouanet, Vander-

---

* Lenin says the vote was 128 to 110, with 10 abstentions. The figures given are from Braunthal.

velde and MacDonald. There were differences among them: de la Fontaine and Jaurès dreamt of an international administration of colonies, which van Kol and Bernstein did not accept. There was no agreement on whether the colonies aided the whole of the West European countries or only the capitalists. All the centrists believed that colonialism was a fact and that combatting it was useless. They all denounced "colonial barbarism." But they did not believe that the colonial peoples were to be treated on a par with Europeans.

After the Congress, Kautsky and David produced extended studies on the subject. Kautsky rested his argument largely on ethical grounds; he also contended that colonialism was not a force for progress. Indeed, he said, colonialism does not develop the productive forces nor the means of production; on the contrary, it uses, under various forms of forced labor and looting, the most primitive forms of accumulation and production. The human race is one; democracy and socialism are valid for the colonial areas too. With this point of view Lenin expressed himself in full accord.[68]

The center and the right did not offer any coherent economic analysis at all. The left concerned itself with the birth of movements of resistance in the colonial countries, and the International itself helped to establish Social-Democratic movements in some of them. "Without doubt, as in Persia and in China, it was in the context of the growth of the nationalist movement that Indonesian socialism saw the light of day."

It has been said that even when the International was voting radical-sounding motions against colonialism, its action remained essentially pacifist, liberal and humanitarian.[69] This formulation is misleading on two counts. In the first place, the International did not take any action against colonialism. And in the second place, the writer implies that there is some sort of conflict or inconsistency between radicalism and humanitarianism, whereas radical socialism (revolutionary Marxism) has always been humanitarian in its basic philosophy.[70]

Bebel in 1912 at the Basle Congress proposed a resolution

dealing with the steps to be taken to avoid war. An amendment proposed by Rosa Luxemburg, Lenin, and Martov contained the following passage:

If a war threatens to break out, it is the duty of the working class and of its parliamentary representatives in the countries involved, supported by the consolidating activity of the International Bureau, to exert every effort to prevent the outbreak of war by means they consider most effective, which naturally vary according to the accentuation of the class struggle and of the general political situation.

Should war break out none the less, it is their duty to intervene in favor of its speedy termination and to do all in their power to utilize the economic and political crisis caused by the war to rouse the peoples and thereby to hasten the abolition of capitalist class rule.

This might have been considered by the left wing as a commitment to turn the imperialist war into a class war, but it was not, as was indicated when the resolution, including the amendment, passed unanimously.

An element in the International had been working for recognition of participation in defensive wars as consistent with the principles of socialism. The pitfalls in this position were not sufficiently appreciated, and the Copenhagen Congress of the International in 1910 did grant endorsement to the right of national defense against attack.

In all the European countries, nationalism had become so much a way of life, for the working class as for everyone else, that even the workers who talked about internationalism practiced nationalism as a matter of course. Even violent antipatriots like Hervé turned into nationalists when the chips were down. The only exceptions were a very few complete pacifists—not to be confused with the left-wing "pacifists" who simply withheld support from the war—and a little group of revolutionaries who did not hesitate to come out for defeat of the imperialist fatherland, in the name of international socialism.

VI

EAST EUROPEAN MARXISM AND THE
MULTI-NATIONAL STATE

THE POSSIBLE CONFLICT of the demands of nationalism with
the demands of democracy, and hence socialism, was pointed
out as early as the 1860's not only by Lord Acton, as noted
above, but by writers in Eastern Europe. One such was Bernhard Becker, whose book *Der Missbrauch der Nationalitäten-
lehre* appeared in the late 1860's.

Becker pointed out that human progress was advanced when
Holland, using the nationality principle, won its freedom from
Spain in the 17th century. In the French Revolution and for
some time afterward, nationalism was a popular, democratic
movement. But nationality, which the refugee Greeks, Poles
and Italians were seeking to use as a unifying principle, cut
across other social lines and thus helped to create confusion.
"The national," he said, "is the unreasonable." Also, it was not
realized by the early democrats how soon the nationality principle would be turned against them, as it was within 30 years
after the French Revolution by the Russian Tsar and other
reactionaries. "The belief in the nationality principle is sentimentality and superstition," Becker concluded. He foreshad-
owed the fate of certain of the "succession states" whose
economy and polity are so small as to be hardly viable unless
combined in some sort of unequal treaty with a larger power.
This danger was foreseen by Marx and Engels, who also perceived the danger of the national principle as applied in the
Tsar's Panslavism. But their solution for Austria-Hungary
turned out to be an unreal one, as did, for the time being,

Becker's idea of a Europe reorganized into one single state, or at most three.[1]

However we define nationality, we have to recognize that no map of Eastern and Central Europe can be drawn which does not include considerable numbers of one nationality in the territory of another. The emphasis on loyalty to one's nationality, rather than to the political state as such, is thus bound—and this was Becker's main point—to create division at the same time that it is supposed to create unity. Even the strongest advocates of the nationality principle have no ready answer to this contention, nor to the allied difficulty that the national differences are frequently also class differences. In this latter case, redrawing boundaries along nationalist lines may be catastrophic for the ruling class, or conversely for some other class such as the peasants or the workers if the new state is dominated by a reactionary element.

Polish Self-Determination and Rosa Luxemburg

It was this latter difficulty that was chiefly in Rosa Luxemburg's mind when she took a position in the 1890's opposed to the principle of self-determination. She foresaw that Poland, if given its independence, would be dominated by a reactionary bourgeoisie and reactionary landowners.

The Polish question had indeed changed somewhat since the middle of the 19th century, notably in that an urban proletariat had begun to grow up in the expanding cities; Russian Poland was the most industrialized part of the Russian Empire. Engels recognized this change when he wrote in the preface to the second Polish edition of the *Communist Manifesto* in 1892: "The workers of all the rest of Europe need the independence of Poland as much as do the Polish workers. . . . [The re-establishment of Poland] can only be won by the young Polish proletariat, and in their hands it is safe." In London in February, 1896, a memorial service was held, under the chairmanship of Edward Aveling, with the participation of M. Beer, Tom Mann, Eduard Bernstein and Eleanor Marx-Aveling; it adopted a resolution to the same effect and in almost the same words.[2]

But meanwhile, a group of Polish Socialists including Rosa Luxemburg had re-thought the whole problem of Polish independence and had come to the conclusion that the ends of justice and the interests of the proletariat would be best served if Poland were not to become independent but were to obtain recognition as an autonomous province of Russia. Their point of view was set forth by Rosa Luxemburg in two articles in the *Neue Zeit*.

According to her, the Polish bourgeoisie, although it was economically dominant and would probably be able to seize power in an independent Poland, did not especially favor independence, because its economic relations with the respective annexation-lands (Russia, Germany, Austria) were more important than would be the economic relations within an independent Poland. Likewise the big landlords in Galicia and in Prussian and Russian Poland were wary of independence precisely because a separate Poland would be dominated by the bourgeoisie. Thus the most important classes economically were not pushing independence, which would result in a setback for the economy as a whole.[3]

The Polish Social-Democrats had just split off from the Social-Democratic parties of their respective lands and had set up a Polish Socialist Party which had as its main plank the agitation for Polish independence. Rosa Luxemburg's group had seceded from the Polish Socialist Party. Her group maintained that the emphasis on nationalism would give the workers the idea that their exploitation and bad conditions were the result of the nationality of their oppressors rather than of the capitalist system. In Austria where the Poles enjoyed national freedom, the Polish Socialist Party's appeal would have to be to the patriotic sentiment as such, thus diverting attention from socialist agitation and dividing the forces of the proletariat. If the Polish proletariat is strong enough to bring about the reconstitution of Poland against the opposition of the ruling classes of all three parts of the country, it could equally well establish socialism, said Rosa Luxemburg.[4]

Rosa Luxemburg's analysis of the class composition of Poland around 1890 is of much interest for our purposes. She wrote:

The freeing of the serfs in 1864 cut the ground from under the nationalist agitation of the Polish nobles since these could count on the support of the serfs against the Tsar only so long as the serfs could see in Polish independence the way to their liberation. Since the removal of the tariff boundary between Poland and Russia (1851) and the freeing of the serfs, industry in Poland, including heavy industry, has mushroomed and tied Poland closely into the Russian economy, on which it depends for its market. The Polish textile industry is one-quarter of all Russia's, its iron and steel industry one-sixth. Thus there is no class in Poland that has an economic interest in Polish independence. The landed nobility has been taken in tow by the [big] bourgeoisie. The middle landowners are engaged in a ceaseless struggle for existence. Their economic program calls for more credit so that they can engage in intensive production. The petty bourgeoisie is not a unified group. Some handworking businesses depend on the Russian market and seek to start marketing cooperatives. These and many others gain by their access to Russian markets and follow the lead of the big bourgeoisie. The small industry that is being ruined by the Russian-connected big industry is the natural home of Polish nationalist agitation, but it is economically powerless. The peasantry has no discoverable political physiognomy. Their traditional hatred for the landowners has had pro-Russian overtones since the Tsar freed the serfs. *The intellectuals who have not been absorbed into industry complain about their exclusion from the civil service and form the heart of nationalist agitation.* But to bring the parts of Poland together again would disrupt the economy of the cities and a large part of the countryside too.[5]

When they first split off, continued Rosa Luxemburg, the Polish Socialists had professed the same aims as the Social-Democratic parties of the annexation lands, but later they tended to concentrate more on nationalist agitation. They appealed to the handworkers in the towns, who were strongly influenced by the petty bourgeoisie, the chief mass base of nationalist sentiment. Thus the Polish Socialists, deprived of their contact with the class-conscious workers of the German and Austrian proletariat, tended to fall under the influence of the petty bourgeoisie and to adopt their psychology.[6]

Marx and Engels used to talk of the Russian menace to Europe, said Rosa Luxemburg, but today (1896) things are different. Engels himself had pointed out only a short time before that contemporary Russia was hardly capable of waging even a defensive war and was politically bankrupt.[7*] The argument that a democratic Poland would stand as a dike between Europe and reactionary Russia had ceased to apply. A reconstituted Poland might just as well make common cause with Tsarist Russia.

When the proletariat gains power in a modern capitalist state, it makes the splitting up of that state less likely, said Rosa Luxemburg; centralization of the economy and growth of power of the proletariat go together. Taking it for granted, as everybody did, that a victory for socialism would lead to the granting of the demands of the oppressed nationalities, she advised the Polish Socialists to renounce the Utopia of a Polish state and join wholeheartedly in the work of the Social-Democratic Parties of the countries in which they respectively found themselves.[8]

Rosa Luxemburg was indeed so much opposed to recognizing the rights of the small nationalities in Eastern Europe that even after the victory of the Russian Revolution in 1917, she referred to such nationalist movements as that of the Ukrainians as "a nothing, a soap-bubble, a droll conceit of a few dozen professors and lawyers," and advocated nipping their separatist movements in the bud.[9] This period falls outside of the scope of the present study. But Rosa Luxemburg's status as a Marxist theoretician is above dispute, and she was taken very seriously by her contemporaries, including Lenin.

S. Häcker undertook to answer in the *Neue Zeit* the contentions of Rosa Luxemburg, whom he accused of pursuing factional and disruptive activities in the Polish Socialist move-

* Cf. Chapter II, p. 50.

ment. Denying that the Polish Socialist Party had followed a policy different from that of the Social-Democratic Parties in the other countries, he pointed out that the SDP's of Germany and Austria had raised no objection to the formation of a separate Polish party and had accepted its affiliation. With regard to the economic development of Poland, he conceded that Russian Poland especially had made great strides, and had become the most industrialized part of Russia; but, he said, Tsarist policy had recently tended toward the encouragement of industry in other parts of Russia, with the idea of dispensing later with Polish industry.[10]

Rosa Luxemburg returned to the attack with a more detailed analysis of the class structure in Poland, and insisted that for the proletariat to adopt nationalist slogans would be harking back to the precapitalist era; it would be adopting the program of the dying petty bourgeoisie in the present era and of the landed nobility in the previous era. The working class, she contended, should stand for autonomous liberties for Poland within the Russian empire.[11]

Kautsky agreed with Rosa Luxemburg that Panslavism had ceased to be a menace to Western Europe, partly because the Western Slavs had got more liberties, and partly because the Tsar's government was less interested in campaigning for Constantinople since it had been expanding into Central Asia and China. Thus the reconstitution of Poland had ceased to be the burning issue for West European Social Democracy that it had been in Marx's time. But he still thought that a demand for the independence of Poland should be part of the demands of the International. He answered Rosa Luxemburg's arguments seriatim, as follows:

1. Rosa Luxemburg had said that the demand for Poland's reconstitution was unrealizable. Kautsky retorted that the question was whether the demand was consistent with a socialist program and with the interests of the class struggle of the international proletariat.

2. Polish industry may be closely integrated with Russian,

but that is a passing phase. Russian industry, said Kautsky, is already challenging Polish industry in the Asian market, and the Tsarist government is levying higher taxes and railroad rates on the Poles.

3. Rosa Luxemburg had spoken disparagingly of the petty bourgeoisie, but Kautsky stressed its *political* importance—they might well throw in their lot with the proletariat, as prophesied in the *Communist Manifesto*. Kautsky also charged that Rosa Luxemburg had underestimated the role of the intellectuals, who fulfilled an important function, especially in politics.

But further, said Kautsky, no European state stands closer to a revolution than Russia. Thus an independent Poland could be a (proletarian) class state, in spite of Rosa Luxemburg.

While he wished to see Poland's right to independence affirmed, Kautsky did not believe that national independence should be sought "unconditionally, under all circumstances."[12] He thus modified Engels' forthright position of 1882 (see above, pp. 17–18).

In the end, the International Socialist Conference of 1896, at London, refrained from demanding independence specifically for Poland but affirmed the *right* of all nations to self-determination. Thus the way was left open to the Poles and other like-situated peoples to push their demands for independence or not to push them, as the occasion might demand, but the democratic right of self-determination was unconditionally endorsed.

The number of those who opposed the right of self-determination as such was not great even in Rosa Luxemburg's time, and has diminished since, so that her views on the subject have mainly historical importance. However this importance is not negligible for as important a Marxist theorist as she was. The content of her later articles on the subject is known to Western readers only indirectly, through Lenin's discussion of them.[13] It is to be hoped that some translation or summary will be presented in time.

The Theory of the Multi-National State

Bernstein, as we have seen, had sought guidance from Engels in 1882 on the question of what attitude to take to the problems of the Austro-Hungarian Slavs. He was advised that the Slavic peoples of Austria-Hungary had no future and were destined to be absorbed by the more highly developed Germans and Magyars.[14] Kautsky, who was half Czech, dutifully accepted this point of view.

In an extended essay on "The Modern Nationality" in 1887, Kautsky traced the economic basis of modern nationality, which he found to be essentially a bourgeois idea. The organization of the nation was indispensable to the merchants since an agency was needed to regulate the internal market and to support the interests of the merchants abroad; nowhere, he contended, is chauvinism greater than among merchants abroad.[15]

The idea that the *modern* nation is the creation of the bourgeoisie is implicit in the *Communist Manifesto* and was adopted by later Marxist writers, for example, Stalin. But the idea that state-building began with the modern nation is inconsistent with the theory of historyless peoples which Marx and Engels never repudiated. In Hegel's conception the early empires were examples of state-building. The Poland of 1772, which Marx and Engels were so eager to see recreated, was not a bourgeois state. Militaristic landed aristocracies were quite capable of creating a state in their own image, in Marx's view. The ruling class sought to interest the masses of the people in fighting for the enrichment and expansion of the masters. Marx and Engels did not hesitate to speak of "barbarian nations."[16]

The most important factor in the formation of nations has been language, said Kautsky. "In proportion as modern economic development has proceeded, there has grown the need for all who spoke the same language to be joined together in a common state."[17] This emphasis on language as the major force in nation-building had been specifically rejected by Marx and Engels,[18] and was to continue to give Kautsky trouble, as is indicated by the number of times he returned to it and modified it. It seems hard to combine with his other statement, made at the same time, that the more the modern methods of production develop, the larger must the national state become if it is to make good its claims.[19] Suppose the size dictated by economics outruns the boundaries indicated by language—as indeed in places it already had? Kautsky's answer was simple— too simple: the less developed nationality must disappear, and therewith its language. Capitalism, said Kautsky, is developing faster than the Czech nation could; the Czech language is doomed to extinction, though not necessarily in favor of the German language.[20] Kautsky thought that the situation called for the development of an international language; and indeed an international language was proposed in the same year (1887) by an East European, Dr. Zamenhof, writing under the name of Esperanto.

Or suppose the state contains people speaking many different languages? Should it be broken up into as many states as there are languages? Evidently Kautsky had not thought this part of his theory through. The eventual dissolution of the Austro-Hungarian Empire along the lines of language differences meant sacrifices from the point of view of economic viability, and Kautsky was to wrestle long with the implications of his definition, especially after the international-language idea failed to develop rapidly.

The contradiction between linguistic atomism and economic centralization was solved for Kautsky by the concept of proletarian internationalism. In an article published in 1905, Kautsky argued that since capitalism has created the world market, one nation cannot any more exist by and for itself alone. "The ultimate goal of the international socialist society and the movement of national liberation are not to be distinguished; they are one and the same. The individual and the nation must subordinate themselves to the needs of the international liberation struggle."[21]

In the *Manifesto* Marx and Engels had described eloquently how capitalism breaks down national barriers. Kautsky agreed that this was the ultimate effect of technological changes in communication such as the railroad; but, he said, the first effect may be just the reverse. The railroad by revolutionizing productive techniques in Ireland and Central Europe had forced millions of Irish and South Slavs to leave the land and seek their livelihood in the cities of England and Germany respectively; and the reception of the new arrivals was anything but cordial. Thus "the railroads are the mightiest means of the modern period to arouse national hatred."[22] Yet Kautsky followed Engels in predicting that economic unification would consolidate the Austro-Hungarian Empire, and continued to do so long after the nationalist movements in the Slavic provinces of the dual empire had reached the point of no return.

Kautsky in 1903 gave a good analysis of the reason why Eastern Europe had not followed the same path as Western Europe in the matter of national consolidation.

The history of Western Europe seemed to show that commerce has the effect of assimilating languages. The bourgeoisie has every interest in bringing about the complete unification and consolidation of the national state, and in Western Europe this amalgamation did in fact take place; the claims of the French provinces to autonomy in the matter of language were overridden in the French Revolution.[23*] But capitalism came to Eastern Europe bringing with it militarism and nationalism.

Having gone thus far, Kautsky might have been expected to advocate the abolition of all privileges for the dominant nationality, and recognition on the basis of equality for all languages in the dual empire, with autonomy for the several language sectors. Somehow the Austrian Social-Democratic

* Kautsky takes this point (without credit) from Engels' "Polendebatte," in *NRZ*, III (Sept., 1848); see *Werke*, V, 354–355. Cf. above, Chapter II, p. 33.

Party, though it came out for national-cultural autonomy in 1899, never got to the point of demanding abolition of all privileges for all nationalities, though the protection of minorities was supposed to be guaranteed by law.

The Nationality Movement of the Czechs

Some of the standing grievances of the Austro-Hungarian Slavs against the ruling German and Magyar groups have already been mentioned. These had to do largely with language—the use of the official language in government offices, courts and schools made life difficult for anyone who spoke a different language and who aspired to be an official, or to plead a case in court, or to become a schoolteacher, or write for the general press.

The nationality problem was given its mass character by certain developments connected with the industrial revolution, which came to Austria-Hungary in the period beginning with the 1860's. The dual monarchy was never very completely industrialized, and the pace of development for the country as a whole was slow; but Vienna and Prague grew rapidly, Bohemia was becoming an industrial area, and the frictions incident to this transformation had much to do with the fact that the nationality problems of the Czechs were particularly acute.

The defeat of Austria by Prussia in 1866 had determined the future of the labor movement in Austria in that it cut off Austria organizationally—though not ideologically—from the main German movement. At that time the best jobs were in the hands of the German-speaking workers in the cities. The German workers were the first to organize, and they made overtures to the Czechs, at first unsuccessfully. There was some interest among the politically minded in the successes of the anarchist terrorist group in Russia, especially after the illegalization of the German Social-Democratic Party in 1878. However the suffrage was broadened, and the Czech workers, who had supported the bourgeois Czech candidates, perceived that these when elected were working with their employers; the bourgeoisie was the real enemy. A united political and labor movement was established, including both German and Czech-speaking workers. After 1886 the anarchist element disappeared and several hard-fought strikes were conducted, marked by exemplary unity and solidarity on the part of the working class.[24] A number of Social-Democratic representatives were elected to the Vienna City Council (*Reichsrat*), some German-speaking and some Czech.

Big industry developed under German auspices. In Prague in 1890 three percent of the firms employed 54 percent of the workers. The competition of big business resulted in ruining a considerable number of small and medium-sized enterprises; but those that remained constituted an appreciable part of the whole population. Just as in the rest of Europe the local producers sought to guarantee themselves the home market by means of protective tariffs, so in Austria-Hungary the surviving businesses launched nationalist campaigns, as: "Buy Czech," or "Cut Loose from Vienna" (*los von Wien*). A Czech bourgeoisie, which had been lacking earlier, appeared on the scene and led the agitation. It was not very successful; down to 1914 only one-sixth of the cotton industry and one-fourth of the (woolen) cloth industry (*Tuch*) were in Czechish hands. But the Czechs infiltrated the government offices and entered the professions, to the point where there was an oversupply of Czech lawyers.[25]

The Austrian nobility and big landowners, in contrast with those in Prussia, were deeply involved in industry and worked with the industrialists. The land-owners had their own special reasons for wanting to keep the provincial land laws as they were.[26] The early Social-Democrats had thought that the dual monarchy might be drawn together into an integral state by the improvements in transportation and pressures for unification of the market. It will be recalled that Marx and Engels had speculated on this possibility. But history decided otherwise. Not only did the empire tend increasingly to split along nationalist lines—the lower middle class, instead of dissolving into the proletariat, developed into a vocal small-trading element which peddled anti-Semitic and nationalist sentiments, and was not even particularly helpful in the fight for the liberalization of the political machinery.

The nationalist agitation of the Czechs, then and later, had three aspects: economic, political and cultural. The economic aspect was the effort of the bourgeoisie to keep out foreign goods and assure themselves of the domestic market, which comprised not only the rural areas of Bohemia (outside the Südetenland) but most of Moravia and Slovakia as well; in fact the whole of the Slav-speaking area of Austria-Hungary might be considered part of its territory. The political aspect was the campaign for equal (or superior) rights for the Slavic nationalities, and this movement coincided with the granting of the franchise to larger groups of the working class and the peasantry. The cultural aspect was the spread of literary national education among the broad masses of the people, and the official use of the vernacular in government offices, the legislature, the courts and the schools. The German Social-Democratic spokesmen looked on this national movement with a friendly eye at first, and expressed their willingness to help the realization of these justified demands, in which the working class also had a stake.[27]

The establishment of a unitary state in Austria-Hungary was not likely to take place because this would mean the eclipse of the ruling German-Hungarian minority. In the part of the dual monarchy administered by Austria, the Slavs outnumbered the German-speaking population, and even in Hungary the Magyars made up only 40–45 percent of the population. So the logical outcome of the agitation of the Slavs for equality was separation—the breaking up of the dual monarchy—and this was early appreciated, and deplored, by the German Social Democrats who favored large, viable economic units as recommended by Marx and Engels.[28] It was realized that the proletariat, being still in the minority, would be unable to vindicate its political rights in succession states where the bourgeoisie would make common cause with the church, the military, and the landed interests. The peasants could not be counted on as a progressive force.[29]

The first solution advocated in the Austrian Social-Democratic Party was federation, with the boundaries of the several states drawn according to nationality. This program, adopted at Brünn in 1899 as a compromise, satisfied nobody, and the agitation of the Slavs continued. As a matter of fact, federation was right in the Bohemian tradition, since it had been advocated by Palacky and Rieger in 1848–49. It was charged that the Czech nationalists gave up federalism because they thought they saw a chance for national conquest.[30] But since a small Slav Bohemian state could not stand alone, it would probably seek Russian protection. There was some evidence that certain Czech intellectuals were interested in Panslavism under the leadership of the Russian Tsar—just what Marx had feared.[31]

The tendency in Austria-Hungary and Turkey was indeed for economic development not to bring about national consolidation as in Western Europe, but rather for it to create ever new minorities. Kautsky explained this result as coming about through internal migrations, especially the peasants moving to the city; instead of being absorbed, as immigrants from abroad usually are, they retained their sense of their own origins, so that frictions simply increased.[32] Pannekoek, on the other hand, believed that the dynastic state comprising different language groups tends to break up into different nationalities because competition is the law of bourgeois society, and the businessmen seek to develop national consciousness because this gives them a ready-made market. Thus, he said, the nationality struggle in such a state does not necessarily testify to the existence of national oppression; it is the natural result of language differences. He thought that except where skilled workers have a special monopoly of skill to protect—which obviously was not the case with the Slav workers—they have no special economic incentive toward building a separate nation.[33]

The workers, then, had been warned that they had no special advantages to be gained by forming a separate state, unless it were that of ousting the workers of another nationality from their privileged positions. They still preferred to join the nationalist movement; and eventually the trade unions and even the cooperatives in Bohemia were split along national lines. Were there special organizational problems that disposed them to form separate unions?

There is no question that there were such problems. Not that the Czech workers liked domestic capitalists so much more than foreign, though there had been a time, in 1868, when a public meeting of workers in Prague had adopted a resolution stating, "We hate capital only insofar as it is foreign capital."[34] But by 1896 complaints were heard in Vienna that organization of the Czech workers was being neglected; only 4,000 out of 18,000 *organized* Czech workers were affiliated to the German-led Central Labor Union, which they felt was culturally foreign to them. So the Czech workers founded their own Czechish trade-union federation, whose program called for close collaboration with the Austrian Trade Union Commission. It was practically impossible for the Czech groups under the leadership of the Vienna Commission to function, or so it was maintained. The literature was either in German, or if it was in Czech, was in "unintelligible gibberish." There was no full-time Czech leader of stature in the office. If the Czech groups proposed one, the German leaders would quite likely refuse him because he had been active in the separate Czech organization.[35]

Some Czech-speaking workers believed that where the employer was German he tended to prefer German-speaking workers for advancement; they believed that they got a better deal from Czech-speaking employers. The nationality struggle crossed class lines and found Czech workers supporting nationalist organizations of the middle class, which had their own axe to grind, economically speaking.

It was plainly the differences in the political field that rendered impossible the continued functioning of the union federation as a united group, although it was generally conceded that a united labor movement would have been stronger; indeed for many years it was believed that a united union movement could continue in spite of the existence of separate nationalist political parties. The Czech union leaders who wished to cooperate with the German-speaking political and union leaders—the "centralists," as they were called—were expelled and discriminated against by the purely Czech organizations.

The German-speaking unions were extremely bitter at the tactics used by the separate Czech unions, which they accused of using anti-Semitism, strike-breaking, and the deliberate fostering of national antagonisms among the workers. The employers, they pointed out, were not split along national lines. Gustav Eckstein, writing in the *Neue Zeit*, concluded that "social democracy has no more dangerous enemy today than nationalism."[36]

The writers for the *Neue Zeit* underestimated the progressiveness of the Czech trade-union movement taken as a whole, and indeed of the whole Czech separatist movement. Although this was led by the bourgeoisie, it had a strong popular following among the workers and peasants; it was a modern version of the phenomenon of progressive nationalism such as that exemplified by the French Revolution. But whereas early French nationalism had been committed to vindicating the rights of private property (when that was a progressive movement), the new nationalism of the Czechs had socialist overtones. Although Lenin did not realize it at the time, Czechoslovakia was to become an example of the successful application of working-class (Communist) cooperation with the progressive bourgeoisie, developing eventually (after the Second World War) into socialism.*

The question before the Czechs in the period to the First World War was indeed one not of nationalism or no nationalism, but of which nationalism they should adopt—that of the Czechs, or that of the Germans, or rather of the German-speaking element in Austria-Hungary. For what the Austro-Germans were offering them was in effect a modified version of the Austro-Hungarian Empire, not essentially a progressive state. The decision of course did not depend on the Czechs alone; the agitation for splitting up the dual monarchy was even more active outside than inside its boundaries. But the case of the Czechs is especially interesting because their nationalism was strictly home-grown; it developed within the core of the dual empire itself.

A writer in *Der Kampf* (Vienna) said that it was "vulgar socialist prejudice" to think possible the elimination of the nation and national struggle from a consideration of the causes of political struggle.[37]

Otto Bauer and National-Cultural Autonomy

A major work on nationalism was Otto Bauer's book *Die Nationalitätenfrage und die Sozialdemokratie* (1907), which remains to this day the most pretentious Marxist treatise in the field.[38] Bauer was concerned with the problem of how the several nationalities in the dual monarchy of Austria-Hungary could receive their rights without exercising the ultimate sanction of secession. The effort to preserve the dual monarchy of course failed, but Bauer's efforts, and those of his co-religion-

---

* The left wing of the Czech union movement was Communist by the end of the First World War, and during the Second World War a united union movement with progressive leadership was to be established underground. The union movement was to play a key role in the transition to socialism in 1948.

ary Karl Renner, later president of Austria, made a contribution to an understanding of the subject.*

The somewhat limited scope of Bauer's interests is apparent
already in his definition of the subject. The nation is defined
as the totality of people who are united by a common fate so
that they possess a common (national) character. The common fate is shown in the discussion to signify primarily a
common history; the common national character involves
almost necessarily a uniformity of language. Conspicuously
absent from the definition is a common territory, except insofar
as such common territory is involved in the development of a
common character and a common fate. The requirement that
a nation should comprise only people with a common history
would of course exclude from consideration those numerous
nations which have emerged since 1945, in Africa and Asia,
whose unity extended no further back than their arbitrary
grouping by the imperialist powers in the 19th century—
nations which were formed in the struggle for independence.
Even in Europe it is a question whether the Swiss, with their
trilingual setup and correspondingly varying "cultural person-
alities," would qualify as a nation in Bauer's definition; yet
they have maintained an independent national existence for
many centuries.[39]†

The concept of "national character" has been subjected to
attack by sociologists since Bauer's day. While they are not
unanimous, they have quite generally concluded that the term
is too vague and shifting to serve as a basis for sociological
analysis. Professor Karl Deutsch, whose researches since 1940
have added considerably to our knowledge of the problems of
nationalism, does accord importance to national character; but
he points out that Bauer's use of the term was somewhat

* Renner wrote under the name of Rudolf Springer before the First
World War.

† Cf. above, Chapter II, pp. 27–28, on the different definitions of a
nation in use in Western Europe and Eastern Europe respectively.

equivocal and that Bauer was not consistent in his application of the concept.[40]

Even more lacking in precision is the concept of a "community of fate." "Fate" is both forward-looking and backward-looking. In its forward-looking aspect it refers to the future of the ethnic group. Then, the group has a common fate if its members share a common psychology and are acting together in furtherance of joint aims. So conceived, a "nation" is a "corporate soul" (Renan); or, in the more sophisticated language of Bauer's time, "a nation exists if its component parts believe it to be a nation." This concept has much to recommend it. But it is not Bauer's concept. Bauer's idea is backward-looking quite as much as forward-looking: the group has an idea of what its future should be *because* the group has a common history and a common language.

Residence in a given territory and possession of a common language do not in themselves furnish a sufficient or correct definition of nationality, according to Bauer; it is necessary that the group in question would have common reactions to specific stimuli, common customs, and a common conception of the group's future. These reactions, customs, and conceptions together make up national character and national "fate." But these are precisely the constituent parts of what was then usually considered to be a nationality. Bauer added nothing new to current definitions. He defined nationality in terms of itself.

This circularity of reasoning finds expression in passages like the following, which incidentally highlight Bauer's non-materialist, almost mystical approach: "For national materialism, the nation is a piece of unique material substance, which has the secret power to create national community of character out of itself."[41]

In Austria-Hungary, for practical purposes (though not for all purposes according to Bauer's definition) nationality and language have been taken as coterminous. Certain areas have

been predominantly German-speaking, while in certain others
the Magyar (Hungarian) language has predominated, and
there are, or rather were, Slavic, Rumanian, and Italian-speak-
ing areas. Kautsky said that Austria was composed of nine
nationalities, with no one predominating. But even if the
attempt were made to divide these areas by language, the task
would have proved impossible, since the populations were too
much mixed in with each other. Bauer and Renner recognized
this difficulty, and proposed that for certain purposes broadly
defined as cultural, the population should be classified according to nationality regardless of residence, and within each
autonomous locality—this autonomy had been a demand of the
Social Democrats since 1899—the several nationalities should
constitute separate juridical public corporations for the administration of schools and for representing their nationality ad-
herents before the courts and public authorities.[42] Individual
members of a nationality who resided outside the areas in
which that nationality predominated would vote with their
respective national groups on cultural matters.

The personality principle was to involve the setting up of
a countrywide register of nationalities, person by person, a
task beset with difficulties, as Bauer and Renner recognized.[43]*

The principle of federalism in government as a solution of
the nationality problem was indeed more fundamental than
the over-advertized personality principle. On federalism too
there was no general agreement, at least outside of the Austro-
Hungarian Social Democrats.

Bauer deserves much credit for demonstrating, from the
history of the Czechs, how it is possible for a people which has
never had a "history" (in Hegel's sense), or which once had
such a history and lost it, to develop a nationality. Engels had
held the South Slavs in low esteem, partly because they had

---

* When their party came to power in Austria after the First World
War, they nevertheless set about to implement the proposal, which by
then had been modified somewhat; but the whole idea was out of date
since federalism had not been adopted, and the dual monarchy was no
more.

been kept in subjection so long by the German, Magyar and Turkish ruling classes. Yet he held the proletariat in the West, which had been downtrodden even longer, in the highest possible esteem.

The Czech-speaking lords of Bohemia had been largely wiped out in the Hussite wars, and replaced by German-speaking lords. Engels thought that the Czech language would hardly survive; he expected the peasants in Bohemia and Moravia to adopt the language of their conquerors and eventually to be absorbed culturally. Instead, the Slavic peasants in Austria-Hungary migrated to the cities and came to constitute the bulk of the working class in whole areas of the dual empire; eventually they developed a middle class, too, and showed their capacity for nation-building by actually building several nations.

Did the South Slavs constitute nationalities during the period when they were subjected to domination by an alien group? Engels had, in effect, denied that they did; in his writings over a period of half a century we find disparaging references to the "ruins of small nations" in Southeast Europe. Bauer's answer to the question is somewhat equivocal. It emerges most clearly in his discussion on the Jews.

By Bauer's definition, it would seem that the Jews should have been considered a nationality. They seemingly had a common "fate" and were in possession of a national "character" too, in Bauer's sense. They had no specified territory and no unique language, but these were not necessary attributes of a nationality as Bauer defined it.

In the Middle Ages, said Bauer, the Jews did constitute a separate nationality. They were the only brokers, money-lenders, and usurers—the only representatives of the money economy in a society that was generally agrarian. They were united by a common fate.

But with the advance of capitalism, said Bauer, this ceased to be true. The Jewish upper bourgeoisie became assimilated into the Christian bourgeoisie which was entering the money economy. As Marx had put it: "The Christians themselves became Jews." Later the assimilation movement affected the intelligentsia and gradually the petty bourgeoisie too. According to Bauer, insofar as the Jews may still be called a nation they are a historyless nation, since their middle class, those capable of maintaining and perpetuating a culture, have been largely assimilated. In spite of the attempt to bring about a rebirth of nationality among the Jews, they seemed destined to be absorbed, in Bauer's view, because there was no reserve source from which national traits and sentiments might be renewed.[44] He refers here to the peasantry, who had kept flowing to the city a steady stream of migrants with no knowledge of any language but the Slavic, and who had thus prevented the Slavic working class from being absorbed. There was of course no Jewish peasantry. Some Jews came into Austria-Hungary from the East, but this was a trickle, and Bauer thought that assimilation would not be long delayed.

Bauer evidently overstressed the extent of Jewish assimilation. But the point here is that although he emphasized again that it is only the middle class, in modern times, which is capable of building or maintaining a national culture, he referred to the peasantry with their distinctive language and customs as a "reserve" of nationality.

Bauer here throws in question his whole contention that the bourgeoisie is alone capable of building a national culture. Do not the folk songs, folk tales, and folk dances of the country folk, along with their language, constitute a culture in the anthropological sense, even if not a highly developed culture? Is not the failure of the Slavic peasants to adopt the culture of their ruling class over a thousand-year period enough reason for crediting them with a certain toughness of resistance? Even with his narrow subjective definition of nationality, Bauer cannot make nationality the exclusive attribute of one social class. Peasants and workers as individuals have a nationality in both the narrow and the broad sense.[45]

Bauer minimized the distinctiveness of the "national" culture of the Czechs. He said that aside from a few reminiscences about Hus and the White Mountain battle, the Czechs had got their culture from the Germans.* Modern Czech intellectuals challenge this approach; while Bauer's statement may have been more nearly true in the time of Palacky and Havlicek, 20th-century Czech culture has had access for many years not only to the rich Slavic culture but to the West European culture generally; it is far from a reproduction of German culture.

Bauer gave an extended analysis to show that aggressive, expanding nationalism was, and had been throughout the modern period, the work of the exploiting capitalists. His analysis ran primarily in terms of the need to keep capital moving—the need, that is, for quick turnover.[46] Later, having studied Hilferding's *Finanzkapital* (which came out soon after his own essay), he realized that he had overemphasized the purely monetary aspects.[47] But he noted the importance of the concentration of capital and the building of monopolies in the growth of imperialism.

In the heyday of English liberalism, says Bauer, the English merchants controlling the government welcomed the independence of peoples from their feudal oppressors, so that the peoples might trade and serve as markets for British goods— though to be sure the British were not interested in seeing the new states become industrialized. Today (1907), he finds that imperialism is interested not in the freedom of nations, but in the subjection of nationalities, so that the leading group may exploit others within its protected economic sphere. "The ideal of modern capitalism is thus no longer the national state, but the nationality state: a nationality state, however, in which only the population of the dominant country exploits and dominates, and the other peoples are delivered over to it

---

* The Bohemians were subjected to the House of Hapsburg from 1526. In 1620 they made an armed attempt to regain their independence, but their forces were scattered at the White Mountain, near Prague. Bauer's statement is on p. 118.

defenseless. Its model is no longer the English national state, but the British world empire. . . . Now freedom is a childish dream, the will to power a moral duty."[48]

The country that Bauer had in mind in this analysis was evidently Germany; Austria-Hungary was so torn with internal dissensions of a nationalist nature that it was incapable of working out and following an expansionist policy except as a satellite of the more powerful German Reich. Bauer and Renner were "internationalists," as all socialists professed to be, but they were objective enough observers to note the growth of a sentiment in favor of imperialism on the part of the workers. Indeed the chauvinist wing of the German Social-Democratic Party was too noisy to be disregarded. Bauer went even further and found reasons why imperialism might benefit the working class, a point that was anathema to certain writers of the left. Bauer thought that expansion was "good" for all classes of the population, including the workers. With regard to imperialism as such, the favorable results to the working class might outweigh the unfavorable, or just balance them.[49] Bauer eventually concluded that imperialism was against the interests of the working class.[50]

The attitude of the working class to imperialism becomes hostile, said Bauer, not because of the economic effects but by reason of the menace to democracy implied in the subjection of ever greater numbers of foreign peasants and workers to military rule, and the development of national as opposed to international interests. Bauer cited a number of examples from recent history of working-class opposition to imperialism, and concluded that the workers were on the whole hostile to it.[51]* Renner, by contrast, took very seriously the pro-imperialist strand in working-class thought and later dubbed it "social imperialism."[52]

In Marx's thinking, national differences would cease to be a source of friction after the socialist revolution. There would

* Cf. below, Chapter VII, on early AFL opposition to imperialism.

be contradictions among the socialist nations, but they would not be antagonistic contradictions.

Bauer thought that the spread of literacy and general education in the working class would tend to sharpen nationalist differences and would lead to a decline in international working-class solidarity, not only before but after the advent of socialism. He wrote:

> Modern capitalism slowly demarcates more sharply the lower classes of the various nations from each other, for they, too, gain a share in national education, national cultural life, and the national standard language. . . . [The] socialist society, . . . through the differences in national education, . . . will mark off entire peoples sharply from each other, as today only the educated strata of the different nations are separated.[53]

Bauer and Renner recognized the right of nationalities to self-determination, as almost all branches of the socialist movement did at this time; but they sought to avoid secession. An enlightened nationalities policy applied from the middle of the 19th century might have saved Austria-Hungary as a state; but coming when it did, the proposal of Bauer and Renner for national-cultural autonomy was open to the criticisms that were levied against it by Lenin and Stalin.

Criticisms of Bauer, and His Rejoinder

Bauer as an evolutionist evoked an impatient reaction from the revolutionary left wing, and indeed his contention that control of the schools was the most immediate issue facing the Social Democrats, seems in retrospect somewhat childish. But Bauer was quite aware that the struggles for national autonomy were basically power struggles rather than cultural struggles. His program called for a cultural revolution after the workers should by peaceful evolution have won the power.[54]

Kautsky made an extended evaluation and criticism of Bauer's work. His main points are summarized herewith.

(1) Kautsky disagreed with Bauer's definition of nationality. According to Kautsky, any social creation or organization
is a community of fate—the gens or clan, the community, the
state, the guild, the trade union, the party, even the corpora-
tion. Many of these organisms create a common culture for
their members and even a common character. But community
of fate and culture do not create anything that separates one
nation powerfully from another. The German and French Swiss
in spite of the difference of their nationalities are bound more
closely together than the German Swiss is bound to the native
of Vienna or the native of Holstein. Class differences within
a nation, Kautsky finds, are often deeper than the cultural
differences. Bauer's conclusion that only those parts of the
nation who have a share in its culture constitute the nation
Kautsky finds paradoxical, and inconsistent with Bauer's mentioning the peasantry as a reserve of nationality. He also notes
that national sentiment at the present time is characteristic of
all classes and not merely the ruling or exploiting class.[55]

Kautsky finds difficulties with the concept of "national character." When the different parts of a nation or nationality are
developing unevenly, with one part continuing to live under
semi-feudal conditions while another part is developing into
advanced capitalism, which part represents the national character? Kautsky's own definition of nationality, as we have
seen, emphasized language very strongly—not that every person speaking a given language belongs to the same nationality
but that every nationality has but one language. He chides
Bauer for understating the role of language in uniting a nation.
He also thinks, in opposition to Bauer, that national existence
is only possible where there is a common territory. But national
character, in Kautsky's view, is plainly *not* the prerequisite for
the formation of a nation, since it is characteristic primarily of
small undeveloped groups and tends to disappear the more
the nation extends and splits into different occupations and
classes. Kautsky foreshadows the development of a common
culture and common language for all peoples.[56]

(2) Kautsky discusses in turn the problems of several "nationality states," of which Austria-Hungary is only one example, and concludes that each one is unique; the nationality state is not a type, as Bauer implied it is. All the nationality states have remained backward or abnormal in their inner constitution.

(3) Kautsky thinks that Bauer and Renner make too great concessions to the idea of national autonomy, which is inconsistent with the centralization that modern economic conditions demand. He doubts whether national cultural autonomy and the personality principle will commend themselves to the ruling Germans and Magyars in Austria-Hungary; he thinks that only a proletarian revolution will create the conditions for nationality freedom plus centralization.

(4) But the basic weakness of Bauer's book, according to Kautsky, is his enormous overestimation of the national and his complete neglect of the international impulse.[57]

Bauer defended himself against Kautsky's criticisms, and at the same time drew closer to Kautsky's position. The nation (nationality), said Bauer, is a community, in the sense that it has a common psychological make-up leading to common motives and manners of thought, whereas the groups cited by Kautsky (state, trade union, etc.) are all societies, or groups united only for certain purposes.

Bauer, without specific reference to Tönnies, made the distinction between *Gemeinschaft* and *Gesellschaft* which was implicit in Marx's discussion in *Zur Judenfrage*. The nationality was a *Gemeinschaft* (community); the political state on the other hand, and the trade union, the cooperative, the church, etc., were all types of *Gesellschaft*, or structured association. As one interested in the nationality as such, Bauer gave it a good character; he endowed it with those traits of brotherliness which are discussed in ethical writings more often than they are met with in practice.[58]

It was natural, in a way, that the explicit introduction of these terms into Marxist literature, should have come by way of a discussion of the nationality rather than the nation. For the nation is so often confused with the state that the terms are used interchangeably, and it requires a deliberate effort to sort them out for purposes of analysis. But the nationality was not a state, at the time that Bauer wrote, at least not in Austria-Hungary and the other so-called multi-national states. Thus it was possible to discuss the respective attributes of the state and the nationality without fear of confusion.

Bauer accepted the idea that the members of a nationality must have a common language, as the instrument of a common culture, and maintained that that was what he had said in the first place—in his book, though not in his formal definition. As for the peasantry and their antiquated "national" characteristics, Bauer said that he was not thinking of them when he spoke of the bourgeoisie building a national culture; he was thinking of the modern *nation*, in which antiquated local peculiarities would be obliterated. Bauer agreed with Kautsky that the proletariat fights for the possession of international culture, but emphasized that this culture is not an abstraction— it must be the international element in the several national cultures.

Both Kautsky and Bauer sensed that in stressing internationalism they were swimming against the stream which was running strongly in the direction of nationalism. But there were also forces making for internationalism, including one described elsewhere by Kautsky. The workers, as the lowest class, can in his view best improve their lot by increasing the productivity of their labor, but this can best be done through mass production by the development of a world economy, and this in turn presupposes and requires international solidarity.[59]

Bauer failed to point out that Tönnies, who had given the classic treatment of the distinction between *Gemeinschaft* and *Gesellschaft*, was no Marxist.

It is true that Tönnies sympathized with the working class and took its part as against the bourgeoisie. It is also evident that Tönnies admired Marx greatly and leaned on him and on

Engels in his interpretation of history. In criticizing the modern state and calling for a reintroduction of the community spirit Tönnies might have seemed to echo the similar criticisms by Marx and the similar demands by Engels, especially in Engels' *Origin of the Family, Private Property and the State*. Not that Engels contemplated a return to the stage of primitive communism. But he did urge humanity forward to a modern version of communism in which classes would be abolished and general equality established. Communism was looked on as the highest stage of socialism.

Tönnies stopped far short of advocating communism. What he described as a *Gemeinschaft* or community, and what Bauer apparently also contemplated as the alternative to the existing state or *Gesellschaft*, was still a class society. Tönnies even described the caste society of the Middle Ages as a *Gemeinschaft*, on the ground that it depended on the natural will or *Wesenwille* rather than the rational will or *Kürwille*.

Tönnies, who linked his concept of *Gemeinschaft* with the class state, failed to follow up the lead suggested by Marx in *Zur Judenfrage*. Marxist sociology could consider the concept of *Gemeinschaft* as fruitful only if it were redefined and made to embody true equality. Right-wing Social-Democrats, who had come to accept the class state, might talk glibly of *Gemeinschaft* in their future society, but all they would mean would be that the workers should develop a feeling of community with their masters. Left-wing socialists and communists would insist on something better.

Bauer spoke of "a community of education, of work, of the enjoyment of culture, which binds the nation together."[60] If this is all he intended to imply in the way of internal equality for his nation of the future, then he may have been in the spirit of Tönnies but surely not in that of Marx. The nation as it now exists is not a *Gemeinschaft* at all but a *Gesellschaft*, Tönnies pointed out.[61]

The continuing viability of the nation as an organizing principle, even after the demise of the exploitative state, was recognized, as we have seen, by Marx. Said Renner: "Nations existed before states and will continue to exist after the state has disappeared."[62] But if the nation that would rise from the ruins of the state were to be something really different, something having claims to permanence as an institution, it would need to be purged not only of national exploitation but of class exploitation as well, in the Marxist view.

Bauer strongly deprecated the swing to nationalism in Austria and Germany. He said that "the struggle against nationalism is today [1909–1910] our most important task." He believed this to be true even though an "intransigent internationalism" might frighten away from the ranks hordes of fellow-travelers, as he assumed it would. Even this conclusion was challenged by Josef Strasser, another Austrian internationalist, who pointed to his experience in Reichenberg, just across the border from Germany in the Südetenland of Bohemia. There, he recounted, an uncompromising attack on the then current nationalism had indeed scared away some who would otherwise have been fellow-travelers, and even some feeble Social-Democrats. But the outcome had been a membership schooled in the dangers of chauvinism, and eventually an increase in the Social-Democratic vote—"if not because of the party's intransigent stand, then anyway in spite of it."[63]

An illustration of the extreme difficulty of solving nationality problems within the framework of the old Austro-Hungarian "nationality state" is furnished by the debate between Renner and Alfred Meissner on the subject of separate schools for Czech children. Renner had suggested that the national minorities should have the right to set up separate schools if they could show that they were financially able to maintain them. Meissner retorted that the function of the central government was supposed to be to protect the weak, and insisted that equality of treatment should be assured out of the central purse.[64]

By 1914, the several nationalities in the dual empire had reached a kind of impasse where constructive legislation was reached a kind of impasse where constructive legislation was all but impossible. Each of the major nationalities was strong enough, by itself or in combination, to block any major proposal brought in by another faction. This situation was ruefully described by Bauer as "negative autonomy."[65]

Stalin's Redefinition of the Problem

Stalin, in a study of the national question which appeared in 1913, defined the nation as follows: "A nation is an historically evolved, stable community of language, territory, economic life, and psychological make-up manifested in a community of culture."[66] This definition, which refers to the nationality and not the nation-state, is different from Bauer's primarily in that it insists that community not only of language but of territory, and fairly contiguous territory at that, is an essential part of the picture.

Stalin is especially concerned to refute the theory of national-cultural autonomy, both the version promulgated by Bauer and Renner and the modified version adopted as a compromise at Brünn in 1899, by the Austrian Social-Democratic Party. Stalin, while accepting the idea of national self-determination, thought that national-cultural autonomy was both unworkable and undesirable. As for the practicability of national-cultural autonomy, Stalin wrote, with reference to Russia: "Is it conceivable that the Germans of the Baltic Provinces and the Germans of Transcaucasia can be 'welded into a single nation'?"[67]

Stalin found that national-cultural autonomy was undesirable for several reasons. First, national-cultural groups are inter-class groups, in which proletariat and bourgeoisie are supposed to find more in common with each other than with the people of their respective social classes in the rest of the population. Nationality, he declares, is a bourgeois principle. "Implanted among the workers, it poisons the atmosphere and spreads noxious ideas of mutual mistrust and aloofness among

the workers of the different nationalities." Second, Stalin finds
that national-cultural autonomy is a halfway house on the road
to federalism and ultimately to separation, which he deplores;
he cites the Czechs as a horrible example.[68] Like Bauer, he
would prefer to have the tribes and smaller nationalities remain
within the multi-national state; but the mechanism that he
favors, supposing that the latter do not exercise their right of
secession, is *regional* autonomy.

Stalin's booklet was written in January, 1913, and published
in *Prosveshcheniye* in March-May, 1913. Lenin made his own
refutation of Bauer, in terms very similar to Stalin's, in May
and June, 1913. He pointed out that even Bauer had favored
the unity of Social-Democratic Party organizations at the local
level, and called the Bauer-Renner idea of national-cultural
autonomy "an opportunistic dream picture of people who have
lost the hope of building consistent democratic institutions."[69]

Stalin's other conclusions, and indeed his essay as a whole,
were quite acceptable to Lenin; and this fact, and the related
circumstance that Stalin became the accepted theoretician of
the Bolsheviks on the subject of nationality, elevated Stalin's
1913 essay into the role of a textbook on nationality problems
for the world communist movement. This is an honor that it
hardly deserves. Both Bauer and Lenin wrote more comprehensively
than Stalin, and Lenin especially was more incisive
and at the same time more flexible in his approach.

Stalin's definition of nationality, while superior to Bauer's,
shares some of the shortcomings of the latter, for both are
directed to the particular problems of Eastern Europe in the
period before the First World War, and neither is broad
enough to cover the whole field. It was true already at that
time that nationalities were developing which did not have
unity of language, or territory, or history; and many other
nationalities with similarly disparate composition were to
develop later. John H. Kautsky points out: "Speaking of under-developed
countries in general, there would seem to be no
positive factor [in nationalism] at all, but rather the dislike

of a common enemy, the colonial power."[70] In this respect the nationality is like the social class. Marx had pointed out: "The separate individuals [in the proletariat] form a class only insofar as they have to carry on a common battle against another class; otherwise they are on hostile terms with each other as competitors."[71]

Even for East-European conditions, the difficulties that confront both definitions are formidable. For, as has been pointed out before, every state that has been or could be set up in that area, must contain substantial minorities from some other "nationality." Hence the growth of the practice of exchanging minorities, or simply expelling those who do not belong to the dominant ethnic group.

Bauer's definition of nationality in its original form required the acceptance of the Jews as a nationality; but Bauer, as we have seen, in a rather labored argument, had convinced himself that the Jews were moving out of that category. Besides, Bauer in his concessions to his critics drew so close to them as virtually to adopt their position that both a separate language and a distinct territory were necessary attributes of a nationality. Stalin, who specified community of both language and territory as necessary attributes of a nationality, thereby excluded the Jews from the outset.

VII

NATIONALISM, IMPERIALISM AND THE LABOR AND SOCIALIST MOVEMENTS IN THE UNITED STATES

THE UNITED STATES as a country of heavy immigration was related to the nationalist movements of Europe in a special way. Not only ideas came across the ocean, but men, whole groups of them, who organized themselves after their arrival into societies using the language and continuing the traditions of the homeland. Especially significant were, in the second half of the 19th century, the Germans. Their workers' circles, political and economic as well as social in character, formed the first centers of Marxist discussion and agitation in the country. Some of their leaders, such as Wilhelm Weitling, Joseph Weydemeyer and F. A. Sorge, who kept up a correspondence with Marx and Engels, were pioneers in the American union and socialist movement.

In the 1880's, the German anarchist groups took the lead in several important battles such as the eight-hour movement in Chicago. The majority of the Haymarket martyrs were of German extraction; the leaflet announcing the meeting on the evening of May 4, 1886, was printed in German as well as English. The industrial union of the brewers was organized by the Germans in Milwaukee so strongly that it was able to influence municipal politics for many years; Milwaukee became famous for its Socialist administration, the backbone of whose support was the brewers' union.

After the turn of the century the German national groups had lost their revolutionary orientation, but new Marxist groups were organized on a nationality basis among the immigrants from Eastern and Southern Europe. It was the language federations which supplied a large part of the membership and finances to the Socialist Party in the period 1911 to 1917, although the leadership and the bulk of the membership were home-grown.

The old-timers who think of the European nationality groups in the Socialist and Communist movement recall them in their latest phase, when they were already marked for the discard. Such people easily forget that in their day these groups combined an active socialist consciousness with a continuing interest in their respective "home" countries. The European nationality differences meant little to the typical American-born worker, but their influence in building the Socialist movement should not be forgotten. The spark of altruism and dedication without which no social movement can flourish was by no means absent from their proceedings.

The American labor and socialist movement contributed to the development of the Marxist theory of nationalism by giving expression to a deep-seated popular opposition to imperialism. The trade union movement, incredible as it seems today, went through a phase of active opposition to the imperialistic activities of the United States. Samuel Gompers, President of the AFL, in the 1890's also repeatedly voiced organized labor's opposition to war. When the Venezuelan boundary dispute raised the specter of possible war between England and the United States, he said:

Who would be compelled to bear the burden of war? The working people. They would pay the taxes, and their blood would flow like water. The interests of the working people of England and the United States are common. They are fighting the same enemy. They are battling to emancipate themselves from conditions common to both countries. *The working people know no country. They are citizens of the world.*[1]

Gompers and the AFL leadership campaigned against imperialism, by which they understood the annexation of foreign territory. During the 1890's the proposal was advanced for the United States to annex the Hawaiian Islands. Organized labor voiced strong disapproval, and the first attempt at annexation was defeated in the U.S. Senate.

Gompers was interested in the problems of Cuba, which was struggling in the 1890's to throw off the Spanish yoke. The 1896 Convention of the AFL expressed hearty sympathy to the Cuban people in their striving for independence, and called on the President of the United States to recognize the belligerent rights of the Cuban revolutionists. Before the Cubans had secured their freedom, the United States went to war with Spain, promising the Cubans that they would be granted their independence. After the U.S. had won the war, Gompers called for the prompt implementation of this promise.[2]

To be sure, Gompers's motives with regard to Cuba were mixed. The Cigarmakers' Union to which he belonged was in competition with the labor of the Havana cigarmakers. Cuba was the chief source of imported U.S. tobacco and finished cigars. "It was important for us," wrote Gompers later, in his autobiography, "that we should spread the gospel of unionism in Cuba. But a labor movement was practically impossible under Spanish rule."[3]

The union movement was by and large opposed to the U.S. going to war with Spain, but supported the war after it had begun—on the Cuban issue. The *Railway Conductor* said in its issue of May 1898: "There can be no question as to the right of this country to intervene between Spain and the land she had so horribly devastated."[4] And in the same month the *Locomotive Engineers Journal* added its opinion: "We shall feel assured that there will be no faltering, and that there will be an end to Spanish misrule in Cuba."[5]

The Knights of Labor were at this time still active, though not nearly so important as the AFL. The Knights even upbraided President McKinley for not going to war sooner—on the Cuban issue.[6] Unions which did not specifically pick out

Cuban freedom for endorsement nevertheless endorsed the war after it had started; thus the *Coast Seamen's Journal* of the Sailors' Union of the Pacific said in an editorial (April 27, 1898): "Having got into a war, no matter how or why, we want to win out as speedily as possible."*

But labor leaders were far from accepting without criticism the publicly announced war aims of the McKinley administration. I. D. Chamberlain of the Knights of Labor, who as General Worthy Foreman was second in the organization only to General Master Workman Henry A. Hicks, warned the membership already in May, 1898, that it was the intention of Congress to make the pillage of Cuba legal.[7] He also feared that there might be created in the United States a great standing army which would mow down strikers.

Eugene V. Debs denounced the war while it was in progress, a step which practically no other labor leader dared to take, though some privately agreed with Debs.[8] *The Monthly Journal* of the International Association of Machinists hinted darkly after the war that the "capitalistic system" had been responsible.[9]

When it was proposed to annex not only Puerto Rico but the Philippines as well, organized labor moved into open opposition. Imperialism became for a time (1898–1900) a burning issue. It was taken for granted by "imperialists" and "anti-imperialists" alike that Cuba would be given a somewhat circumscribed independence. The battle raged over the fate of the Philippines, and to a lesser extent of Puerto Rico.

The 1898 convention of the AFL went on record against imperialism. Samuel B. Donnelly of the International Typographical Union endorsed the U.S. acquisition of Hawaii and called for the annexation of the Philippines, for conventional nationalistic reasons: to keep pace with colonial Great Britain. But the prevailing sentiment at the convention was opposed to colonial annexations on the ground that this would involve

* The Railroad Trainmen's *Journal* wholeheartedly endorsed the war; see issue of June, 1898, p. 446.

competition from cheap native labor. The resolution adopted read as follows:

WHEREAS, as a result of the war with Spain a new and far-reaching policy, commonly known as "imperialism" or "expansion" is now receiving the attention of the National Government, and if ratified by the United States Senate will seriously burden the wage-workers of our country, thrust upon us a large standing army and an aristocratic navy, and seriously threaten the perpetuity of our Republic, therefore be it

RESOLVED, that this convention offers its protest against any such innovation in our system of government, and instructs our officers to use every honorable means to secure its defeat.[10]

Only three delegates voted against this resolution.

With labor in the campaign for Philippine independence were ranged (said the *Nation* in an editorial) all the leading authorities on statecraft and political morality—men of the caliber of Carl Schurz, Senator Hoar of Massachusetts, Samuel W. McCall, Senator Pettengill of South Dakota, and many others, joined later by Samuel L. Clemens (Mark Twain).[11] An Anti-Imperialist League was formed in Boston on November 19, 1898, with Gompers as a vice-president. In October 1899 a convention in Chicago attracted delegates from nearly every state in the union. It was estimated that 150,000 persons signed the card for membership in the League. Gompers was a vice-president of the national Anti-Imperialist League, and worked actively in its campaign.

The 1899 convention of the Knights of Labor passed a resolution opposing (1) the subjugation of the Philippines by military conquest and (2) the extension of U.S. territory beyond the limits of the American continent. "It is clearly the interest of all wage-earners to oppose imperialism root and branch," wrote Ernest H. Crosby in the *American Federationist* for September 1900.

Gompers shared the general view that America's productive capacity was outrunning the ability of American markets to absorb the output, but thought that it was ridiculous to attribute the limitation of domestic markets to the saturation of America's consuming power, when so many millions of Americans were "workless, ahungered and ragged."[12] He advocated extending American commercial might, but for other reasons; he thought that U.S. economic penetration of foreign territories would contribute to "the attainment of the highest pinnacle of [American] national glory and human progress."[13] He agreed with Carl Schurz in condemning "the barbarous notion that we must own the countries we are to trade with," but did not oppose economic imperialism.[14] His economic analysis was more realistic, though less moral, than that of the American Socialists.

If he opposed colonialism as such, then known as "imperialism" or just "expansion," this was primarily in order to forestall an erosion of American standards such as might take place if the U.S. acquired colonies. He opposed the annexation of Puerto Rico "with its semi-nude people," and especially of the Philippines, whose "half-breeds and semi-barbaric people" were, he contended, "perhaps nearer the condition of savages and barbarians than those of any islands possessed by any other civilised nation on earth."[15]

The danger to U.S. labor, as he saw it, was partly economic, through the admission of colonial products to the American market in competition with American-made goods, and partly political. In a debate with F. B. Thurber of the U.S. Export Association, Gompers said that the AFL had to oppose annexation because countries becoming part of the United States would share the same legal system as the home country, and laws applied to native labor might set precedents for restrictive legislation against American workers. The AFL feared the results that might follow if insular labor were allowed free immigration to the U.S. Colonial expansion, finally, would violate the American principle that governments derive their just powers from the consent of the governed.[16] It is most interesting to find that the AFL in its stand on early American imperialism reproduced the position, and some of the arguments, that we found the Council of the International using with regard to Ireland in 1866–1870.*

Gompers, in consistence with his idea of protecting American labor from the competition of the labor in the new dependencies, interested himself personally in the condition of labor in the islands, including Hawaii. He claimed at least some of the credit for abolishing "involuntary servitude" in Hawaii and for the establishment of a certain degree of trade-union freedom in Cuba and Puerto Rico.[17] The American military in Cuba had started out in the traditional imperialist style. In the fall of 1899 a general strike for the eight-hour day was broken when General Ludlow threatened to arrest and imprison all the leaders. Gompers personally went to Cuba and protested vehemently. Some years later, direct American rule of Cuba was somewhat reluctantly withdrawn.

In Puerto Rico also, the legality of trade unionism was at first in doubt. Gompers had a conference with President Theodore Roosevelt about the case of Santiago Iglesias, union leader who had been sentenced to three years, four months and a day in prison for his organizing activities. Thereafter Governor Hunt recommended to the legislature that unionism be made legal, and this was done. In 1902 we find the AFL convention recommending that the inhabitants of Puerto Rico be admitted to full citizenship in the United States, and this also was eventually done. Iglesias continued active in Puerto Rico on the payroll of the AFL for something like forty years. His position was that of a right-wing Socialist, opposed to Puerto Rican independence and not differing substantially, as would be expected, from that of the Executive Council of the AFL, which of course abhorred the designation of Socialist. With regard to Hawaii and the Philippines the AFL maintained a somewhat intermittent interest, investigating and protesting from time to time but carrying on no serious organizing.

In 1901 Gompers joined the National Civic Federation. His close association over the years with Ralph Easley, the red-

* Cf. Chapt. III, above.

baiting secretary of the NCF, was to do much to shape his psychology in the imperialist mold and prepare him for intimate cooperation in State Department policies.[18] Already in 1904 an episode illustrated how the anti-imperialist sentiments of the AFL leaders had begun to ebb. The Filipino cigarmakers had expressed a desire to get organized, and the AFL had been asked to aid them in their campaign, but the U.S. leaders turned down the request; the reason was that the "agitation of Philippine independence was very strong among the better class of workers."[19] This attitude may be compared with that of Gompers in relation to the Havana cigarmakers only ten years before.

Gompers paid lip service to anti-militarist movements such as those then popular in labor and socialist circles abroad, as when, in 1907, he strongly attacked militarism and war, including the use of war to open up new markets. With an eye on the powerful left wing in the AFL, he used to describe himself as a "doctrinaire pacifist"; but it turned out that he meant by the term little more than one who advocates peace in time of peace.[20] Most of the time he was a conventional patriot. "American trade-unionists have always shown themselves patriotic when their country needed them," he wrote in 1910.[21]

While it would be incorrect to read a Leninist analysis into the early anti-imperialism of the AFL, it would be even less correct to deny, deprecate, and downgrade the forthright anti-militarism and anti-colonialism of those early days. The IWW at its founding convention (1905) was reviving an honorable tradition when it "[condemned] militarism in all its forms and functions" and voted that anyone joining the militia should be denied membership in the IWW.[22] From 1900 to 1914 the AFL put up a solid front of resistance against every effort to increase armaments.

The first issue of the *International Socialist Review* appeared in July, 1900. For a while the columns were overflowing with discussions of imperialism and foreign policy. The view of most of the writers was that "expansion" was an inherent part of the wage system; an editorial in October, 1900, stated: "Expansion is simply the natural results [sic] of the accumulation of the surplus products of labor in the hands of the capitalist and while capitalism exists, expansion is inevitable."[23]

The economic analysis was on a rather low level, and could be called Marxist only by courtesy. Take the following editorial in the first number:

It is a characteristic of capitalism, which it shares with all life, that it must grow or die. Resting upon the exploitation of the producing classes, who continuously receive little more than their subsistence, the improvement of productive processes brings to the ruling possessing classes an ever larger mass of unearned profits. These cannot be sold to the laborers who produce them. Hence, a market is sought among a less highly developed society, where these finished products can be exchanged for raw materials.[24]

This is not Marxism; it is neo-mercantilist underconsumptionism.

Somewhat more pretentious, but still profoundly unsatisfactory, was the analysis by Boothman. Within the United States, he argued, there is a long-run tendency for the rate of profit to fall. But the *volume* of profit tends to increase, so the capitalists buy up old businesses, especially small ones. To get a higher rate of profit, the need for expansion is obvious. "It is written in the inexorable decree of fate that the United States shall develop into a colonial power. . . . Imperialism is something which must be."

Thus far, the argument recalls that of Hobson, Edward Atkinson, and, many years before, Rodbertus. To be sure, Boothman's presentation is defective in that he states that there is *no* more opportunity for internal investment at a profit: "Investment has gone about as far as it safely may." Also, he leaves out of his figures on imports and exports the invisible items—a serious omission. But the worst is yet to come.

We are approaching the stage where the capitalization of the industries of the United States must rise to infinity. . . . The percent of interest will sink to zero. . . . Under expansion [meaning the

acquisition of colonies] we may for a little while avert the
threatened consolidation of big capital. . . . From the point of view
of the working class expansion is, or rather ought to be, something
absolutely devoid of charm; something not worth talking about.
Our new foreign policy has no concern, one way or another, with
the material interests of this class.

When the rate of profit had sunk internationally to the level
of zero, "forces would spontaneously evolve themselves" that
would "bring about a disintegration of the existing order, and
inaugurate a new era of social advance."[25]

It is indeed surprising that when foreign expansion is considered to be so intimately bound up with the future, indeed
with the survival, of the economic order, such expansion should
be set down as of no importance to the working class. Surprising is Eugene V. Debs' acceptance of this analysis; he wrote
that imperialism was an issue of no concern to the working
class—a "meaningless phrase."[26] Most surprising of all, however, is the attitude of certain modern American scholars who
profess to find in the socialist analysis a "radical challenge" to
all those who said that expansion abroad was a prime necessity.[27] Quite the contrary was the case. By withdrawing from
the battle over imperialism and concentrating (supposedly)
on building the cooperative commonwealth at home, the
Socialists were shirking their responsibilities.

Boothman's rather extreme position was not shared by all
the Socialist writers. Thus A. M. Simons took the realistic position in 1901 that "there will be no breaking down of American
industrial machinery because of a plethora of capital" for a
generation to come; "there are opportunities in yet undeveloped portions of the earth to absorb the surplus capital of
America."[28] Simons still thought that socialism would come to
the United States rather quickly, though not for the reason of
a glut of capital. Hence he endorsed the Party's position that it
was unnecessary and undesirable to carry on a campaign
against imperialism.

The Socialist Party shared the general opposition in the

working class to war and militarism in all its manifestations. Maurice F. Eldridge in the *ISR* in 1907 called for the education of the militiamen so that they should not shoot down their brothers.[29]

By 1909 some Socialists had discovered the oppressive and exploitative nature of the operations of American investors in Mexico. "Uncle Sam has gone to slave-driving in a foreign country," wrote John Kenneth Turner in an article, "The American Partners of Diaz," in 1910; and an editorial in the *ISR* at the same time described "Mexico, Our Capitalists' Slave Colony."[30]

But this interpretation of events in Mexico did not go unchallenged in left-wing circles, and after the first cordial greeting to the Mexican Revolution in 1911[31] the editors of the *International Socialist Review* backed water: "The capitalists have their necessary work to do in developing the natural resources of Mexico and organizing its industry along modern lines."[32] The editors showed no awareness of the neo-mercantilist policies of the capitalists of advanced industrial countries and their governments, nor of the chronic inability of this group to develop industries in backward countries as long as raw materials, mining resources, and foodstuffs remained to be exploited. Thus the greeting to the Chinese Revolution of the same year lauded the "modernization and Westernization of China," mentioning Standard Oil as a shining example.[33]

The silence of the Socialists on the "dollar diplomacy" of the Taft administration, which had drawn the unfavorable notice of certain liberals, is very conspicuous. But the left wing shortly returned to the attack in the columns of the Socialist theoretical organ. Arturo Giovanitti in an article on Tripoli condemned "colonial expansion" by all advanced capitalist states, including the United States.[34] And Bill Haywood presented a resolution to the Socialist Party Convention calling for a general strike in case of a war against Mexico, and for the expulsion from the SP of any member taking part in such a war.[35] Herbert Sturges also opposed American intervention in Mexico.[36]

In 1912 the convention of the AFL adopted a resolution, proposed by Andrew Furuseth of the International Seamen's Union, opposing any intervention in Mexico, and extending cordial greetings and best wishes to the "men in Mexico now struggling to abolish age-long wrongs by striking the shackles from the limbs and minds of men and women and to abolish the present land tenure."[37] This position, incidentally, revived the early tradition in the U.S. of applauding popular revolutions against reactionary governments abroad, and hailing economic reforms as a gain to humanity.

At the 1913 convention of the AFL, a relatively innocuous administration resolution (no. 163) calling for a one-year moratorium on the building of naval armaments was amended from the floor so that it "condemn[ed] the attempts . . . by American and foreign corporations, and certain jingo newspapers, to force armed intervention by the U.S. government in Mexico." (*AFL Convention Proceedings, 1913*, p. 364.)

The anti-militarist forces in the AFL came to be led by the Socialist Party union leaders, who year in and year out managed at this time to muster perhaps a third of the votes in AFL conventions. In 1916, when the jingoist "preparedness" fever was sweeping the country and had already enlisted the support of the group of labor leaders around Gompers, a group of Socialists at the head of various AFL unions was strong enough to defeat the Gompers group in the AFL convention on this issue and to reaffirm labor's opposition to peacetime military training (conscription).

In mid-1915 the Socialist Party membership overwhelmingly ratified both a Peace Manifesto and Program of "aggressive . . . uncompromising opposition to the whole capitalist system, and to every form of its more deadly fruits—militarism and war," and a constitutional amendment providing for expulsion of any Socialist office-holder voting funds for any military purpose. In 1916 the general strike against war was incorporated into the Party platform.[38] A midwesterner named Allan Benson wrote for the *Appeal to Reason* a series of articles against preparedness, which were so well received that they won for him the Party's nomination for president of the United States in 1916, although he had been unknown previously.[39]

The 1916 convention of the IWW continued even more forcefully the policy of anti-militarism and anti-nationalism which had marked its whole existence. One resolution said in part:

With the European war for conquest and exploitation raging and destroying the lives, class consciousness and unity of the workers, and the ever growing agitation for military preparedness clouding the main issues and delaying the realization of our ultimate aim with *patriotic and, therefore, capitalistic* aspirations, we openly declare ourselves the *determined opponents of all nationalistic sectionalism, or patriotism,* and the militarism preached and supported by our enemy, the capitalist class. We condemn all wars and, for the prevention of such, we proclaim the anti-militarist propaganda in time of peace, thus promoting Class Solidarity among the workers of the entire world, and, in time of war, the General Strike in all industries.[40]

The delegates were confident that their anti-war position expressed the true feeling of the great majority of American workers.

When war was declared in 1917, the IWW did not indeed call a general strike—its numbers were far too small for that—but its head office sent out a statement of strong opposition to the war: "All class conscious members of the Industrial Workers of the World are conscientiously opposed to spilling the life blood of human beings . . . because we believe that the interests and welfare of the working class in all countries are identical."[41]

On July 28, 1917, shortly before the top leaders were rounded up by the federal government and the movement effectively squelched, the General Executive Board issued from Chicago a "final statement" which said in part:

Since its inception our organization has opposed all national and imperialistic wars. We have proved, beyond the shadow of a doubt, that war is a question with which we never have [compromised] and never intend to compromise. . . .

The principle of international solidarity of labor to which we have always adhered makes it impossible for us to participate in any and all of the plunder-squabbles of the parasite class. . . .

All members of the I.W.W. who have been drafted should mark their claims for exemption, "I.W.W., opposed to war."[42]

When it became evident that war would be declared, the Socialist Party called an emergency convention in St. Louis for April 7–14, 1917. A small group headed by John Spargo attempted to lead the party into support of the war, but it received only five votes out of 177. The resolution adopted reaffirmed "its allegiance to the principle of internationalism and working class solidarity the world over," and proclaimed its "unalterable opposition to the war just declared by the government of the United States." Continuing, the resolution said:

The wars of the contending national groups of capitalists are not the concern of the workers. The only struggle which would justify the workers in taking up arms is the great struggle of the working class of the world to free itself from economic exploitation and political aggression, and we particularly warn the workers against the snare and delusion of so-called defensive warfare. As against the *false doctrine of national patriotism* we uphold the idea of international working-class solidarity. In support of capitalism, we will not willingly give a single life or a single dollar; in support of the struggle of the workers for freedom we pledge our all.[43]

After the entry of the United States into the war, the isolated Socialist Party organizations in the Mississippi Valley area fell apart, like the IWW, under the pounding of federal government prosecutions, including suppression of the press, indictments for conspiracy to commit sabotage, and various trumped-up charges.* The center of gravity of the Party then shifted to

* According to Roger Baldwin's compilation, during the first year of the war most of the socialist papers were either held up by the Post Office Department or had their second class mail privileges revoked.— N. Fine, *Labor and Farmer Parties in the United States, 1828–1928* (New York, 1928–1961), p. 318.

the militant city workers, especially in the Eastern cities, where the East European language federations had been less affected than the American-born by the pro-war propaganda. The Socialist Propaganda League, organized in Boston in 1915, was the creature of the Lettish Federation, which, although affiliated with the American Socialist Party, still functioned as a branch of the Latvian Socialist Party.[44] It issued a manifesto in that year which declared that the worker had no country, disparaged political activity, called for mass action, and pledged support to the new International forming in Europe. The East European language federations were much excited by the issues of war and internationalism, and carried the ball in the American Party for the left-Marxist point of view.

But the Party's anti-war position was originally developed independently of the language federations, which had not affiliated until the period 1911–1915.

Popular opposition to American involvement in the First World War was associated in the midwest and the plains states with a particular kind of provincialism not connected with race or national origin, and not necessarily with socialism. The farmers of the Mississippi Valley had long felt exploited by the Eastern capitalists, who they thought were charging them too much in interest, in railroad freight rates, and in monopoly prices on manufactured goods, while the Eastern middlemen realized an excessive profit from their dealings in grain. This sentiment crystalized in the "Granger" agitation for regulation of railroad rates in the 1880's, found expression in the Sherman Anti-Trust Act of 1890, and underlay the Populist revolt of the 1890's. When war was declared in 1917, the first reaction of many workers and farmers in the great central section of the United States was that this was a rich man's war, specifically a war of the Easterners, some of whom had already made a good thing businesswise of the European War and stood to make still more in war profits from American involvement.

This point of view found expression in the propaganda of the Non-Partisan League, a farmers' organization which arose

in North Dakota in 1916 and succeeded in capturing control of
that state's politics while spreading its organization to a dozen
neighboring states. Under the leadership of A. C. Townley, a
former Socialist, the League campaigned against the war
profits of the "pay-triots" and expressed doubts about the draft,
then a new departure.

But while the rumblings of dissent sometimes reached
formidable proportions, as in the "Green Corn Rebellion" in
Oklahoma, the isolationism of the midwest presently began
to wear off. The publication of the Lichnowsky Memorandum,
for example, convinced some people that Germany really was
the aggressor. In the end North Dakota and the other states
of the Mississippi Valley swung into line and supported the
war.

This shift in attitude had its echo in the ranks of the Socialist
Party. Leaders like Debs remained staunch in their opposition
to the war and the draft. But the influential *Appeal to Reason*
of Girard, Kansas, had supported the war from the outset; and
in time the zeal for the St. Louis resolution cooled appreciably
in large sections of the membership. Nathan Fine was moved
afterwards to state that the Party had not lived up to the
implications of its declared position.[45] The Socialist Party was
not far removed from the sentiment of the masses on the war
issue down to the end of 1917.[46]

The anti-war sentiment in the United States, of which the
Socialist Party was for a short time after the St. Louis convention the only spokesman, was made up of many strands; no
doubt the most important was America's geographical isolation.
This isolation—which was always relative and has long since
disappeared—helps explain how it was that in all the warring
countries there was only one significant union federation which
opposed the war before, during, and after its country's involvement: the IWW.

The followers of Marx in the European countries had been
insufficiently alerted to the perils of unthinking nationalism.
The followers of Bakunin, who of course were more numerous

in Italy, Spain and the Latin countries generally, came off on the whole better in this respect. But close attention to the doctrines of Marx could yield, as in Lenin's case, a strongly anti-patriotic line of thought. In the United States, where Bakunin's influence was clearly less than that of Marx, the anti-patriotic stand of both the Socialists and the IWW in the First World War cannot be attributed to their theoretical antecedents, but must be sought in the particular conditions of the country.

VIII

LENIN AND THE FORMULATION OF A
MARXIST NATIONALITY THEORY

THE OBVIOUS SHORTCOMINGS of Stalin's treatment of nationality questions have led in recent years to renewed study of Lenin's writings on the subject. It is now seen that while Lenin did not correct Stalin's definition of the problem at the time, he made room in his handling of the subject for other places and times than Eastern Europe before the First World War. He filled in many of the gaps in Stalin's treatment; furnished materials for an understanding of the new role of nationality in the 20th century; and in the application of Marxist theory to the problems of the Soviet Union—a subject which unfortunately lies outside the scope of this study—he diverged completely from Stalin.

Lenin had participated in the formulation of the Russian Social-Democratic Party's position on nationality problems in 1903, and for a number of years the statement then adopted continued to command the approval of all factions in the party; Plekhanov and the Mensheviks supported it no less vigorously than did Lenin and the Bolsheviks. The Party's position was one of unqualified support for the principle of self-determination as applied to the nationalities of Tsarist Russia, of equality for all the nationalities in the empire, and of unconditional guarantees for the protection of the rights of national minorities. It opposed the organization of unions on the basis of nationality.[1]

However the nationality question arose in the Russian party, where the ideas of Otto Bauer and Karl Renner gained ground

among the Mensheviks, to the point where a conference of
right-wingers in August, 1912, declared for "national-cultural
autonomy." Lenin, who up to that time had considered the
national question chiefly in its relation to the rising movement
for colonial independence, now gave the subject of self-
determination in Europe the most serious consideration, and
in a series of articles and theses, extending from the middle
of 1913 to the end of 1916, he reviewed the position of Marx
and Engels and formulated his own proposals.

Nationalism as a Historic Category

Since Lenin (following Marx) believed that general principles were relative to time and place, he discussed Marx's ideas
on nationalism and nationality problems as of three distinct
epochs, all of them modern. The first epoch, 1789–1871, represents the ascending line of the bourgeoisie, of bourgeois-democratic movements in general and of bourgeois-national
movements in particular—an epoch of the rapid breakdown of
obsolete feudal absolutist institutions. The second epoch,
1871–1914, is the epoch of full domination and decline of the
bourgeoisie, and of its transformation from a progressive class
to a reactionary, even rabidly reactionary class, under the
leadership of finance capital. Some historians, including some
Marxists, would call this the epoch of imperialism, and Lenin
occasionally wrote as if imperialism reached its apogee around
1900; but in his formal classification the epoch of imperialism
began only in 1914 with the outbreak of the First World War,
which he expected, correctly, to usher in a period of convul-
sions ending in the overthrow of capitalism in one country after
another.[2]

Imperialism as a *system*, identical with colonialism, of course
long antedated even the first of these epochs. Thus Lenin used
the term "imperialist war" to characterize the French and
Indian Wars (known in Europe as the Seven Years' War) in

1756–1763; he remarked that an imperialist war "is as possible on the basis of slavery, or of primitive capitalism, as on the basis of highly developed modern capitalism."[3]

Lenin thought that in the first of the epochs he listed (1789–1871), nationalism was a progressive force, as it is wherever the rising capitalist class seeks to throw off the chains of feudalism; it then makes use of the form of the national state. He assumed that all nations would go through the same development, and that India and China would follow "the national road," and be organized into national states, although this had not yet happened.[4] In the epoch that had ended in 1871, "it was perfectly natural that the elements of modern democracy, with Marx as their representative, should have been guided by the undisputed principle of supporting the progressive bourgeoisie . . . against feudalism."[5]

Engels in *Po und Rhein* had contended that the "great and virile European nations" had absorbed a number of small and devitalized nations, and that the boundaries of the great nations had been determined "more and more" by the "language and sympathies" of the population. Engels, as we have noted, was somewhat of a great-power imperialist in his early days, and Lenin excuses him partly on the basis that the great powers were then progressive, and partly on the ground that the "language and sympathies" of the populations had supposedly been followed—a means of fixing boundaries which Lenin found to be democratic.[6] This is a rather unsatisfactory way of disposing of a troublesome question, since it is not clear that Engels was really recommending the principle of self-determination which Lenin in general favored. Lenin endorsed the judgment of Marx and Engels that the Czechs were to be condemned for the reactionary role they had played in 1848, but refrained from unfavorable judgments on the South Slavs generally, or on the Czechs of a later period.

Lenin made no defense of Engels' first treatment of Algeria, nor of the treatment of the Mexican war of 1847 by Engels and Marx. The first he did not discuss at all; on the second, the best that he could say for Marx and Engels was that they had changed their minds.

The basis on which he arrived at this opinion was to be sure somewhat shaky, and could have involved him in difficulties if he had pursued it to its logical conclusion. He agreed with Kautsky that Marx's address to the First International on the Franco-Prussian War constituted a condemnation of aggressive wars, hence, by implication, of the U.S. aggression against Mexico.

The awkward thing about this interpretation is that although Marx did at first condemn Napoleon III for aggression (Marx did not then know about the Ems telegram), and although he warned the German workers not to support the annexation of Alsace-Lorraine, Marx did not have a general philosophy of opposing aggressive wars. The general opinion of democratic society was opposed to aggressive wars, and Marx played up to this opinion. But the Marxist theory of war is that each must be judged on its merits; those wars that contribute to progress are to be supported, others not.

It may happen, as Marx was well aware, that the side which actually starts a war is working for progress. For example, Marx and Engels would hardly have approved the conquest of Ethiopia by Italy in 1896; certainly all anti-imperialists sided with Menelik when he attacked the Italian garrison and drove it out. But the question of defining wars of aggression is full of pitfalls, as was discovered at the time of the First World War, and Lenin shrank, quite correctly, from developing too far the implications of his not very happy idea. In any case, Lenin did not endorse retrospectively the U.S. conquest of Mexico in 1847.

On some other points, Lenin said that Marx was right at the time but that his position had to change with the changing times. This was his explanation of Marx's shift on the Irish question, which was discussed in Chapter I. In the 1840's Marx and Engels had thought that Ireland would gain more than it would lose by association with advanced England, especially as they then expected the Chartist Feargus O'Connor to lead the working classes of both England and Ireland into democracy and eventually into socialism.[7] Later, in the 1860's, Marx and Engels reversed their position and worked hard for Irish independence.

Lenin endorsed this reversal, on the grounds (1) that the expected social revolution in England, which would have rendered a bourgeois-democratic and general national movement in Ireland superfluous, had not materialized; and (2) that a general national movement had by the 1860's developed in Ireland, and the British workers had the duty of supporting it, or at the very least of supporting what was progressive in it.[8]

Students of Irish history may question whether there was not already in the 1840's a general national movement in Ireland which was in principle no different from that of the 1860's, and no less worthy of support. There was even a revolutionary movement ("Young Ireland"). Marx by the 1860's had pretty well decided that his earlier attitude had been in error; the passages cited by Lenin make plain this shift.[9] In stating that Marx and Engels were consistent in their approach to the Irish question, that they had pursued a "consistently proletarian policy," Lenin was, to say the least, giving them the benefit of any doubt. Lenin was sure that Marx and Engels were not content merely to act as the tail to the kite of the petty-bourgeois Fenians; he believed that they had favored a revolutionary movement, to be conducted by the (whole) Irish people and supported by the British workers.[10] This might be called a constructive interpretation. Perhaps the most important point for later times is Lenin's view that the attitude which the proletariat of an advanced nation should take on the question of whether a colony should be independent depends on whether or not there is a movement for national liberation in that colony.

The case of Poland is highly suggestive of Lenin's attitude, since it shows that he himself did not hesitate to adopt an

attitude different from that which Marx and Engels had
adopted, when he was satisfied that the fundamental conditions
had changed. Marx and Engels had lived in a time when nearly
the whole Polish aristocracy had been willing to support the
demands of the republican separatists in setting up a democratic, free Poland. But now, said Lenin, the aristocracy has
taken to supporting the ruling class of the countries in which
they respectively find themselves. Thus the only way to Polish
independence is by a socialist revolution. Lenin quoted with
approval Mehring, who had said in 1902: "Today the
renascence of Poland is possible only through the social revolution, in which the modern proletariat will break its chains."[11]
Lenin also quoted with approval Kautsky, who had written in
favor of Poland's independence, but had added: *"National
independence is not so inseparably linked with the class interests of the militant proletariat as to make it necessary to strive
for it unconditionally, under any circumstances."*[12] Lenin himself put it thus:

Class antagonism has now [1903] undoubtedly relegated national
questions far into the background, but . . . it cannot be categorically
asserted that some particular national question cannot appear temporarily in the foreground of the political drama.[13]

The Polish Social-Democratic Party had a right to agitate
for complete independence, and was advised to do so; but
Lenin added: "We subordinate to the interests of the proletarian struggle our support of the demand for national
independence."[14]

France, Germany and Italy were examples of countries in
which nationalism had been a progressive force in the period
1789–1871, said Lenin. Nationalism might still be a progressive
force in other parts of the world after this epoch if conditions
were analogous to those specified. While the European bourgeoisie has become reactionary, in Asia the bourgeoisie *"still*
goes with the people and against reaction," he wrote in 1913.[15]

As far as Lenin's theory of nationalism was concerned, there was no reason why nationalism could not be a progressive force in any other part of the world where socio-economic developments had reached the stage then exemplified by China and India. For Eastern Europe, the development of separate national states seemed to him a natural phenomenon. He pointed out that to achieve complete victory for commodity production the bourgeoisie must capture the home market, and must have a politically united territory with a population speaking the same language, while all obstacles to the development of that language and to its consolidation in literature are removed. "The formation of *national states* is therefore the tendency of every national movement. . . . A heterogeneous national state represents backwardness or is an exception."[16]

Lenin was quite aware of the existence of nationalism as a growing, even progressive force in Eastern Europe. He wrote:

As far as the Ukrainians or White Russians are concerned, the national movement has not yet been consummated; . . . the awakening of a desire among the masses to possess their native tongue and native literature . . . is *still* in progress there. . . . In these countries "defense of the fatherland" may still be defense of democracy, of the native tongue, of political freedom against oppressing nations, against medievalism.[17]

Lenin brushed aside Bauer's proposal for "national-cultural autonomy" as a bourgeois device which would tend to split the workers. "We favor *international* culture and not the national culture of the several bourgeoisies." However he came out for "far-reaching self-government and autonomy of the several regions, which among other things should have boundaries according with nationality differences."[18] What was meant was *cultural* autonomy, such as would not hamper the economic development of the country as a whole.[19] Considering that Lenin was in general a strong centralist, this concession shows how seriously he took the nationality problem. On federation, the attitude of Lenin and of the Bolshevik Party underwent a change. Until 1917 they were firmly opposed to federation; but in the summer of 1917 Lenin spoke for the first time of the permissibility of federation, and the way was thus prepared for federation as a guiding principle in the Soviet Union when this was set up.[20] On assimilation, Lenin answered a spokesman for the Jewish Bund by saying that the best Jewish spokesmen had never feared assimilation, which was taking place all the time through the migration of the peasants to the cities.[21]

Concerning some of the problems with which the Austro-Marxists had been concerned, Lenin offered the following: the local population determines the boundaries of the autonomous units, and the state government confirms them. General school councils should be democratically elected.[22] The local organs of administration and the autonomous legislatures determine the language in which the business of all state and social institutions will be conducted. In legal proceedings every minority has a right to an answer in the language in which a request was made.[23]

Lenin was opposed on principle to having "nationality sections" of the Party, but showed his statesmanship by suggesting that a certain number of seats be reserved in the national congress to those areas where such separate organizations were actually in existence.[24] He also believed that centralization in the Party was needed in the interests of the national struggle itself.

The Right of Self-Determination

Lenin was not in favor of self-determination as an absolute principle. He contended that none of the democratic demands were absolute; "a democratic demand must be considered not in isolation but on a world scale." "Every democratic demand (including self-determination) is, for the class conscious workers, subordinated to the higher interests of socialism." He also contended: "The interests of a number of big and very big nations in Europe stand higher than the interests of the movement for liberation of small nations"; and he reprimanded the Polish Social-Democrats for adopting nationalism and secession as part of their program.[25]

It was in connection with the Polish question that Lenin sharpened up his position on the right of nations to self-determination, a right which Rosa Luxemburg had questioned, as we have seen.* She had argued: By supporting the right to secession you are supporting the bourgeois nationalism of the oppressed nations. Not so, said Lenin:

To the extent that the bourgeoisie of the oppressed nation struggles against the oppressing one, *to that extent*, we are always, in every case, and more resolutely than anyone else, *for* it, because we are the staunchest and the most consistent enemies of oppression. . . . The bourgeois nationalism of *every* oppressed nation has a general democratic content which is directed *against* oppression, and it is this content that we *absolutely* support, strictly distinguishing it from the tendency toward one's own national exclusiveness, fighting against the tendency of the Polish bourgeois to oppress the Jews, etc., etc.

The proletarians, said Lenin, are against special privileges for any nation, hence also for the bourgeoisie of an oppressed nation. "The proletariat . . . evaluates every national demand, every national separation *from the angle* of the class struggle of the workers." But Lenin had no doubts that the maintenance of the right of secession and the general principle of self-determination of nations, was right: "A thousand factors which cannot be foreseen will determine whether the Ukraine, for example, is destined to form an independent state. And without attempting idle '*guesses*,' we firmly uphold what is beyond doubt: the right of the Ukraine to form such a state."[26]

The general principle, the "absolute right" for which Lenin was contending, was thus not any "natural right" of self-determination, but the right of resistance to oppression, which always coincided with the interests of the workers in their struggle for freedom and socialism. So the "patriotic" Heinrich Cunow, who twitted Lenin for believing in "natural rights" in

* See Chapt. VI.

the 18th century sense, is seen to have missed Lenin's main point.[27]

Indeed, in Lenin's view, there were certain limitations on the "right" of self-determination.

In his "Theses on the National Question," written in June 1913, Lenin had said that Social-Democrats (meaning the party of the larger unit, in this case Russia) must make a judgment in each individual case whether it is in the interests of the international proletarian movement that any given national group should exercise its right of self-determination and withdraw from the larger nation. He added that the Poles and the Finns were "the most developed culturally and the most emancipated" of the nationalities making up the Russian Empire and could most easily and "naturally" exercise their right of separation.[28] This sounds too much like the arguments of the conventional apologists for colonialism, who usually contend that any given colony is "not ready" for self-government. However, Lenin backed independence in practice for Finland, and eventually became reconciled to Polish independence too.

Lenin mentioned still another limitation on the right of self-determination. Suppose, he said, that "a number of nations were to start a socialist revolution . . . while *other* nations serve as the chief bulwarks of bourgeois reaction—then we would have to be in favor of a revolutionary war against the latter, in favor of 'crushing' them, in favor of destroying all their outposts, no matter what small national movements arose there" (Georgia?).[29]

But Lenin stated flatly, and repeated many times, that the Social-Democrats of the large countries are duty bound to fight every form of national oppression, and to support the right of every nationality to self-determination.[30] Marx and Engels had not gone this far.

This insistence was not inconsistent with Lenin's emphasis on the idea of large national units. As explained in a pamphlet printed during the war: "To defend this right [of self-determination] does not mean to encourage in any way the formation of small states; on the contrary, it leads to a freer, more fearless and therefore wider and more universal formation of larger governments and unions of governments."[31]

The union of states must take place voluntarily, "on a truly democratic, truly internationalist basis, which is *unthinkable* without the freedom of separation."[32] "A socialist of a great nation or a nation possessing colonies who does not defend this right is a chauvinist."[33]

Lenin of course believed with Marx that true international- ism could come only with socialism; but he advocated the right of separation also in advance of the socialist revolution. He was aware before 1917 that the success of the Russian Revolution might turn on the attitude of the smaller nationalities of Tsarist Russia, and he sought to have at best their active cooperation and at worst their friendly neutrality. But his posi- tion on this point was based on more than opportunism; it was a matter of principle.

The Theory of the "National" Class*

Lenin, writing on behalf of the revolutionary proletariat, was not opposed on principle to all coalitions, but only to those with reactionary groupings. Where the working class party entered into a union with the progressive bourgeoisie, it was always to be with the perspective of *leading* the coalition rather than of following the lead of the bourgeoisie. This part of his theory he proceeded to put into practice when he returned to Russia in April 1917, and the history of the world was influenced by the result. To follow in the wake of the bour- geoisie would be an example of "tailism," which he always condemned. Lenin did not interpret Marx's passing references to the "national class" to mean that the workers' party should surrender its independence or its power of initiative.

Consistent with his idea that all nations have the same road

* Cf. above, Chapter III.

to travel, Lenin considered the Asian countries to be just entering the phase in which the bourgeoisie is a progressive class,
with which the proletariat could suitably be allied. Specifically,
in China "there already exists a liberal bourgeoisie," which in
alliance with "peasant democracy" has won some gains, though
the proletariat is either non-existent or quite impotent (1912).
Incidentally in Lenin's remarks on China there is no trace of
any patronizing attitudes; in speaking of Sun Yat-sen's ideas
he wrote: "What we have before us is a really great ideology
of a really great people."[34]

It has been suggested that where an underdeveloped country
has no bourgeoisie, the correct Marxist policy is to help create
one and then follow its lead. We have not seen any writings
of Lenin which advocate this policy; indeed it seems to us to
be contrary to the spirit of his teachings. Where there is not
only no bourgeoisie but even no wage-earning class, it is still
correct, according to Lenin, to advance the slogan of self-
determination. Such slogans are advanced "for the whole
working population, for the whole people. . . . Even for those
colonial countries where there are no workers, where there are
only slave-owners and slaves, etc., it is not only *not* absurd but
obligatory for every Marxist to advance the slogan of 'self-
determination.' "[35]

That such policies can be not only advanced but put into
practice had been shown many years before by Toussaint
l'Ouverture!

Wars of Resistance Against Imperialism

When the bourgeoisie is a progressive class, building the
nation, destroying feudalism, and either fighting off imperialism or trying to get rid of it, Lenin unquestionably felt that it
deserves support both from the working masses in the country
in question and from those in the imperialist country. When,
however, the resistance to imperialism is offered by a reactionary class, the case is not so simple.

The espousal of the principle of self-determination creates a presumption in favor of national rebellion. "We are in favor of *national* rebellion," wrote Lenin, but not in favor of *all* rebellion—specifically, not that of the Southern states of America in 1863.[36] Even rebellions against imperialism must be truly national in order to gain the right to support. Lenin wrote: "It is *not* our duty to support every struggle against imperialism. We will *not* support the struggle of the reactionary classes against imperialism; we will *not* support an uprising of the reactionary classes against imperialism and capitalism."[37]

However in the same article it develops that "[we cannot] *withhold* support from any *serious popular* struggle against national oppression."[38] The implication is clear that even if reactionary classes initiated an anti-imperialist struggle in a colonial, or semi-colonial country, from the time that considerable masses of the people supported it, the duty of the workers in both the underdeveloped country and the imperialist country would be to support the struggle too.

Would Lenin have withheld support from Abd-el-Kader, the reactionary Bedouin chief, in Algeria at the time the French captured him in 1848? It will be recalled that Engels withheld his support. Or would Lenin have attacked the French as imperialists, as Engels did ten years later?* Would Lenin have refrained from supporting the Indian uprising of 1857–1859, on the ground that it was led by the reactionary classes? R. P. Dutt, the contemporary Indian-British Marxist seems to withhold his support retrospectively, as Marx himself did. Or would Lenin have hailed it as a war of independence and given it sympathetic treatment, as the Marx-Engels-Lenin Institute of Moscow was to do a hundred years after the event?† We are given no specific guidance, except the extent of the popular support for the respective movements in question.

Lenin would certainly not have wished to see the Communists for whatever reason put themselves under the command

* See above, Chapter III, pp. 64–65.
† See above, Chapter III, p. 67.

of some potentate who would disarm them and later shoot their leaders, as happened recently in one country of the Middle East. But we cannot refrain from remarking that Marxism in the 20th century dictates opposition to imperialism as a system and to imperialist aggression even when that opposition is led by a reactionary class. Not support of the reactionary classes but opposition to imperialism should surely be the slogan appropriate to such occasions. We should turn from Engels the imperialist apologist to Engels the anti-imperialist, as Lenin turned from the judgment of Marx and Engels at the time of the United States aggression against Mexico in 1847 to the First International's condemnation of aggressive war 23 years later.* Lenin strongly favored national wars against the imperialist powers; he considered such wars to be *progressive* and *revolutionary* (Lenin's italics).[39]

One of the strongest arguments in favor of colonial wars of liberation, and in favor of anti-imperialist movements generally, has been that such movements mean attacking capitalism at its weakest point. But the theory of the weakest link belongs to a later period. Before the Russian Revolution it was generally believed that capitalism had to run its course—that is, reach its highest stage of development—before it turned into socialism. Thus the question in the period under discussion was: will colonial anti-imperialist movements hasten capitalist development or interfere with it? Revisionists tended to argue that since such movements interfered with capitalism's full development, they actually tended to postpone the arrival of socialism, in which the revisionists still pretended to believe.† Lenin argued that, on the contrary,

the opposition against the colonial policy and the international thievery through the organization of the proletariat, through the defense of freedom for the proletarian struggle does not limit the development of capitalism, but hastens it, since it compels capitalism to use more civilised and technically developed methods.[40]

* See above, pp. 63, 188.
† Cf. Chapter IV, above, pp. 97 and *passim*.

Rosa Luxemburg had argued that the form of the state that best suited the development of capitalism was a predatory state. Lenin retorted that this argument was contradicted by the experience of Asia, where it was precisely in Japan, which managed to retain its independence, that capitalism developed most rapidly.[41]

The Working Class and Nationalism

While Lenin recognized, in theory, that there were certain situations where the working class would have not only the right but the duty to participate in movements for national separation, his attitude in specific cases was nearly always to deprecate working-class participation in nationalist movements, if not to condemn them strongly.

Already in 1903 Lenin had noted the existence of nationalist "estrangement" among the working classes, and had considered it to be part of the legacy of autocracy.[42] Ten years later, he drew up for the Central Committee of the Party a directive, to be addressed to the workers of all nationalities in Russia, calling "for the most determined opposition against the aggressive nationalism of reaction, for struggle against any and every appearance of nationalism among the working masses."[43] In his discussion of Marx's ideas on the Irish question, he remarked that the working class "should not make a fetish of the national question." In his "Critical Remarks on the National Question" (December 1913) he described Marxism as being "incompatible with nationalism."[44] And in 1914 he reminded the proletariat of its task "to fight against all nationalism, and above all against Great Russian nationalism."[45]

There was a special reason why Lenin found nationalism to be a nuisance organizationally. It split the centralized, unified party which he was trying to build, into national sections, warring against each other and each coming under the sway (as he thought) of its respective bourgeoisie. He tended to look on nationalism as primarily a bourgeois prejudice, and

paid more than lip service to Bauer's idea that modern nationalism is the creation of the bourgeoisie.

In Western Europe Lenin thought that the national movement had ceased to be a constructive force; it could not "produce anything progressive, anything capable of rousing new
masses of people to new economic and political life."[46] "Now
the bourgeoisie fears the workers, seeks alliance with . . .
reaction, betrays democracy, favors the suppression of nations
or opposes their equality, and demoralizes the workers with
nationalistic slogans."[47] The bourgeoisie had become "a sinking,
decaying, internally dead, reactionary class," and the bourgeois-national framework of states had become a hindrance to
the free development of the productive forces.[48] Since the
official spokesmen of the Marxist movement in the West used
this same analysis and vocabulary, it seemed inconceivable to
Lenin that the class-conscious proletariats would march off to
war under the leadership of the bourgeoisie, as they did.

Kautsky had tried to counterpose the "international impulse"
of the workers to the nationalist impulse. He was not very
successful. Lenin also was of course interested in internationalism, but at the outbreak of the war he courageously faced up
to the fact that the decision on what attitude to take to the
war would have to be made locally, and launched the slogan
of "Defeat of the Fatherland," and of turning the imperialist
war into a civil (class) war. This approach was not without
precedent, since the Russian Social Democratic Party had
refused to interest itself in the Russo-Japanese War; Lenin had
referred to the Tsar's "shameful and criminal Manchurian
adventure" in 1904.[49]

This attitude of opposition was shared by the Mensheviks;
Plekhanov was an outspoken defeatist. The Bolsheviks and
Mensheviks at this time both claimed to be revolutionists; both
were pursued and persecuted by the Tsarist regime, not less
because of their attitude toward the war. It is reasonable to
think of this attitude as a carryover to the international field of

attitudes of hostility to the regime developed in two decades of internal strife. But Plekhanov by 1914 had become a Russian patriot—so much so that he was favored for a cabinet post by General Kornilov.[50]

In August 1914 the issue was thus squarely joined between two of the three great forces of the 19th century. As Rosa Luxemburg put it, the question was: *either* imperialism *or* socialism. Nationalism won the first round, as Engels had predicted; however, Engels' pessimistic prediction about the effect on the revolutionary movement in Russia was not borne out, and nationalism did not have the last word.

Both Marx and Lenin recognized the existence of love of country, and did not condemn it as such, but rather approved it as a worthy sentiment, provided always that it was not put at the service of an exploiting class. The international working class has no contact with the individual worker except indirectly. The internationalism of labor proposed by the Second International could be implemented only by national organizations, and was easily defeated in the loyalty contest by the claims of the nation.

On the question whether Marxism before the Russian Revolution had developed any philosophy about patriotism in a socialist state, the answer must be in the negative. Both Marx and Lenin thought that the socialist revolution would take place more or less simultaneously in the advanced industrial countries, which would then have no immediate problem of defense.

National Self-Determination Under Socialism

Lenin was rather impatient with those who questioned whether socialism would consult the wishes of the population in drawing boundaries. His first reaction was: "Of course!" His second reaction was that it did not especially matter anyway:

Socialism by organizing production *without* class oppression and by ensuring the well-being of *all* members of the state, gives *full scope* to the "sympathies" of the population, and precisely by virtue of this facilitates and enormously accelerates the establishment of intimacy among and amalgamation of nations.[51]

Lenin thought that the attraction of a big state under socialism would be so great that the question of secession would hardly arise. But, he added, with that remarkable balance which was characteristic of all his work: "The hatred—and perfectly legitimate hatred—of an oppressed nation for its oppressor will *continue* for a while."[52] Marx and Lenin were suspicious of patriotism, which Bakunin had called "a narrow, exclusive, anti-human, and quite often simply a cruel sentiment."[53] Lenin pointed out time and again that the social and economic conditions engendering the petty proprietor impart special stability to one of "the most deep-seated of petty-bourgeois prejudices, namely: prejudices of national egoism, of national narrow-mindedness."[54]

Man's loyalty tends to be basically toward the group to which he belongs as a whole, rather than for some particular purpose. Kautsky, criticizing Bauer, had tried to make out that the trade union, the government, the guild, in fact any human association, was a *Gemeinschaft*. Bauer answered that Kautsky had misunderstood the meaning of the term, and Bauer was right. If self-preservation is the first law of nature, then in time of crisis men tend to act together in that way that will most effectively preserve themselves and their families. The union, and the other organizations mentioned by Kautsky, are structured for a particular purpose, and have no claim to man's total loyalty.

But does the nation have such a claim? It is plain that a modern nation, in the sense of the inhabitants of a given state, has no such claim in the sense that the primitive classless tribe did. For the modern capitalist state is a class state, and loyalty to it, or to the nation which is the alternative expression of it, is loyalty to the purposes and methods of the ruling class, in Marxist theory. If, then, workers show loyalty to a particular state, it is class loyalty limited as to time and place.

Marx proposed that members of the working class owe their principal loyalty to the workers' International, and Bakunin accepted this idea. But this concept is a difficult one. The original idea of a *Gemeinschaft* is that of a face-to-face association, whose members know each other personally in all aspects. Lenin called for loyalty to the working class in its revolutionary aspect, to the proletarian revolution; hence his slogan for the Defeat of the Fatherland, which in his view was working against the interests of the proletariat. By the same token, the loyalty of the workers after the revolution would be first of all to the interests of the revolution. Lenin could not understand that the workers of any country, such as Poland, would put their loyalty to their (bourgeois) country ahead of their loyalty to the revolution.

For the rest, Lenin made no special advance over the position which we found to be implicit in Marx's concepts, as summarized at the end of Chapter III.

Nationalism in the Epoch of Imperialism

Lenin was writing in the age of imperialism, and was conscious of the fact. Marx and Engels wrote the *Communist Manifesto* when the trading bourgeoisie was conquering the world market, breaking down national barriers in order to do so. Lenin wrote in an age when the bourgeoisie, while continuing its expansive rush, was becoming more exclusive, more nationalistic; List, the champion of the protective tariff, was coming into style, replacing Adam Smith and free trade. The business classes might on occasion gang up to fight the working classes on an international scale, as Marx and Engels had described; but they were also making ever more of an appeal to the working classes of their respective countries for aid in their struggles against the bourgeoisies of other countries. The nature of the national question had changed fundamentally. Marxism was not backward in perceiving this change; Rudolf Hilferding's *Finanzkapital* showed the economic basis of modern nationalism as no other writer of his time had done. Lenin drew heavily on the philosophy of this work when he wrote his famous essay on imperialism in 1916.

Hilferding in a superb passage had shown how the whole ideology of racism and nationalism was related to the emergence of the integrated, protectionist-imperialist state. The victory of protectionism, said he, is a victory for the employing class. Accompanying protectionism are: quicker and stronger cartelization, strengthening of business organizations, the sharpening of national rivalries, the increase of armaments, the growth of the pressure of taxes, increase in the cost of living, the enlarging of the power of the government, the weakening of democracy, and the emergence of an anti-labor, power-oriented ideology.[55]

Capitalism, he added, cannot pursue any policy other than imperialism.*

The power of the state being needed for the competitive struggle on the world market, the attitude of the bourgeoisie to the state undergoes a fundamental change. The national idea, which found its natural boundary in the state's borders, is now transformed into the idea that one's own nation is superior to the others.[56] The idea of equality is transformed by the growth of monopoly into the idea of privilege; the superiority of a nation economically is attributed to its racial qualities. "The dedication of self-interest to a superior social interest, which is the condition of every viable social ideology, is won; the anti-popular state and the nation itself are combined in one unit and the national idea is put at the service of politics as its driving power."[57]

Lenin's famous essays, *Imperialism: The Highest Stage of Capitalism* and *State and Revolution* do not directly include a theory of the nation and nationalism, but they imply such

---

* Those who are accustomed to quote Hilferding as saying that imperialism is a policy of capitalism rather than an immanent necessity are invited to take note of this passage (p. 471).

a theory, and thus furnish a final refutation of those who say that Marxism was *incapable* of handling the national question.

Imperialism, and also Lenin's highly significant theory of uneven development, which is formulated more exactly elsewhere, show how clearly Lenin understood the complete shift which had taken place in the bourgeois attitude to the state in the epoch of monopoly and neo-colonialism. Hilferding's work summarizing the new reasons for emphasis on the state as such, is approved and much new material is added.

State and Revolution is significant for what it leaves out as well as for what it includes. It is hardly possible to think of Marx or Engels producing a programmatic statement of this kind without including somewhere a statement of the case for international action by the proletariat, such as was contained in *The Communist Manifesto.* Lenin was not at this time (1917) disillusioned with the prospects of such international action, but he was shortly afterwards to reach the point of not considering it absolutely essential; the class struggle was *"in the first instance,"* as Marx and Engels had put it, national. The picture of the proletariat laying hold of the state machinery and destroying it in order to rebuild it on a new basis, is intended to apply internationally, and indeed Lenin never expected that the latter part, the withering away of the state, would or could take place where the socialist state was surrounded by hostile capitalist states.

Marx constantly stressed the growth of monopoly and departures from free competition which were apparent already in his day; but he did not foresee the rise of highly integrated imperialist states, each with its own protective tariff, dominated by finance capital and driven to invest its surplus abroad and thus run foul of other imperialist states. This whole concept, which was summed up so well by Hilferding in 1910, was not part of Marx's approach, though not alien to it either. Thus Hilferding, and Lenin after him, were going far beyond Marx and Engels when they worked out the driving forces in modern imperialism. By the same token, the national state, which played a rather subordinate role in the thinking of Marx and Engels, comes into focus almost for the first time.

When the state does wither away, what is left? This is a question on which neither Marx nor Lenin was explicit; neither had much time for constructing Utopias or blueprints for the distant future. But it is clear from the writings of both (Lenin in *State and Revolution* and Marx in *Zur Judenfrage*) that the chief historic reason for the bourgeois state as such was policing the system of private property. With the disappearance of that system and the introduction of full socialism on a world-wide scale, the political state would have passed, and with it national rivalries, alienation, war and poverty. Nationalism would have lost its sting; the national cultures would remain, and would be productive of an interesting diversity. Lenin wrote:

> The overthrow of the bourgeoisie will tremendously accelerate the collapse of every kind of national *partition* without decreasing, but on the contrary increasing millions of times, the "differentiation" of humanity, if we are to understand by this the wealth and variety of spiritual life, trends of ideas, tendencies, shadings.[58]

Lenin admitted to feeling love of country, though not of the kind described as "collective egoism." Discussing the National Pride of the Great Russians in 1914, Lenin wrote:

> What we witness is a broad and very deep ideological current whose origins are closely interwoven with the interests of the landowners and capitalists of the great nations. . . .
> Are we enlightened Great-Russian proletarians impervious to the feeling of national pride? Certainly not! We love our language and our motherland. . . . We are filled with national pride, and therefore we *particularly* hate *our* slavish past . . . and *our* slavish present.[59]

We noted earlier a disagreement among Marxist writers on the question of whether the ruling class and the working class have the same culture or different cultures—whether they constitute "Two Nations" in the sense that Disraeli gave to the terms in his well-known novel. The revisionists believed that the culture was the same for all classes, or that it tended to become so, while some extremists like A. B. Soep contended that the culture and even the language of the working class were different.[60] While not denying that working-class forms of expression were frequently different from those of the rulers, Lenin in his remarkable essay, "What Is To Be Done?" (1902) had advised the workers to get as much culture—genuine culture, not the spurious variety—as they could. The best, he said, is none too good for the working class. Working class intellectuals must get used to standing on their own feet; they must avoid being patronized. At the same time, Lenin was quite clear in his own mind that the working class culture of the future was to be, not national in any narrow or exclusive sense, but international.

Is it then true that Lenin left no clear and cogent directives for his successors in the matter of how to deal with nationalism?* Lenin's strong opposition to great-power nationalism might be considered a clear and cogent directive, and something like that policy of opposition is coming increasingly to the front as the only alternative to general disaster. But those of Lenin's successors who were not satisfied with the negative approach could revert to the philosophy of an earlier period, and take the position of Marx and Engels, that nationalism was a tool that could suitably be used in a good cause; and this was of course to be done on a big scale in the Soviet Union during the Second World War.

Lenin at first, down to the Russian Revolution, underestimated the depth of nationalist feeling among the European workers, as is shown by the surprise and chagrin that he felt at their reaction to the outbreak of the First World War. He also may have underestimated the constructive possibilities of the nationalist movements in Eastern Europe, in that he discouraged the separatism of the constituent nationalities in

---

* As asserted by Louis Fischer in *Columbia University Forum* (New York: 1964), p. 6.

Austria-Hungary. But Lenin learned from experience, and before his death he had made the discovery, which Stalin in spite of his supposed expertise had not grasped, that "the oppressed nationals are not as sensitive in regard to any other matter as in regard to their equality."[61] While he usually counterposed "bourgeois nationalism" and "proletarian internationalism," he had shown by his cordial welcome of the nationalist movements in the colonial countries that he had room in his thinking for a third category: proletarian nationalism. In countries where the nationalist movement was still young, it might still, as in the early days of the 19th century in Europe, "walk hand in hand" with democracy and socialism. Lenin also remarked, very acutely, that nationalism might be capable of swinging the otherwise conservative peasantry into the track of progress and social revolution.

For what concerns the incompatibility between the socialist and nationalist movements, we can do no better than refer to Lenin's ideas on *State and Revolution*. This essay, written just before the Bolshevik takeover, shows clearly enough what Lenin thought about the future of the national state, and of the nationalist sentiment attaching to it—both would "wither away" some time after the proletarian revolution. Since Lenin did not foresee the protracted period of competition between capitalist and socialist states, many problems have arisen which were not covered by Lenin's treatment. For this Lenin can hardly be blamed, any more than he can be accused of having had a wrong *theory* of nationalism in that he failed to appreciate how powerful a force nationalism was becoming before 1914, or how deeply it had penetrated the consciousness of the European working class.

Indeed Lenin's persistent optimism concerning the prospects of the proletarian revolution furnished an essential corrective to Engels' pessimism of some years earlier. Jingoism and chauvinism, the effects of which Engels so much feared, do indeed overwhelm opposition at the outbreak of a war; but the effects are not as lasting as Engels depicted. The loyalty to the state which uses such tactics is likely to be of the brittle variety; disillusion may follow patriotic overexcitement.

The state, said Hegel, is necessary because of the system of private property. Under a regime of general selfishness, without a strong central government society would fly apart. Or as Engels put it:

This society . . . is cleft into irreconcilable antagonisms which it is powerless to dispel. But in order that these antagonisms, classes with conflicting economic interests, may not consume themselves in sterile struggle, a power apparently standing above society becomes necessary, whose purpose is to moderate the conflict and keep it within the bounds of "order"; and this power arising out of society, but placing itself above it, and increasingly separating itself from it, is the state.[62]

Marx had begun to work out the philosophy of how to hold society together once society had rid itself of the exploitative state. The force that Marx mentioned—though Lenin seems to have missed this part of his approach—was the nation: the people considered as an organic whole, apart from the machinery of government, in a classless socialist (communist) society.

Cedric Belfrage wrote in a book review in the *National Guardian*, Dec. 18, 1964:

The first revolution on a world scale is making the customary backward as well as forward steps, but its end will be the burial of *that outdated and noxious institution, the nation-state as now known.* . . . Experience leads many to the conclusion—especially after Nazism and its nightmares, and the postwar witch-hunt—that the only treason one can now commit is to oneself as a member of the human race. [Emphasis added]

A correspondent says: "This is good, basic, fundamental, elementary Marxism."[63] But true Marxism would retain the distinction between the nation and the state. For Marx and Lenin the real enemy was the system of private property—capitalism. Nationalism was a tool of the system of privilege—or alternatively, of course, it could be a tool of some other system, or could be discarded when it no longer served a useful purpose. Lenin considered the main mistake of the Social-Democrats before the First World War to have been, not that they failed to fight against nationalism (though perhaps they should have done that too) but that they failed to fight, or to fight hard enough, *against capitalism and for socialism*—Marxian socialism, that is.

Lenin may not have written out a set of directives for his successors, but he left them something much more valuable—a precedent. Although it is not strictly within our purview, we cannot refrain from mentioning the famous case of the recalcitrant Georgians, whose aspirations for independent nationalism were so ruthlessly curbed by Stalin in 1922. The incident is especially significant because no question of theory was involved; Lenin and Stalin supposedly had the same ideas on nationalism; the only point at issue was one of administration. Lenin castigated Stalin unmercifully, in a document which was given to the public only in 1956, three years after Stalin's death. Some passages are so relevant to our topic that we must perforce quote at length:

An abstract concept of nationalism is absolutely worthless. Distinction should be made between the nationalism of an oppressing nation and the nationalism of an oppressed nation, the nationalism of a large nation and the nationalism of a small nation.

. . . We, the nationals of a great nation, show ourselves almost always in historical practice guilty of untold numbers of outrages and, what is more—we do not even observe that we are perpetrating untold numbers of acts of violence and abuse. . . .

For this reason the internationalism of the oppressing nation, or of the so-called "Great" nation (even if it is great only through its violence, great only as an overlord can be "great") should depend not only on the formal observation of equality among nations, but also of such inequality which actually exists in life. He who does not understand this does not understand the true proletarian approach to the national question, actually still retains the petit bourgeois outlook and, for that reason, cannot but fall into the bourgeois position.

. . . The oppressed nationals are not as sensitive in regard to any

other matter as in regard to their equality. . . . It would be preferable to sin by too much rather than too little concession and
indulgence toward national minorities.[64]

Summary

Marxist nationality theory as it had developed up to the
time of the Russian Revolution bore little resemblance in
several respects to the ideas of Marx and Engels. The changes
were partly in the way of dropping out formulations that were
inadequate or incorrect, and partly by way of bringing the
theory up to date. The new emphasis on self-determination
was the result less of rethinking basic positions—Lenin's basic
approach was *in form* hardly different from that of Marx and
Engels—than of according recognition to the development of
nationalist movements in the interim. The adoption of the idea
that nationalist movements are worthy of support when they
represent actions by a progressive class against oppression is
a step in advance, as is the opposition against imperialism as
such and the explicit support for colonial nationalist movements.* The emphasis on the internal class struggle rather
than the international class struggle was adopted somewhat
regretfully, as a result of the collapse of the First International,
and, later, also of the Second International. But Marxist theory
had already prepared itself for this change by its fundamental
discussion of the nature of the state in the new era of imperialism. National rivalries arising out of the struggle for markets
and colonies had finally come to the focus of attention. Monopoly and protectionism were seen to have reinforced the new
emphasis on nationalism. But the implications of the rising
importance of nationalism were not fully developed.

Halfway measures would not do in the struggle against
capitalism in the imperialist era. The general strike against
war, the demand for a citizens' militia, and the endorsement of
disarmament were ideas with which the Marxists had toyed,

---

* The shift from acceptance of imperialism to opposition was of
course made by Marx himself; cf. above, Chapter III, p. 69.

as had the rest of the labor and socialist movement; these were
now to be discarded as mere gestures. The definition of defensive war was modified, or rather superseded, thus signalling
another break with Marx and Engels.

The greatest change in Marxist theory was the recognition
that "internationalism" as preached by the Second International was a will-o'-the-wisp. This shift might indeed be
considered a reversion to "pure" Marxist theory, since Marx's
conception of internationalism involved, as we have seen,
direct action by the proletariat on an international scale,
whereas the spokesmen for the Second International continued
to talk about internationalism when the specific proposals for
implementing action were being rejected one after the other;
they were thus talking about a capitalist international, which
as Lenin showed was a completely unrealistic, non-Marxist
approach.[65] But proletarian internationalism, in which the
working class in different countries would combine to fight
imperialism, remained a part of Marxist theory.

Marx and Engels had never quite made up their minds about
what attitude to take toward nationalism as such. Engels
particularly retained a warm appreciation for the national
culture of Germany, though Marx preferred to speak of himself
as a citizen of the world. Lenin, like Bakunin, felt attachment
to the language and the soil of Russia, though his long periods
of exile and his active participation in and knowledge of the
socialist movements of several countries and continents made
him a practical internationalist as Marx and Engels had been.
He made great efforts to avoid letting his feelings as a Russian
overweigh his judgment of what was in the interests of the
world revolutionary movement.

Bauer and Renner labored hard to salvage Austria-Hungary
as a national state; they were frankly nationalists, but not in
the exclusive, bellicose sense; there was no trace of jingoism
or chauvinism in their writings. Some pseudo-Marxist
"socialist" writers by their adoption of militant bourgeois
nationalism read themselves out of the Marxist movement.

But while the authentic Marxists continued to profess a nationalist sentiment at the cultural level, they had by 1917 come close—perhaps temporarily—to the pre-war anti-patriotic stance of Hervé, the CGT, and the IWW, as far as the capitalist countries were concerned. Lenin's Defeat-of-the-Fatherland slogan cannot be interpreted in any other way. This was not "national nihilism"; it referred to a particular time and place, and served a highly important purpose in sharpening up the distinction between real and pseudo-patriots.

It is indeed ironic that in this field as in others Marxism should have had to travel such a long way around in its search for the goal of a super-national classless society. Just as the leaders of the Soviet Union were to find themselves obliged to stress the *inequality* of incomes in practice after the revolution, as the most direct way to communism, so the same leaders were to emphasize nationalism as strongly as anyone when it was used in a worthy cause. We have already noted that this was a Marxist position, in that Marx did not accord any specific value to the nation as such in the epoch of capitalism—the whole question was the usefulness, or otherwise, of the idea, in furthering the aims of the international proletarian revolution. After capitalism should have disappeared for good, nationalism would continue, but not nationalism of the "collective egoist" type—instead, we would see emulation, in a friendly way, over the whole range of human culture.

The acceptance of the principle of self-determination by Marxists like Lenin was never complete; Rosa Luxemburg, as we have seen, did not accept it at all. But so far as the idea was adopted, it involved a weakening of the emphasis by Marx and Engels on the superior claims of the large nations, and a closer approximation to the idea of formal equality of nations. The limits of this idea were still to be found in the paramount interests of the international proletarian revolution.

Marxist writers on nationalism too often think that when they have found an economic explanation of the phenomenon, their task is finished. Actually there is more to it than that, as

our discussion should have made plain. But the Marxist literature on nationalism will stand comparison with that of any
other school of thought in our period, for incisiveness of
analysis, for comprehensiveness, and of course for its basic
value system. If Marxism did not solve all the problems in
advance of their arising, that is nothing for it to be ashamed
of. A theoretical system stands or falls, not on past dogmas, but
on its ability to tackle new problems as they come up, and to
provide workable solutions. In this sense, Marxism and the
dialectic method have been abundantly vindicated. The question is not whether Marxists ever make mistakes, but whether
they have the apparatus and the will to correct them. The
vitality of the Marxist school and its ability to survive errors
which at the time seemed overwhelming give ground for
thinking that with the aid of a correct Marxist analysis this
greatest of all problems can be surmounted and nationalism
can be made to serve useful purposes instead of destroying
humanity.

SOURCE NOTES

Notes to Foreword

1. (Oxford: 1939), pp. xvi ff. The chairman of the Study Group was Prof. E. H. Carr.

2. *Ibid.*, p. xvii.

3. Quoted from Channing, "A Catechism for the Constituencies," in H. J. Ogden, *The War Against the Dutch Republics* (Manchester: 1901), p. 167.

4. F. W. Coker, "Patriotism," in *Encyclopaedia of the Social Sciences*, XII (New York: 1934), 28.

5. V. I. Lenin, "On the National Pride of the Great Russians" (1914), in *Collected Works* (London: 1930), XVIII, 99.

6. Article of May 22, 1857, in Karl Marx-Friedrich Engels, *Werke* (Berlin: 1957 and later), XII, 214; English in *Marx on China, 1853–1860* (London: 1951), p. 50. Emphasis added.

7. Fritz Pappenheim, *The Alienation of Modern Man* (New York: 1959), pp. 50–51.

Notes to Chapter I

1. G. W. F. Hegel, in *Encyclopaedia der philosophischen Wissenschaften* (2d. ed., Leipzig: 1905), p. 459.

2. Herbert Marcuse, *Reason and Revolution: Hegel and the Rise of Social Theory* (2d. ed., London: 1954), pp. 214, 236.

3. Hegel, "Grundlinien der Philosophie des Rechts," in F. Bülow (ed.), *Hegel: Gesellschaft-Staat-Geschichte* (Leipzig: n.d. 1932?), p. 133.

4. Herman Heller, "Hegel und die deutsche Politik," *Zeitschrift für Politik*, XIII (Berlin: 1924), 133.

5. Marcuse, *Reason and Revolution*, p. 215.

6. Adam Ferguson, *Essay on the History of Civil Society* (3d. ed., London: 1778), p. 31.

7. Letter of January 21, 1966, to the author from Wolfgang Mönke, of the Deutsche Akademie der Wissenschaften zu Berlin, who carried out the research establishing this point.

8. F. Engels, "Ernst Moritz Arndt," in *Marx-Engels Gesamtausgabe* I, Vol. II (Berlin: 1930), 108. This series hereafter referred to as *MEGA*.

9. Engels, "Glossen und Randzeichnungen zu Texten aus unserer Zeit," in *ibid.*, p. 299.

10. Gustav Mayer, *Friedrich Engels: Eine Biographie* (Haag: 1934), I, 53–55.

11. *MEGA* I, Vol. I(1) (Frankfurt: 1927), 572.

12. Auguste Cornu, *Karl Marx und Friedrich Engels: Leben und Werk* (Berlin: 1954), I, *1818–1844*, 463–464.

13. Marx, "Zur Judenfrage," *Deutsch-Französische Jahrbücher*, 1843–44; in *Werke*, I, 376.

14. Marx & Engels, *The German Ideology* (Moscow: 1964), p. 45.

15. *Ibid.*, pp. 89, 90, 91.

16. *Ibid.*, p. 86.

17. See Marx's "Speech on Protection, Free Trade, and the Working Class" of September, 1847. This speech was not delivered, but Engels published fragments from it in the *Northern Star* of October 9, 1847. English in *MEGA* I, Vol. VI (Berlin: 1932), 428–431; German in *Werke*, IV, 305–308.

18. "Protection and Free Trade," preface to U. S. edition of Marx's speech on Free Trade (Boston, 1889). First published in *Neue Zeit*, July, 1888. *Werke*, XXI, 360-375. Excerpt in Marx and Engels, *On Colonialism* (New York: 1972), pp. 266–269.

19. Marx, "Contribution to the Critique of Hegel's Philosophy of Right: Introduction" (1843), in Karl Marx, *Early Writings*, trans. and ed. by T. B. Bottomore (London: 1963), p. 49. Marx's view on protectionism is in *Capital* (Moscow: 1959), I, 756–757. Cf. *Werke*, I, 378 ff.

20. R. Rosdolsky, Note in *Science & Society*, Summer, 1965, p. 335; H. Cunow, *Die Marxsche Geschichts-, Gesellschafts-, und Staatstheorie* (Berlin: 1921), II, 30.

21. "Manifesto of the Communist Party" (1848), in Marx and Engels, *Basic Writings on Politics & Philosophy*, ed. by Lewis S. Feuer (New York: 1959), pp. 11, 26; *Werke*, IV, 462, 481.

22. *Ibid.*, p. 26.

23. *Ibid.*, p. 18.

24. Bloom, pp. 24–25.

25. *I. F. Stone's Bi-Weekly* (Washington, D.C.), June 10, 1963, p. 1.

26. E. Bernstein in *Die Neue Zeit*, XV, Bd. 1 (October, 1896), pp. 111–112.

27. Michael Bakunin, *Gesammelte Werke*, III (Berlin: 1924), 123.

28. Bloom, pp. 25–26.

29. Engels, "Gewalt und Oekonomie bei der Herstellung des neuen Deutschen Reiches," written in 1887 or 1888, posthumously published in *Neue Zeit*, XIV, Bd. 1 (February, 1896), p. 679.

30. Bloom, p. 33.

31. Lord Acton, *The History of Freedom and Other Essays* (London: 1919), pp. 298, 299.

32. *Werke*, II, 611–614. Emphasis in original.

33. F. Mehring, *Karl Marx: The Story of His Life* (New York: 1935), p. 349.

34. Benedikt Kautsky (ed.), *Friedrich Engels' Briefwechsel mit Karl Kautsky* (Vienna: 1955), pp. 50–53.

35. Speech of Engels at a meeting in London for the freedom of Poland, Nov. 29, 1847; see *Werke*, IV, 417–418.

36. *Werke*, IV, 417.

37. *Ibid.*

38. Engels, "Marx und die Neue Rheinische Zeitung, 1848–1849" (1884), *Werke*, XXI, 19–20.

Notes to Chapter II

1. See Engels, "Die Polendebatte in Frankfurt," *Neue Rheinische Zeitung*, Sept. 3, 1848; in *Werke*, V, 354.

2. *Werke*, V, 80.

3. *Ibid.*, 82.

4. Roman Rosdolsky, "Friedrich Engels und das Problem der 'Geschichtslosen Völker,'" *Archiv für Sozialgeschichte*, IV (Hannover, 1964), 98–99. Emphasis in original.

5. Letter to Weydemeyer, April 12, 1853. Cf. below, p. 38.

6. F. Mehring (ed.), *Aus dem literarischen Nachlass von Karl Marx, Friedrich Engels, und Ferdinand Lassalle* (Stuttgart: 1902), III, 238. This work referred to hereafter as *Nachlass*.

7. Herman Wendel, "Der Marxismus und die Südslawenfrage," in *Die Gesellschaft* (Berlin: 1924), p. 159.

8. H. Wendel, "Marxism and the Southern Slav Question," in *Slavonic Review*, II (London: 1923–1924), 294.

9. S. Harrison Thomson, "A Century of a Phantom: Panslavism and the Western Slavs," *Journal of Central European Affairs* (Boulder, Colo.), XI (Jan.-April, 1951), 60.

10. R. Schlesinger, *Federalism in Central and Eastern Europe* (London: 1945), pp. 160, 161.

11. Wendel, in *Slavonic Review*, II, 261.

12. Rosdolsky, "Friedrich Engels . . . ," p. 108.

13. *Ibid.*, pp. 99–101.

14. George Lichtheim, *Marxism: An Historical and Critical Study* (London: 1961), p. 74.

15. R. Schlesinger, *Marx: His Time and Ours* (London: 1950), p. 334.

16. "Der Anfang des Endes in Oesterreich," *Werke*, IV, 508.

17. *New York Tribune* article of Jan. 9, 1857; see *Werke*, XII, 85.

18. Rosdolsky, "Friedrich Engels . . . ," pp. 115 ff.

19. Schlesinger, *Federalism* . . . , p. 157, n. 2.

20. Letter of Feb. 22, 1882; *Die Briefe von Engels an Ed. Bernstein* (Berlin: 1925), p. 55.

21. Letter of Nov. 17, 1885; W. Blumenberg (ed.), *August Bebels Briefwechsel mit Friedrich Engels* (The Hague: 1965), p. 244.

22. Letter of Feb. 7/15, 1882; *Friedrich Engels' Briefwechsel mit Karl Kautsky* (Vienna: 1955), p. 53.

23. Engels, "Gewalt und Oekonomie bei der Herstellung des neuen Deutschen Reiches" (written 1887/88), *Neue Zeit*, XIV, Bd. 1 (Feb., 1896), p. 687.

24. Engels, article in *New York Tribune*, April 21, 1853; see *Werke*, IX, 33–35.

25. Engels, "Deutschland und der Panslawismus," *Werke*, XI, 197. The article appeared first in *Neue Oder-Zeitung*, Breslau, April 24, 1855. The reprint in the *New York Tribune*, May 7, 1855 ("Austria's Weakness") alters the argument.

26. *Werke*, XI, 193, 194 (the first part of the article quoted above, reprinted in the *New York Tribune*, May 5, 1855, also with some alterations).

27. P. W. Blackstock and B. F. Hoselitz (eds.), *The Russian Menace to Europe* (Glencoe: 1952).

28. J. A. Doerig (ed.), *Marx vs. Russia* (New York: 1962), esp. pp. v–viii.

29. Letter of May 23, 1851.

30. April 24, 1852; *Werke*, VIII, 81. Emphasis not in original. Retranslated from the German.

31. Marx, *Însemnări despre Romăni* (Bucharest: 1964), p. 39. The original notebook from which this excerpt is taken may be consulted in the archives of the International Institute for Social History, Amsterdam.

31a. Engels in *The Commonwealth* (London), Mar. 31 and May 5, 1866; in Grünberg's *Archiv*, VI (1915), pp. 215–217, and *Werke*, XVI, 157–161.

32. M. Bakunin, "Aufruf an die Slawen," in *Zwei Schriften aus den 40er Jahren des XIX. Jahrhunderts, Internationale Bibliothek für Philosophie*, Bd. II, Nr. 11–12 (Prague: 1936), p. 27.

33. *Ibid.*

34. Samuel Rezneck, "The Political and Social Theory of Michael Bakunin," *American Political Science Review*, XXI, No. 2 (May, 1927), 291–292.

35. M. Bakunin in *Kolokol* (A. Herzen, ed.), No. 122–123 (London, Feb. 15, 1862), p. 1027.

36. Quoted in Rosdolsky, "Friedrich Engels . . . ," p. 234, n. 47.

37. Bakunin, *Gesammelte Werke*, III, 92.

38. Bakunin, "Aufruf . . . ," p. 39.

39. V. Cejchan, *Bakunin in Bohemia* [Czechish] (1928), pp. 193, 196, 198; quoted by Rosdolsky, "Friedrich Engels . . . ," p. 228, n. 30. (From Bakunin's *Zweiten Aufruf an die Slawen.*)

40. H. Lagardelle, "Les Oppositions Nationales de Marx et de Bakounine," *Le Mouvement Socialiste*, No. 251–252 (May-June, 1913), p. 297; quoting M. Bakunin, letter to *La Réforme*, Jan. 27, 1845.

41. Bakunin to Katkow, Jan. 2, 1861 (Julian calendar); in Viacheslav Polonskii, *Materialy dlia biografiii Bakunina* (Materials for Bakunin's biography), 3 vols. (Moscow-Leningrad: 1929?), vol. 2, p. 512.

42. M. Bakunin, *Confession* (4th ed., Paris: 1932), trans. by Brupbacher, p. 166. Emphasis in original.

43. *Ibid.*, pp. 87–88. For a view of Bakunin different from that presented in the text see Rezneck, "The Political and Social Theory . . . ," p. 272.

44. Arthur Lehning (ed.), *Michel Bakounine et les Conflits dans l'Internationale: 1872* (Leiden: 1965), pp. xiii–xiv.

45. Edith Riemerschmid, *Der Einfluss Bakunins auf die Italienische anarchistische Bewegung*, excerpts from doctoral dissertation at the Univ. of Zürich (Winterthur: 1956), p. 24.

46. *Letopisi Marksisma* [Russian], II (Moscow: 1926), 94.

47. Letter of April 16, 1856.

48. Engels, *The Peasant War in Germany* (1850), in *Werke*, VII, 329–413. There exist several English editions.

49. Cf. Bert F. Hoselitz, Preface to *The Political Philosophy of Bakunin: Scientific Anarchism*, ed. E. P. Maximoff (Glencoe: 1953), p. 13; and Rosdolsky, "Friedrich Engels . . . ," p. 233.

50. Bakunin, "Lettres à un Français, &c." (1870), *Oeuvres*, IV (Paris: 1910), p. 34.

51. Jacques Freymond (ed.), *La Première Internationale: Recueil de Documents* (Geneva: 1962), II, 207.

52. *Werke*, XVIII, 187.

53. J. Guillaume, *Karl Marx: Pangermaniste, et l'Association Internationale des Travailleurs de 1864 à 1870* (Paris: 1915), pp. iii–iv, 85.

54. See Engels' third article in *The Commonwealth*, May 5, 1866, in N. Riazanov, "Marx und Engels über die Polenfrage," Grünberg's *Archiv für die Geschichte des Sozialismus und der Arbeiterbewegung*, VI (1916), 217; in *Werke*, XVI, 159–163.

55. Cf. G. M. Stekloff, *History of the First International* (International: 1927), p. 85.

56. Engels to Marx, August 15, 1870.

57. N. Riazanov, in notes to ed. of articles by Marx and Engels in the *New York Tribune*; in N. Rjasanoff (ed.), *Gesammelte Schriften von Karl Marx und Friedrich Engels 1852 bis 1862*, I (Stuttgart: 1917), p. 472.

58. Letters of April 16, 1856, and Aug. 15, 1863.

59. See Bloom, p. 194 and Chapter 14 generally.

60. For a collection of the writings of Marx and Engels on the nature of the Prussian government, see *Reactionary Prussianism* (pamphlet, International: 1944).

61. Quoted from an unpublished MS (1872), in Arthur Lehning's Introduction to *Michel Bakounine et l'Italie*, II (Leiden: 1963), p. xvi; cf. Bakunin's *Werke*, III, 118.

62. Marx, *The Civil War in France*, in Marx & Engels, *Selected Works* (Moscow: 1950), p. 490; see *Werke*, XVII, 361.

62a. Friedrich Engels, Preface to the Second Edition of *The Peasant War in Germany*, July 1, 1874 (International: 1966), pp. 29–30.

63. Letter of Dec. 22, 1882, in Werner Blumenberg (ed.), *August Bebels Briefwechsel mit Friedrich Engels* (The Hague: 1965), p. 143.

64. Engels, "Socialism in Germany," in *Werke*, XXII, 248–260. Written, in October, 1891, in French, and first published in the *Almanach du Parti ouvrier pour 1892* (Lille: 1891), this article has been published by the leading socialist papers in Europe, and also in the *People* of New York, in 1892.

65. Letter of Oct. 13, 1891, to Bebel; in *August Bebels Briefwechsel mit Friedrich Engels*, pp. 450–453.

66. *Ibid.* Emphasis in original.

67. Samuel Gompers, *Seventy Years of Life and Labor* (New York: 1925), p. 388.

68. Engels, *Kann Europa abrüsten?* (Feb., 1893); see *Werke*, XXII, Chapts. V and VI, pp. 387–392.

69. On Engels' national pride in his later years see Mayer, *Friedrich Engels*, II, 455–456.

70. Hermann Oncken, *Lassalle: Eine politische Biographie* (4th ed., Stuttgart and Berlin: 1923), p. 372.

71. Quoted by Carlton J. H. Hayes in "The History of German Socialism Reconsidered," *American Historical Review* (New York), vol. XXIII, #1 (Oct. 1917), p. 66.

72. Ferdinand Lassalle, "Die Indirekte Steuer und die Lage der arbeitenden Klassen" (1863), in E. Bernstein (ed.), *Gesammelte Reden und Schriften* (Berlin: 1919), II, 484. Emphasis in original.

73. Miklos Molnar, "Die Londoner Konferenz der Internationale 1871," *Archiv für Sozialgeschichte*, IV (1964), 303–304.

74. Letter of Engels to Sorge, Sept. 12/17, 1874, in Marx & Engels: *Letters to Americans* (International: 1953), p. 114.

75. Cf. Robert Grimm, "Klassenkampf und Nation," *Neues Leben* (Bern), I, 1 (1915), p. 11.

76. "Tell the Truth," editorial in *Monthly Review*, XVII, 2 (June, 1965), pp. 1–3; article by Chinese Defense Minister Lin Piao, as published in *New York Times*, Sept. 4, 1965, p. 2.

Notes to Chapter III

1. Cf. Engels, *Origin of the Family, Private Property and the State* (1884), in *Werke*, XXI, Chapt. IX, pp. 152–173, on slavery. On the same subject see also Marx, *The Poverty of Philosophy* (1847), in *Werke*, IV, 65–182; and especially Engels, *Anti-Dühring* (1877/78), in *Werke*, XX, 167–169 (in the English edition [2nd ed., Moscow: 1959] pp. 249–251).

2. Engels, "Der Schweizer Bürgerkrieg," article published Nov. 14, 1847; in *Werke*, IV, 392.

3. Grimm, "Klassenkampf und Nation," p. 4.

4. Engels, "Po und Rhein," in *Werke*, XIII, 267. Emphasis in original.

5. *Ibid.*, 227.

6. Letter Marx to Engels, Feb. 16, 1857; letter Marx to Engels, Nov. 20, 1862; Marx and Engels, *The Civil War in the United States* (International: 1937), p. 262.

7. Marx, "Revolution in China and in Europe," (published in *New York Tribune*, June 14, 1853); in *Werke*, IX, 96; and in English in *Marx on China* (London: 1951), p. 3.

8. Letter Engels to Marx, May 23, 1851.

9. Engels, "The Real Issue in Turkey" (published in *New York Tribune*, April 12, 1853); in *Werke*, IX, 15.

10. Bloom, p. 49.

11. Engels, "Der demokratische Panslawismus" (published in *Neue Rheinische Zeitung*, Feb. 15, 1849); in *Werke*, VI, 273.

12. K. Kautsky, "Die Befreiung der Nationen," *Neue Zeit*, 1916–1917, Bd. 2, p. 148.

13. Julius Braunthal, *Geschichte der Internationale* (Hannover: 1961), I, 157–158.

14. Engels, "Socialism in Germany" (1891); in *Werke*, XXII, 253.

15. [F. Engels] Correspondence, in *The Northern Star* (London), Jan. 22, 1848; in *MEGA* I, Vol. VI, 387; [F. Engels] "Algeria," in *The New American Cyclopedia*, edited by George Ripley and Charles A. Dana, I (1865; copyright 1857), 350, 351; *Werke*, XVI, 724, n. 82.

16. Cf. Marx to Engels, Nov. 30, 1867; and Marx to S. Meyer and A. Vogt, April 9, 1870.

17. See *Werke*, XVI, 461–500, 675.

18. R. Palme Dutt, *The Internationale* (London: 1964), p. 67.

19. Cf. Marx's interventions in the General Council's meetings of Nov. 9, 16, 23, 30, 1869, in *Documents of the First International. The General Council of the First International 1868–1870. Minutes* (Moscow: 1966), pp. 176–194.

20. Marx, *Letters to Kugelmann* (London: 1935), p. 108.

21. Marx & Engels, *Letters to Americans* (International: 1953), p. 79. Original in library of International Institute for Social History, Amsterdam (letter of April 9, 1870).

22. Marx, "The Future Results of British Rule in India" (published in *New York Tribune*, Aug. 8, 1953); in *Werke*, IX, 224.

23. Marx, "Ein Londoner Arbeitermeeting" (published in *Die Presse*, Vienna, Feb. 2, 1862); in *Werke*, XV, 455.

24. R. P. Dutt, Introduction to Marx, *Articles on India* (2d. ed., Bombay: 1951), pp. 17–18.

25. Marx to Danielson, Feb. 19, 1881; in Marx & Engels, *Selected Correspondence, 1846–1895* (International: 1942), pp. 385–386.

26. Stuart Schram & Hélène Carrère d'Encausse, *Le Marxisme et l'Asie, 1853–1864* (Paris: 1965), p. 19; letter of Marx to the Russian review *Otečestvennye Zapiski*, 1877, in *Werke*, XIX, 108;

preface to the Russian edition of the *Communist Manifesto*, 1882, in *ibid.*, 296; Engels, "Nachwort [zu Soziales aus Russland]," 1894, in *Werke*, XXII, 421–435; letter of Marx to Vera Sasulich, March 8, 1881, in Blackstock and Hoselitz (eds.), *The Russian Menace to Europe*, pp. 278–279.

27. Marx to Engels, Oct. 8, 1858.

28. Engels to Kautsky, Sept. 12, 1882; see Marx & Engels, *Selected Correspondence* (International: 1935), p. 399.

29. Marx, *Capital*, Vol. I, Chapter XXXI and *passim*. Many of the articles on India are reprinted in *K. Marx and F. Engels on Colonialism* (Moscow: 1960).

30. Engels, "Drei neue Konstitutionen" (published in *Deutsche Brüsseler Zeitung*, Feb. 20, 1848); in *Werke*, IV, 516–517.

31. Marx & Engels, *The German Ideology* (written 1845/46) (Moscow: 1964), p. 174.

32. Engels, "Der dänisch-preuszische Waffenstillstand" (published in *Neue Rheinische Zeitung*, Sept. 10, 1848); in *Werke*, V, 394.

33. Marx, "Zur Judenfrage" (1843); in *Werke*, I, 374–376.

34. Dagobert Runes, Introduction to Karl Marx, *A World Without Jews* (New York: 1959).

35. "Zur Judenfrage," in *Werke*, I, 375.

36. Riazanov, "Marx und Engels über die Polenfrage," p. 186.

37. Letters of Engels to Marx, Aug. 7, Oct. 2, Oct. 3, 1866.

38. Marx, "Prospects in France and England" (published in *New York Tribune*, April 27, 1855); in *Werke*, XI, 182.

39. Engels, letter to the editor of the *Northern Star* (published March 25, 1848); in *Werke*, IV, 532.

40. *The German Ideology*, p. 518.

41. Engels, "Das Fest der Nationen in London" (written 1845 and published in *Rheinische Jahrbücher zur gesellschaftlichen Reform*, 1846); in *Werke*, II, 614.

42. *The German Ideology*, p. 518.

43. Marx to Engels, July 28, 1870.

44. Hubert Lagardelle, "Der Nationalismus in Frankreich," *Die Neue Zeit*, XX, Bd. 1 (1901–1902), 47.

45. Engels, "Protection and Free Trade" (written and published in 1888 as a preface to the American edition of Marx's speech on Free Trade); in *Werke*, XXI, 362.

46. Bloom, p. 58.

47. Marx, "The London Press" (published in *New York Tribune*, April 11, 1853); in *Werke*, IX, 20.

48. Bloom, p. 60.

49. *Ibid.*, p. 61, citing Engels, *Germany: Revolution and Counter-Revolution* (New York: 1933), pp. 141–142.

50. Lichtheim, *Marxism: An Historical and Critical Study*, p. 88.

51. Benedetto Croce, *Historical Materialism and the Economics of Karl Marx*, trans. Meredith (London: 1914), p. 15.

52. See the author's "Imperialism and Labor: An Analysis of Marxian Views," *Science & Society*, XXVI, No. 1 (1962).

53. *Werke*, XXII, 231. Emphasis in original.

54. Letter Engels to Marx, Oct. 7, 1858.

55. II. B. Davis, "Imperialism and Labor . . ."

Notes to Chapter IV

1. Cf. *Nieuwe Tijd* (Amsterdam), *passim*.

2. Cf. Abraham Ascher, "Imperialists Within German Social Democracy Prior to 1914," *Journal of Central European Affairs*, XX, No. 4 (Jan., 1961), 397. On Ascher see further below, pp. 91 ff.

3. Herman Heidegger, *Die deutsche Sozialdemokratie und der nationale Staat, 1870–1920* (Göttingen: 1956), p. 33.

4. *Ibid.*, p. 36, quoting stenographic reports.

5. Wilhelm Liebknecht, *Weltpolitik, Chinawirren, Transvaalkrieg* (pamphlet, Dresden: 1900), pp. 8–9.

6. Roger Morgan, *The German Social Democrats and the First International, 1864–1872* (Cambridge: 1965), p. 187.

7. Letter Engels to Cuno, May 7–8, 1872; in *Letters to Americans*, pp. 103–106.

8. Bebel, *Aus meinem Leben* (Stuttgart: 1907–1910), III, 167–168.

9. A. Winnig, *Das Reich als Republik, 1918–1928* (Stuttgart-Berlin: 1929), pp. 82–83.

10. Heidegger, p. 56.

11. *Ibid.*, pp. 46, 66, and *passim*.

12. W. Jansson, "Gewerkschaftliche Randbemerkungen zum kommenden Frieden," in *Arbeiterinteressen und Kriegsergebnis* (Berlin: 1915), ed. by Jansson for the General Federation of German Unions (ADGB), p. 150.

13. Rosa Luxemburg, "Gewerkschaftskampf und Massenstreik," in *Gesammelte Werke* (Berlin: 1928), IV, especially pp. 410–479.

14. Karl Liebknecht, *Militarismus und Antimilitarismus* (Berlin: n.d. [1907]), p. 14.

15. *Ibid.*, p. 106.

16. Rosa Luxemburg, "Der Wiederaufbau der Internationale," in *Ausgewählte Reden und Schriften* (Berlin: 1951), II, 517 ff.

17. Rosa Luxemburg, "Die Krise der Socialdemokratie" (Junius pamphlets), in *ibid.*, I, 258–399.

18. *Ibid.*, p. 399.

19. Abraham Ascher, *National Solidarity and Imperial Power: The Sources and Early Development of Social Imperialist Thought in Germany, 1871–1914*, MS (Ph.D. thesis) in Columbia University Library, 1957 (microfilm, Ann Arbor, 1958) and quotes from the following: A. Pannekoek, "Massenaktion und Revolution," in *Neue Zeit*, vol. XXX, 1912, pp. 541–550; Paul Lensch, "Miliz und Abrustung," in *Neue Zeit*, vol. XXX (1912), pp. 770–771; Lensch, speech in SPD Convention, 1912—see *Protokoll*, 415–419.

20. Kautsky, "Die Indianerfrage," *Neue Zeit*, III (1885), 17–21, 63–73, and 107–115.

21. Kautsky, "Kamerun," *Neue Zeit*, VI (1888), 26.

22. Braunthal, *Die Internationale*, I, 313.

23. Kautsky in *Neue Zeit*, April 26, 1912, pp. 97–109.

24. Paul Lensch, "Miliz und Abrüstung," *Neue Zeit*, Aug. 23, 1912, pp. 769–772.

25. E. Bernstein, "Die deutsche Sozialdemokratie und die türkische Wirren," *Neue Zeit*, XV, 1 (1896–1897), p. 110; E. Bernstein, *Evolutionary Socialism* (London: 1911), p. 171.

26. Wendel in *Slavonic Review*, II, 303–304; Ascher in *Journal of Central European Affairs*, XX, 401.

27. Bernstein, "Einiges über das indische Problem," *Neue Zeit*, XV, 2 (1896–1897), pp. 651–654.

28. Bernstein, *Evolutionary Socialism*, pp. 178–179. Original German ed. published 1899.

29. *Neue Zeit*, XVI (1897–1898), p. 420.

30. Kautsky, "Militarismus und Sozialismus in England," *Neue Zeit*, XVIII, 1 (1899–1900), pp. 587 ff.

31. Bernstein in *Sozialistische Monatshefte* (1900), p. 559.

32. Teut., "National und International," *Der sozialistische Akademiker* (Berlin), I (1895), 249 ff. This periodical was renamed *Sozialistische Monatshefte* in 1897.

33. *Ibid.*, p. 253.

34. *Ibid.*

35. Heidegger, p. 59.

36. Max Schippel, "Kolonialpolitik," *Soz. Mon.* (1908), 3 ff.

37. *Protokoll der Sozialdemokratischen Partei Deutschlands, 1907*, p. 132.

38. E. Kehr, *Schlachtflottenbau und Parteipolitik, 1894–1901* ("Historische Studien" Heft 197 [Berlin: 1930]), p. 332.

39. See R. Calwer, "Kolonialpolitik und Sozialdemocratie," *Soz. Mon.*, March, 1907, pp. 196–198.

40. Kautsky, "Patriotismus, Krieg und Sozialdemokratie," *Neue Zeit*, XXIII, 2 (1904–1905), p. 344.

41. Kautsky, *Patriotismus und Sozialdemokratie* (pamphlet, 1907), p. 12.

42. Bakunin, *Statism and Anarchy* (Russian), preface to Vol. I (Zürich & Geneva: 1873), p. 11.

43. Bakunin, *Oeuvres*, IV (Paris: 1910), 56–57; from "Lettres à un Français sur la crise actuelle" (1870). Emphasis in original.

44. Charles Andler, *Le Socialisme Impérialiste dans l'Allemagne Contemporaine, 1912–1913* (Paris: 1918), pp. 124–125.

Notes to Chapter V

1. M. Rebérioux & G. Haupt, "L'Attitude de l'Internationale," *Le Mouvement Social* (Paris, Oct.-Dec., 1963), No. 45, pp. 8–9.

2. Milorad M. Drachkovitch, *Les Socialismes français et allemand et le Problème de la Guerre, 1870–1914* (Geneva: 1953), p. 34.

3. Paul Louis, *Histoire du Socialisme en France de la Révolution jusqu'à nos jours* (Paris: 1925), pp. 320–322, 328.

4. Jean Jaurès, *Oeuvres*, ed. Max Bonnafous, Vol. IV, "L'Armée Nouvelle" (Paris: 1932), p. 303.

5. Maurice Lair, *Jaurès et l'Allemagne* (Paris: 1935), p. 114.

6. James Joll, *The Second International, 1889–1914* (London: 1955), p. 110.

7. J. Guesde, *L'Antimilitarisme et la Guerre*, p. 43, as quoted in Drachkovitch, p. 93.

8. Samuel Bernstein, "Jules Guesde, Pioneer of Marxism in France," *Science & Society*, Winter, 1940, p. 46.

9. Drachkovitch, pp. 141, 136, 142.

10. *Ibid.*, pp. 136–140.

11. *Ibid.*, pp. 145, 148.

12. Henry Pelling, *The Origins of the Labour Party: 1880–1900* (London: 1954).

13. H. M. Hyndman, *Further Reminiscences* (London: 1912), p. 15.

14. F. J. Gould, *Hyndman: Prophet of Socialism* (London: 1928), pp. 133–134.

15. F. Bealey in *Mouvement Social*, No. 45 (Paris, Oct.-Dec., 1963), p. 46, quoting *Justice*, June 17, 1899.

16. *Ibid.*, pp. 46–48, quoting *Justice*, Oct. 28, 1899; May 11, 1901; and July 20, 1901.

17. *Ibid.*, quoting *I. L. P. Annual Report* (1900), pp. 28, 29; and *Labour Leader*, Feb. 24, 1900.

18. J. R. MacDonald, *What I Saw in South Africa, 1902* (London: n.d.), p. 109.

19. H. J. Ogden, *The War Against the Dutch Republics, &c.* (London-Manchester: 1901), pp. 82–85.

20. *Report of the 33rd Annual Trades Union Congress, 1900* (London), pp. 54–55.

21. Ogden, pp. 85–86.

22. Bealey, p. 70.

23. G. Bernard Shaw (ed.), *Fabianism and the Empire: A Manifesto by the Fabian Society* (London: 1900), pp. 22 ff.

24. Bealey, pp. 42, 44.

25. Sidney Webb, "Lord Rosebery's Escape from Houndsditch," *The Nineteenth Century*, No. ccxcv (Sept., 1901), p. 371.

26. J. A. Hobson, *Imperialism: A Study* (1st ed., London: 1902).

27. T. F. Tsiang, *Labor and Empire* (New York: 1923), pp. 169–170.

28. *Ibid.*, p. 166.

29. *Ibid.*, p. 59.

30. H. N. Brailsford, *The War of Steel and Gold* (London: 1915 ed.), p. 160.

31. *Socialism and Nationalism: A Selection from the Writings of James Connolly*, with introduction and notes by Desmond Ryan (Dublin: 1948), pp. 20–21. Hereafter referred to as "Connolly."

32. R. M. Fox, *Jim Larkin: Irish Labor Leader* (International: 1957), p. 18.

33. Connolly, pp. 67–71, 105, 112, 121.

34. Gould, p. 148.

35. C. F. Brand, *British Labour's Rise to Power* (London: 1941), p. 77.

36. Roberto Battaglia, "Le tradizioni anticolonialiste della classe operaia italiana," *Rinascita*, XV, No. 11–12 (Rome, Nov.-Dec., 1958), pp. 852–853.

37. *Ibid.*, pp. 854–856.

38. Antonio Labriola, "Tripoli, il Socialismo e l'Espansione Coloniale," interview published in the *Giornale d'Italia*, April 13,

1902; see Antonio Labriola, *Scritti Varii, &c.*, ed. B. Croce (Bari: 1906), pp. 432–441.

39. Battaglia, p. 857.

40. Maurice Vaussard, *De Pétrarque à Mussolini: Évolution du Sentiment Nationaliste Italien* (Paris: 1961), p. 182.

41. R. P. Dutt, *Fascism and Social Revolution* (International: 1934), p. 188.

42. "Ontwerp-Program voor de Nederlandsche Koloniale Politik (Congress S. D. A. P. 1901)," *Nieuwe Tijd* (Amsterdam), 1901, pp. 197–220; Henri van Kol in *Soz. Mon.*, II (1904), 606 ff.; W. van Ravesteyn, Jr., in *Neue Zeit*, XXVI, Bd. 1 (1907–1908), pp. 85 ff.

43. J. Saks, "Over de koloniale kwistie," *Nieuwe Tijd*, XII (1907), 882.

44. W. van Ravesteyn, Jr., "Koloniale Propaganda," *Nieuwe Tijd*, XIV (1909), 774–776.

45. H. Gorter, *Der Imperialismus, der Weltkrieg und die Sozial-Demokratie* (Amsterdam: 1915), pp. 54–56, 60, 109.

46. Connolly, pp. 40–41.

47. *Ibid.*, p. 29.

48. *Ibid.*, pp. 2, 25.

49. *Ibid.*, p. 2; see also p. 171.

50. *Ibid.*, p. 108.

51. *Ibid.*, pp. 33–34.

52. *Ibid.*, p. 20.

53. *Ibid.*, p. 57.

54. Fox, pp. 134, 74.

55. Connolly, pp. 11, 12; Fox, p. 74.

56. R. M. Fox, *James Connolly: The Forerunner* (Tralee: 1946), p. 239.

57. C. Desmond Greaves, *The Life and Times of James Connolly* (London: 1961), p. 285.

58. *Ibid.*

59. Connolly, p. 181.

60. Greaves, p. 342.

61. *Ibid.*, p. 344.

62. *Ibid.*, p. 343.

63. Lenin, *Selected Works* (International: 1943), V, 306. Emphasis in original.

63a. Sen Katayama, "Attitude of Japanese Socialists Toward Present War," in *International Socialist Review* (Chicago), vol. 4 (March 1904), pp. 513–514.

64. Braunthal, I, 311.

65. Rebérioux & Haupt, pp. 10–14.

66. Bealey, p. 48.

67. Rebérioux & Haupt, pp. 10–14.

68. *Ibid.*, pp. 17–22, quoting Kautsky, *Sozialismus und Kolonial-politik* (1907), *passim*; and Lenin in *Proletari*, Oct. 16, 1908.

69. Rebérioux & Haupt, pp. 23 ff., 33–37.

70. Cf. Donald Clark Hodges, "Marx's Contributions to Humanism," *Science & Society*, XXIX, No. 2 (Spring, 1965), pp. 173–191.

Notes to Chapter VI

1. Bernhard Becker, *Der Missbrauch der Nationalitäten-Lehre* (2nd. ed., Vienna: 1869), p. 8.

2. S. Häcker in *Neue Zeit* (Stuttgart), XIV, Bd. 2 (1895–1896), pp. 326–328.

3. Rosa Luxemburg in *ibid.*, p. 180.

4. *Ibid.*, pp. 176–177, 208–209.

5. Rosa Luxemburg, "Der Sozialpatriotismus in Polen," in *ibid.*, pp. 464–468. Emphasis not in original.

6. *Ibid.*, pp. 178–179, 211–212.

7. *Ibid.*, p. 212, quoting Engels, *Kann Europa Abrüsten?*, Chapts. V and VI; in *Werke*, XXII, 387–392.

8. *Ibid.*, pp. 213, 216.

9. Grünberg's *Archiv für die Geschichte des Sozialismus und der Arbeiterbewegung*, XIII (Leipzig: 1928), 295.

10. Häcker, pp. 325, 329–331.

11. Rosa Luxemburg in *ibid.*, pp. 467–470.

12. Kautsky, "Finis Poloniae?," *Neue Zeit*, XIV, Bd. 2 (1895–1896), pp. 489–491, 513–520.

13. Rosa Luxemburg, "The National Question and Autonomy," in *Przeglad Sozialdemokratyczny*, Nos. 6, 7, 8/9, 10, 12, and 14/15 (1908 and 1909).

14. Engels to Bernstein, Feb. 22, 1882, in *Die Briefe von Friedrich Engels an Eduard Bernstein*, ed. Bernstein (Berlin: 1925), pp. 54–64.

15. Kautsky, "Die moderne Nationalität," *Neue Zeit*, V (1887), 402.

16. *Manifest der kommunistischen Partei* (1848); in *Werke*, IV, 466.

17. Kautsky, "Die moderne Nationalität," pp. 404–405.

18. Engels, "Die Polendebatte in Frankfurt" (published in *Neue Rheinische Zeitung*, Aug. 9, 1848), in *Werke*, V, 321; see also

Engels, "Der magyarische Kampf" (published in *Neue Rheinische Zeitung*, Jan. 13, 1849), in *Werke*, VI, 171; see also Marx/Engels, *Die deutsche Ideologie* (1845/46), in *Werke*, III, 411–412.

19. Kautsky, "Die moderne Nationalität," p. 446.

20. *Ibid.*, pp. 447–448.

21. Kautsky, "Patriotismus, Krieg und Sozialdemokratie," *Neue Zeit*, XXIII, Bd. 2 (1904–1905), p. 348.

22. Kautsky, in *Neue Zeit*, 1886, pp. 522–525.

23. Kautsky, "Die Krise in Oesterreich," *Neue Zeit*, XXII, Bd. 1 (1903–1904), pp. 41–42.

24. Kautsky, "Die Arbeiterbewegung in Oesterreich," *Neue Zeit*, VIII (1890), 50–56, 97–106, 155–163.

25. Hans Mommsen, *Die Sozial-Demokratie und die Nationalitätenfrage im Habsburgischen Vielvölkerstaat* (Vienna: 1963), I, 24–25.

26. *Ibid.*, p. 44.

27. Kautsky, "Der Kampf der Nationalitäten und das Staatsrecht in Oesterreich," *Neue Zeit*, XVI, Bd. 1 (1897–1898), pp. 520, 516–518.

28. *Ibid.*, p. 724.

29. Kautsky, "Das böhmische Staatsrecht und die Sozialdemokratie," *Neue Zeit*, XVII, Bd. 1 (1898–1899), pp. 296–297.

30. Verus, "Der Kampf der Nationalitäten in Oesterreich," *Neue Zeit*, XVI, Bd. 1 (1897–1898), pp. 665–666.

31. Ignaz Daszybski, "Die Lage in Oesterreich," *Neue Zeit*, XVI, Bd. 1 (1897–1898), p. 719.

32. Kautsky, "Die Krise in Oesterreich," p. 45.

33. Anton Pannekoek, *Klassenkampf und Nation* (pamphlet, Reichenberg: 1912), pp. 12–13.

34. Viktor Stein, "Ein Beitrag zur Parteigeschichte in Oesterreich," *Neue Zeit*, XX, Bd. 2 (1901–1902), p. 531.

35. Rudolf Tayerle, "Die Gewerkschaftsbewegung der tschechischen Arbeiter," *Neue Zeit*, XXIX, Bd. 1 (1910–1911), pp. 728–730, 732.

36. Gustav Eckstein in *Neue Zeit*, XXX, Bd. 1 (1911–1912), pp. 104–106; Paul Umbreit in *ibid.*, pp. 470–473.

37. L. M. Hartmann, "Zur nationalen Debatte," *Der Kampf*, 1911–1912, p. 152.

38. Otto Bauer, *Die Nationalitätenfrage und die Sozialdemokratie* (Vienna: 1907; reprinted with new preface 1924).

39. *Ibid.*, pp. 135, 133.

40. Karl W. Deutsch, *Nationalism and Social Communication* (2nd. ed., Cambridge: 1966), p. 20.

41. Bauer, p. 121.

42. *Ibid.*, pp. 532–533.

43. *Ibid.*, Chapt. XXII.

44. *Ibid.*, pp. 375–376.

45. Cf. criticism by Kautsky, "Nationalität und Internationalität," *Neue Zeit*, XXVI Supplement, Bd. 1 (Jan. 18, 1908), p. 4.

46. Bauer, Chapt. XXVII, "Die Wurzeln der kapitalistischen Expansionspolitik."

47. *Ibid.*, Foreword to 1924 ed., p. xi.

48. *Ibid.*, pp. 474–475.

49. *Ibid.*, p. 487.

50. O. Bauer, "Der Arbeiter und die Nation," *Der Kampf*, 1911–1912, p. 403.

51. Bauer, *Die Nationalitätenfrage*, p. 490.

52. K. Renner, *Marxismus, Krieg, und Internationale* (Stuttgart: 1918), pp. 361 ff.

53. Bauer, *Die Nationalitätenfrage*, p. 135.

54. *Ibid.*, pp. 280, 511.

55. Kautsky, "Nationalität und Internationalität," pp. 2–4.

56. *Ibid.*, pp. 6, 9, 17.

57. *Ibid.*, p. 35.

58. O. Bauer, "Bemerkungen zur Nationalitätenfrage," *Neue Zeit*, XXVI, Bd. 1 (1907–1908), p. 793.

59. Kautsky, *Patriotismus und Sozialdemokratie*, pp. 7–8.

60. Bauer, *Die Nationalitätenfrage*, p. 120.

61. F. Tönnies, *Die Entwicklung der sozialien Frage bis zum Weltkriege* (Berlin-Leipzig: 1926), p. 32.

62. Karl Renner, "Organisation der Welt," *Der Kampf*, 1909–1910, p. 341.

63. Bauer, in *Der Kampf*, III (1909–1910), p. 107; Josef Strasser, in *ibid.*, pp. 152–154.

64. Alfred Meissner, "Löst die nationale Autonomie das nationale Problem?", *Der Kampf*, 1907–1908, p. 273, quoting Rudolf Springer (Karl Renner), *Der Kampf der oesterreichischen Nationen um den Staat*, Tl. I (1902), pp. 188, 207; Meissner, p. 276.

65. Bauer, "Unser Nationalitätenprogramm und unsere Taktik," *Der Kampf*, I (1907–1908), p. 205.

66. Joseph Stalin, *Marxism and the National Question* (International: 1942), p. 12.

67. *Ibid.*, p. 36.

68. *Ibid.*, pp. 39, 65–66.

69. Draft Platform for the Fourth Conference of the Lettish Social-Democratic Party, May, 1913; and "Theses on the National Question," June, 1913; quoted in V. I. Lenin, *Ueber die Nationale und die Koloniale Nationale Frage* (selected writings, Berlin: 1960), pp. 100, 106. This source hereafter referred to as *Nat. & Kol. Nat. Frage.*

70. John H. Kautsky, *Political Change in Underdeveloped Countries: Nationalism and Communism* (New York: 1962), p. 38.

71. Marx & Engels, *The German Ideology*, pp. 68–69.

Notes to Chapter VII

1. Philip S. Foner, *History of the Labor Movement in the United States*, II (International: 1955), pp. 405–406. Emphasis added.

2. *Pres. Gompers' Report . . . to 18th Annual Convention of the AFL*, Dec. 13, 1898, pp. 17–18.

3. Samuel Gompers, *Seventy Years of Life and Labor* (New York: 1925), II, 64.

4. *Railway Conductor*, May, 1898, p. 339.

5. *Locomotive Engineers' Monthly Journal*, 1898, pp. 346–347.

6. *Journal of the Knights of Labor*, April 1, 1898 (editorial).

7. *Journal of the Knights of Labor*, May, 1898.

8. See *Appeal to Reason*, Jan. 14, 1899, p. 1; and Ray Ginger, *The Bending Cross: A Biography of Eugene Victor Debs* (New Brunswick: 1949), pp. 202–203.

9. Machinists' *Monthly Journal*, Oct., 1898.

10. *Report of Proceedings of the 18th Annual Convention of the AFL*, 1898, pp. 94–97.

11. Editorial, *The Nation* (New York), Jan. 12, 1899.

12. AFL *Proceedings*, 1898, p. 20.

13. *American Federationist*, V, No. 7 (Sept., 1898), p. 139.

14. Carl Schurz, *For Truth, Justice and Liberty* (New York: 1900), p. 20; *Am. Federationist*, V, No. 10, p. 207. Cf. Foner, *History*, II, 428.

15. Editorial, *Am. Federationist*, July, 1898; AFL Convention *Proceedings*, 1898.

16. *Am. Federationist*, V, No. 10, p. 207.

17. On Hawaii see AFL Convention *Proceedings*, 1900, Report of the President.

18. Cf. Lewis L. Lorwin, *The American Federation of Labor*

(Washington: 1933), pp. 138–139; and Norman Hapgood, *Professional Patriots* (New York: 1927), Chapt. XII.

19. Foner, *History*, pp. 437–438.

20. Gompers, *Seventy Years . . .* , II, 331 and *passim*.

21. Editorial, "Trade Unionists as Citizen Soldiers," *Am. Federationist*, March, 1910, p. 223.

22. IWW *Proceedings*, 1905, p. 269 ff.

23. Editorial, *International Socialist Review (ISR)*, I, No. 4 (Oct., 1900), p. 254.

24. Editorial, "Expansion and the Chinese Question," *ISR*, I, No. 1 (July, 1900), p. 55.

25. H. L. Boothman in *ISR*, I, Nos. 4 (Oct.) and 5 (Nov., 1900).

26. E. V. Debs, "Outlook for Socialism in the United States," *ISR*, I, No. 3 (Sept., 1900).

27. Ronald Radosh in *Science & Society*, Winter, 1964, p. 99.

28. A. M. Simons, "The United States and World Politics," *ISR*, I, No. 8 (Feb., 1901), p. 461.

29. *ISR*, VII, 364.

30. *ISR*, X, 509–510; and XI, 321–328, 364.

31. J. K. Turner, "The Revolution in Mexico," *ISR*, XI (Jan., 1911), 417–423.

32. Editorial, "The Situation in Mexico," *ISR*, XII (July, 1911), 47.

33. Tioka Yakama, "The Chinese Rebellion," *ISR*, XII (Jan., 1912), 394–396; Mark Sutton, "Standard Oil in China," *ISR*, XIII (March, 1913), 681–683.

34. Arturo M. Giovanitti, "The Brigandage of Tripoli," *ISR*, XII (March, 1912), 572–576.

35. W. D. Haywood, Resolution, *ISR*, XIII (Oct., 1912), 327.

36. Herbert Sturges, "History, Mexico, and American Capitalism," *ISR*, XIII (Oct., 1912), 332–336.

37. AFL Convention *Proceedings*, 1912, p. 256.

38. Gerald Friedberg in *Studies on the Left*, IV, No. 3 (1964), pp. 84–85.

39. James Weinstein in *Studies on the Left*, III, No. 4 (1963), p. 99.

40. IWW, *Proceedings of the Tenth Convention*, p. 138; quoted in John Steuben, *Labor in Wartime* (International: 1940), p. 85. Emphasis added.

41. Wm. D. Haywood, *Bill Haywood's Book* (International: 1929), p. 297.

42. *Ibid.*, pp. 300–301.

43. Steuben, p. 105. Emphasis added.

44. Weinstein, p. 103.

45. N. Fine, *Labor and Farmer Parties in the United States, 1828–1928* (New York, 1928–1961), p. 322.

46. But cf. Friedberg, p. 87.

Notes to Chapter VIII

1. Isaac Deutscher, *Soviet Trade Unions* (London: 1950), p. 9.

2. Lenin, "Under a Stolen Flag," in *Collected Works*, XVIII (London: 1930), 126–127. Written in Feb., 1915.

3. "The Pamphlet by Junius," in *Collected Works*, XIX, 204. Written Aug., 1916.

4. Lenin, "The Proletariat and the War," lecture delivered Oct. 14, 1914; in *Col. Works*, XVIII, 69.

5. Lenin, "Under a Stolen Flag," in *Col. Works*, XVIII, 128.

6. Lenin, "The Discussion on Self-Determination Summed Up," in *Col. Works*, XIX, 270–271. Written Oct., 1916.

7. See the letter of the Association Démocratique of Brussels, to the Fraternal Democrats in London, Feb. 13, 1848, signed among others by K. Marx, vice-president (published in *Northern Star*, March 4, 1848); in *Werke*, IV, 601–603.

8. Lenin, *Sel. Works*, IV, 279.

9. Letter Marx to Engels, Nov. 2 and Nov. 30, 1867; also Marx to Engels, Dec. 10, 1869.

10. Lenin, *Sel. Works*, IV, 279–280.

11. Mehring, Introduction to *Nachlass*, III, 44.

12. Kautsky, "Finis Poloniae?", *Neue Zeit* (1895–1896). Italicized in original. See Ch. VI, n. 12, for full page reference.

13. Lenin, *Col. Works*, VI, 454–463.

14. *Ibid.* The period is 1902–1903.

15. "Backward Europe and Advanced Asia," in *The National Liberation Movement in the East* (Moscow: 1962), p. 62. Written May 1913. Emphasis in original.

16. *Sel. Works*, IV, 250–251, 254. Emphasis in original. Cf. Kautsky in Ch. VI, above, n. 57.

17. Lenin, "The Discussion on Self-Determination Summed Up," in *Col. Works*, XIX, 225–226. Emphasis in original.

18. Draft Programme for the Convention of the SDP of Latvia, 1913; in *Nat. & Kol. Nat. Frage*, pp. 97–98. Emphasis in original.

19. *Nat. & Kol. Nat. Frage*, p. 167; from "Critical Remarks on the National Question," 1913.

20. *Ibid.*, p. 675, n. 55.

21. *Ibid.*, pp. 149–150.

22. Letter to S. G. Shaumyan in Baku, May 19, 1914; in *Letters of Lenin* (New York: 1937), p. 328; also in *Nat. & Kol. Nat. Frage*, pp. 199–200.

23. Draft bill on the equality of rights of nations and on the defense of the rights of national minorities, written 1914. See *Nat. & Kol. Nat. Frage*, p. 202.

24. *Ibid.*, p. 31, Note to resolution at Unity Conference of SDAPR, 1906.

25. "The Discussion on Self-Determination Summed Up," pp. 285–286; "A Caricature of Marxism and 'Imperialist Economism'" (1916), in *Col. Works*, XIX, 243.

26. *Sel. Works*, IV, 265–268. Emphasis in original.

27. See Kautsky, "Die Befreiung der Nationen," *Neue Zeit*, 1916–1917, p. 146, quoting H. Cunow, *Parteizusammenbruch*, p. 36 and *passim*.

28. *Nat. & Kol. Nat. Frage*, pp. 102–103.

29. "The Discussion on Self-Determination Summed Up," p. 287. Emphasis in original.

30. *Nat. & Kol. Nat. Frage*, pp. 126, 129.

31. G. Zinoviev & N. Lenin, "Socialism and War" (pamphlet, 1915), in *Col. Works*, XVIII, 235.

32. "The Revolutionary Proletariat and the Right of Nations to Self-Determination" (1915), in *ibid.*, p. 373.

33. "Socialism and War," p. 235.

34. "Democracy and Narodism in China" and "Regenerated China" (both 1912), in *Sel. Works*, IV, 305–311 and 312–313.

35. Lenin, "A Caricature," p. 251. Emphasis in original.

36. Letter to N. D. Kiknadze, Oct., 1916; in *Col. Works*, XIX, 266.

37. "A Caricature," p. 250. Emphasis in original.

38. *Ibid.*, p. 248. Emphasis added.

39. "The Pamphlet by Junius," p. 206.

40. Letter to A. M. Gorki, Jan. 3, 1911 (first published 1924); see *Nat. & Kol. Nat. Frage*, p. 60.

41. Lenin, "On the Right of Nations to Self-Determination" (Feb., 1914), in *Sel. Works*, IV, 253.

42. Lenin, "The National Question in Our Programme" (1903), in *Col. Works*, VI, 462.

43. *Nat. & Kol. Nat. Frage*, p. 79.

44. *Ibid.*, p. 153.

45. *Sel. Works*, IV, 292.

46. *Col. Works*, XIX, 225.

47. *Nat. & Kol. Nat. Frage*, p. 95; emphasis in original. Written in 1913.

48. *Col. Works*, XVIII, 129.

49. *Sel. Works*, II, 488. Written Nov., 1904.

50. Louis Menashe in *Science & Society*, XXIX, No. 3 (Summer, 1965), p. 342.

51. "The Discussion on Self-Determination Summed Up," p. 271. Emphasis in original.

52. *Ibid.*, pp. 285, 299.

53. Bakunin, *Étatisme et Anarchie* (proof, 1965), p. 11.

54. M. A. Suslov, "Struggle of the CPSU for the Unity of the World Communist Movement," in *Soviet Documents*, II, No. 18 (April 20, 1964), p. 74, quoting Lenin, *Collected Works* (Russian Ed.), XXXI, 128.

55. Rudolf Hilferding, *Das Finanzkapital* (Vienna: 1910), p. 470.

56. Hilferding here gives credit to Bauer, pp. 491 ff.

57. Hilferding, pp. 423–429.

58. *Col. Works*, XVIII, 191; emphasis in original. Written May-June, 1915; published 1924.

59. "On the National Pride of the Great Russians" (1914), in *Col. Works*, XVIII, 99–102. Emphasis in original.

60. A. B. Soep, *Nationalisme of Internationalisme* (pamphlet, The Hague: 1915).

61. Cf. below for whole passage.

62. Engels, *The Origin of the Family, Private Property, and the State*, in *Werke*, XXI, 165; English ed. (International: n.d.), p. 140.

63. Bernard Galitz, Letter to the editor, *National Guardian* (New York), Jan. 2, 1965.

64. Lenin, Memo of Dec. 31, 1922, as quoted in *New York Times*, July 1, 1956; also in *Nat. & Kol. Nat. Frage*, 653–654.

65. Cf. especially Lenin, "The Slogan for a United States of Europe," in *Collected Works*, vol. 21 (Moscow: 1964), 339–343. Written in 1915.

BIBLIOGRAPHY

KARL MARX AND FRIEDRICH ENGELS

Historisch-kritische Gesamtausgabe. ERSTE ABTEILUNG: *Sämtliche Werke und Schriften mit Ausnahme des "Kapital."* Edited in Moscow by D. RYAZANOV (vols. 1 and 2) and V. ADORATSKY (vols. 3–7) and published in Frankfurt-am-Main (vol. 1, first half-vol., by Marx-Engels-Archiv Verlagsgesellschaft), Berlin (vol. 1, 2d half-vol. through vol. 6, by Marx-Engels Verlag) and Moscow (vol. 7, also by Marx-Engels Verlag). Vols. 1–3: "Im Auftrage des Marx-Engels-Instituts." This collection stops with December 1848. Referred to in the notes as *MEGA.*

Aus dem literarischen Nachlass von Karl Marx, Friedrich Engels und Ferdinand Lassalle, ed. FRANZ MEHRING. 4 vols. Stuttgart, 1902. Referred to in the notes as *Nachlass.*

Correspondence. Since there are many editions of the correspondence between Marx and Engels, all arranged chronologically, we have contented ourselves with giving the dates of the respective letters. The reader can then find the letter in whatever source he is using.

Works. The latest (second) Russian edition of the *Works* of Marx and Engels, ed. by Marx-Engels-Lenin Institute, Moscow, appeared beginning in 1955. Twenty-two volumes covering the whole period 1838–1895 appeared in Russian, ending in 1962, and in German, ending in 1963. The Correspondence is in progress; *Capital* is to follow. Some volumes of this edition have appeared in English, but most of our references are to the German edition (*Werke*), with references also, where possible, to an English edition of the specified work.

KARL MARX. *Early Writings,* trans. and ed. T. B. BOTTOMORE. London, 1963.
———. *Letters to Kugelmann,* London, 1935.
MARX & ENGELS. *Basic Writings on Politics and Philosophy,* ed. LEWIS S. FEUER. New York, 1959.
MARX & ENGELS. *Letters to Americans.* International, 1953.
MARX & ENGELS. *The German Ideology.* Moscow, 1964.

Friedrich Engels' Briefwechsel mit Karl Kautsky, ed. BENEDIKT KAUTSKY. Vienna, 1955.

Die Briefe von Engels an Eduard Bernstein. Berlin, 1925.

August Bebels Briefwechsel mit Friedrich Engels, ed. W. BLUMEN-BERG. The Hague, 1965.

Gesammelte Schriften von Karl Marx und Friedrich Engels, 1852 bis 1862, ed. D. RJASANOFF. Stuttgart, 1920. 2 vols.

V. I. LENIN

Collected Works. The Russian edition of the *Collected Works* of Lenin appeared in Moscow in the late twenties and early thirties. A number of volumes were translated into English and published by International Publishers, and where the reference in the present volume is to Lenin's *Collected Works*, this is the edition that is meant. An expanded edition of Lenin's *Collected Works* has recently been published in Russian, and English translations of several volumes are available, published in Moscow. Where this translation has been used it is called *Collected Works* (Moscow).

Selected Works. Twelve volumes of Selected Works, translated from the Russian, were published by International in New York in 1943. These are referred to as *Sel. Works.*

Ueber die Nationale und die Koloniale Nationale Frage (selected writings). Berlin, 1960. The title is usually abbreviated to *Nat. & Kol. Nat. Frage.*

PERIODICALS CONSULTED

American Federationist. Washington, D. C. 1894–

Archiv für die Geschichte des Sozialismus und der Arbeiterbewegung, Carl Grünberg, ed., Leipzig, 1911–1930.

Archiv für Sozialgeschichte. Hannover, 1960–

Der Kampf: Sozialdemokratische Monatsschrift. Vienna, 1907–

Die neue Zeit. Stuttgart, 1885–1917.

International Socialist Review. Chicago, 1901–1918.

Journal of Central European Affairs. Boulder, Colo.

Le Mouvement Social. Paris, 1921–

Le Mouvement Socialiste. Paris, 1899–1914.

Nieuwe Tijd. Amsterdam.

Sozialistische Montashefte. Berlin, 1895–1933.

OTHER SOURCES

ACTON, LORD. *The History of Freedom and Other Essays*. London, 1919.

ANDLER, CHARLES. *Le Socialisme Impérialiste dans l'Allemagne Contemporaine, 1912–1913*. Paris, 1918.

ASCHER, ABRAHAM. "Imperialists Within German Social Democracy Prior to 1914," *Journal of Central European Affairs*, XX, No. 4 (January, 1961).

BAKUNIN, MIKHAIL A. *Oeuvres*. 6 vols. Paris, 1907–1911.

———. *Gesammelte Werke*. 3 vols. Berlin, 1921–24.

———. *Archives Bakounine*, ed. by A. LEHNING and others, for International Institute for Social History (Amsterdam). Leiden. 2 vols. in 3, 1961–1965. More volumes in preparation.

BATTAGLIA, ROBERTO. "Le tradizioni anticolonialiste della classe operaia italiana," *Rinascita* (Rome), No. 11–12 (November-December, 1958).

BAUER, OTTO. *Die Nationalitätenfrage und die Sozialdemokratie*. 2d ed. Vienna, 1924.

———. "Bemerkungen zur Nationalitätenfrage," *Neue Zeit*, XXVI, Bd. 1 (1907–1908).

———. "Unser Nationalitätenprogramm und unsere Taktik," *Der Kampf*, 1907–1908.

———. "Der Arbeiter und die Nation," *Der Kampf*, 1911–1912.

BEALEY, F. "Les Travaillistes et la Guerre des Boers," in *Mouvement Social* (Paris), No. 45, Oct.-Dec. 1963, pp. 39–70.

BEBEL, AUGUST. *Aus meinem Leben*. Vol. III. Stuttgart, 1907–1910.

BECKER, BERNHARD. *Der Missbrauch der Nationalitäten-Lehre*. 2nd ed. Vienna, 1869.

BERNSTEIN, E. *Evolutionary Socialism*. London, 1911.

BLACKSTOCK, P. W. & B. F. HOSELITZ (eds.). *The Russian Menace to Europe*. Glencoe, 1952.

BLOOM, SOLOMON F. *The World of Nations: A Study of the National Implications in the Work of Karl Marx*. New York: Columbia University Press, 1941.

BORKENAU, F. *World Communism*. New York, 1939.

BRAILSFORD, H. N. *The War of Steel and Gold*. London, 1915.

BRAND, C. F. *British Labour's Rise to Power*. London, 1941.

BRAUNTHAL, JULIUS. *Geschichte der Internationale*. 2 vols. Hannover, 1961.

CARR, E. H. *et al. Nationalism: A Report by a Study Group of Members of the Royal Institute of International Affairs*. Oxford, 1939.

CONNOLLY, JAMES. *Socialism and Nationalism: A Selection from the Writings of James Connolly*. With Introduction and notes by DESMOND RYAN. Dublin, 1948.

CORNU, AUGUSTE. *Karl Marx und Friedrich Engels: Leben und Werk*. 2 Vols. Berlin, 1954.

CROCE, BENEDETTO. *Historical Materialism and the Economics of Karl Marx*. Translated by MEREDITH. London, 1914.

CUNOW, H. *Die Marxsche Geschichts-, Gesellschafts-, und Staatstheorie*. 2 vols. Berlin, 1921.

DEUTSCH, KARL W. *Nationalism and Social Communication*. 2nd. ed. Cambridge, 1966.

DEUTSCHER, ISAAC. *Soviet Trade Unions*. London, 1950.

Documents of the First International. The General Council of the First International 1868–1870. Minutes. Moscow, 1966.

DOERIG, J. A. (ed.) *Marx vs. Russia*. New York, 1962.

DRACHKOVITCH, MILORAD M. *Les Socialismes français et allemand et le Problème de la Guerre, 1870–1914*. Geneva, 1953.

DUTT, R. PALME. *Fascism and Social Revolution*. International, 1934.

———. (ed.) *Articles on India* by MARX. 2nd ed. Bombay, 1951.

———. *The Internationale*. London, 1964.

FERGUSON, ADAM. *Essay on the History of Civil Society*. 3d ed. London, 1778.

FINE, N. *Labor and Farmer Parties in the United States, 1828–1928* (New York, 1928–1961).

FONER, PHILIP S. *History of the Labor Movement in the United States*. Vol. 2. International, 1955.

FOX, R. M. *James Connolly: The Forerunner*. Tralee, 1946.

———. *Jim Larkin: Irish Labor Leader*. International, 1957.

FREYMOND, JACQUES. (ed.) *La Première Internationale: Recueil de Documents*. 2 vols. Geneva, 1962.

GINGER, RAY. *The Bending Cross: A Biography of Eugene Victor Debs*. New Brunswick, 1949.

GOMPERS, SAMUEL. *Seventy Years of Life and Labor*. 2 vols. New York, 1925.

GORTER, H. *Der Imperialismus, der Weltkrieg und die Sozial-Demokratie*. Amsterdam, 1915.

GOULD, F. J. *Hyndman: Prophet of Socialism*. London, 1928.

GREAVES, C. DESMOND. *The Life and Times of James Connolly*. London, 1961.

GRIMM, ROBERT. "Klassenkampf und Nation," *Neues Leben* (Bern), I, 1 (1915).

GUILLAUME, J. *Karl Marx: Pangermaniste, et l'Association Internationale des Travailleurs de 1864 à 1870.* Paris, 1915.

HAPGOOD, NORMAN. *Professional Patriots.* New York, 1927.

HAYES, CARLTON J. H. "The History of German Socialism Reconsidered," *American Historical Review,* vol. XXIII, #1 (New York, Oct. 1917), 62–101.

HAYWOOD, WILLIAM D. *Bill Haywood's Book.* International, 1929.

HEGEL, G. W. F. *Hegel: Gesellschaft-Staat-Geschichte,* ed. F. BÜLOW. Leipzig, n.d. (1932?).

HEIDEGGER, HERMAN. *Die deutsche Sozialdemokratie und der nationale Staat, 1870–1920.* Göttingen, 1956.

HILFERDING, RUDOLF. *Das Finanzkapital.* Vienna, 1910.

HOBSON, J. A. *Imperialism: A Study.* 1st ed. London, 1902.

HYNDMAN, H. M. *Further Reminiscences.* London, 1912.

JAURÈS, JEAN. *Oeuvres,* ed. MAX BONNAFOUS. 9 vols. Paris, 1932.

JOLL, JAMES. *The Second International, 1889–1914.* London, 1955.

KAUTSKY, JOHN H. *Political Change in Underdeveloped Countries: Nationalism and Communism.* New York, 1962.

KAUTSKY, K. "Die moderne Nationalität," *Neue Zeit,* V (1887).

——. "Patriotismus, Krieg und Sozialdemokratie," *Neue Zeit,* XXIII, 2 (1904–1905).

——. *Patriotismus und Sozialdemokratie.* Article in *Leipziger Volkzeitung* reprinted as pamphlet. Leipzig, 1907.

——. "Die Befreiung der Nationen," *Neue Zeit,* XXXV, 2 (1916–1917).

LAGARDELLE, HUBERT. "Der Nationalismus in Frankreich," *Die Neue Zeit,* XX, Bd. 1 (1901–1902).

——. "Les Oppositions Nationales de Marx et de Bakounine," *Le Mouvement Socialiste,* No. 251–252 (May-June, 1913).

LAIR, MAURICE. *Jaurès et l'Allemagne.* Paris, 1935.

LASSALLE, FERDINAND. *Gesammelte Reden und Schriften,* ed. E. BERNSTEIN. 12 vols. Berlin, 1919–1920.

LEEUW, A. S. DE. *Het Socialisme en de Natie.* Amsterdam, 1939.

LEHNING, ARTHUR (ed.). *Michel Bakounine et les Conflits dans l'Internationale: 1872.* Leiden, 1965.

LICHTHEIM, GEORGE. *Marxism: An Historical and Critical Study.* London, 1961.

LIEBKNECHT, KARL. *Militarismus und Antimilitarismus.* Berlin, n.d. [1907].

LIEBKNECHT, WILHELM. *Weltpolitik, Chinawirren, Transvaalkrieg.* Pamphlet. Dresden, 1900.

LORWIN, LEWIS L. *The American Federation of Labor.* Washington, 1933.

LOUIS, PAUL. *Histoire du Socialisme en France de la Révolution jusqu'à nos jours.* Paris, 1925.

LUXEMBURG, ROSA. *Gesammelte Werke.* Vol. IV. Berlin, 1928.

——. *Ausgewählte Reden und Schriften.* 2 vols. Berlin, 1951.

MACDONALD, J. R. *What I Saw in South Africa, 1902.* London, n.d.

MARCUSE, HERBERT. *Reason and Revolution: Hegel and the Rise of Social Theory.* 2nd ed. London, 1954.

MAXIMOFF, E. P. (ed.) *The Political Philosophy of Bakunin: Scientific Anarchism.* With a Preface by BERT F. HOSELITZ. Glencoe, 1953.

MAYER, GUSTAV. *Friedrich Engels: Eine Biographie.* 2 vols. Haag, 1934.

MEHRING, F. *Karl Marx: The Story of His Life.* New York, 1935.

MOMMSEN, HANS. *Die Sozial-Demokratie und die Nationalitätenfrage im Habsburgischen Vielvölkerstaat.* 2 vols. Vienna, 1963.

MORGAN, ROGER. *The German Social Democrats and the First International, 1864–1872.* Cambridge, 1965.

NICOLAIEVSKY, BORIS and MAENCHEN-HELFEN, OTTO. *Karl Marx: Man and Fighter.* 1936.

OGDEN, H. J. *The War Against the Dutch Republics.* Manchester, 1901.

ONCKEN, HERMANN. *Lassalle: Eine politische Biographie.* 4th ed. Stuttgart and Berlin, 1923.

PANNEKOEK, ANTON. *Klassenkampf und Nation.* Pamphlet. Reichenberg, 1912.

PAPPENHEIM, FRITZ. *The Alienation of Modern Man.* New York: 1959.

PELLING, HENRY. *The Origins of the Labour Party: 1880–1900.* London, 1954.

REBÉRIOUX, M. and HAUPT, G. "L'Attitude de l'Internationale," *Le Mouvement Social* (Paris), No. 45 (October-December, 1963).

RENNER, K. *Marxismus, Krieg, und Internationale.* Stuttgart, 1918.

RIEMERSCHMID, EDITH. *Der Einfluss Bakunins auf die Italienische anarchistische Bewegung.* Doctoral dissertation at the University of Zürich. Winterthur, 1956.

ROSDOLSKY, ROMAN. "Friedrich Engels und das Problem der 'Geschichtslosen Völker'," *Archiv für Sozialgeschichte* (Hannover), IV (1964).

RUNES, DAGOBERT. Introduction to KARL MARX, *A World Without Jews.* New York, 1959.

SAKS, J. "Over de koloniale kwistie," *Nieuwe Tijd*, XIV (1907).

SCHIPPEL, MAX. "Kolonialpolitik," *Sozialistische Monatshefte*, XII (1908), Bd. I.

SCHLESINGER, R. *Federalism in Central and Eastern Europe*. London, 1945.

——. *Marx: His Time and Ours*. London, 1950.

SCHRAM, STUART and HÉLÈNE CARRÈRE D'ENCAUSSE. *Le Marxisme et l'Asie, 1853–1864*. Paris, 1965.

SHAW, G. BERNARD (ed.). *Fabianism and the Empire: A Manifesto by the Fabian Society*. London, 1900.

SOEP, A. B. *Nationalisme of Internationalisme*. Pamphlet. The Hague, 1915.

STALIN, JOSEPH. *Marxism and the National Question*. International, 1942.

STEKLOFF, G. M. *History of the First International*. International, 1927.

STEUBEN, JOHN. *Labor in Wartime*. International, 1940.

STRASSER, JOSEPH. "Die Werbekraft des Internationalismus," *Der Kampf*, 1909–1910.

THOMSON, S. HARRISON. "A Century of a Phantom: Panslavism and the Western Slavs," *Journal of Central European Affairs*, XI (January-April, 1951).

TÖNNIES, F. *Die Entwicklung der sozialien Frage bis zum Weltkriege*. Berlin-Leipzig, 1926.

TSIANG, T. F. *Labor and Empire*. New York, 1923.

VAUSSARD, MAURICE. *De Pétrarque à Mussolini: Évolution du Sentiment Nationaliste Italien*. Paris, 1961.

WENDEL, H. "Marxism and the Southern Slav Question," in *Slavonic Review* (London), vol. II, #5 (Dec. 1923).

WINNIG, A. *Das Reich als Republik, 1918–1928*. Stuttgart-Berlin, 1929.